Letters from Lynn
A Journey of Faith, Laughter, and Survival

Volume I

Written by Lynn Thomas

Dedicated to my late brother, Tony.

Lynn Thomas spent his life turning hard things into hope—and making people laugh along the way. An Alabama native, he made a career in information technology, earning Microsoft, Novell, and CompTIA certifications and working as an I.T. manager before disability brought him home to be near family. Faith was his compass: saved at thirteen and baptized later in life, Lynn wrote openly about prayer, grace, and everyday kindness.

Born with spina bifida and a tethered spinal cord, Lynn underwent more than thirty surgeries and lived with a colostomy and urostomy—cheerfully nicknamed "Lenny" and "Squiggy." He could walk, garden, drive long country highways for doctor visits, and swap classic-rock trivia with anyone who'd listen. He loved his dog Tommy, The Andy Griffith Show, and the small Southern rituals of diners, church pews, and front-porch talk. Friends called him "a nice guy in a mean world," and he tried to prove them right with simple generosity and a stubborn joy.

Lynn began chronicling his days in a plainspoken journal he called "Walking with Spina Bifida." Those entries—equal parts humor, grit, and gratitude—became Letters from Lynn: A Journey of Faith, Laughter, and Survival. After his passing from complications of spina bifida, his mother gathered these pages so readers could keep walking with him, one honest, hope-soaked story at a time.

Foreword

First and foremost, I am a Christian.

I was saved at thirteen years old and baptized in my early forties.

As you read through my stories, I do hope that you can see God shining through.

I once asked a friend how he describes me to other people.

His answer?

"Describe you? I don't describe you. I introduce you in story form by saying, '…have you ever heard the ballad of Lynn…?'"

I love humor and being funny. I love making others laugh.

According to many, I'm a "sweetheart."

A friend once said, "The fact is, you're a nice guy in a mean world."

I hate conflict.

Many moons ago, I began shying more and more away from it.

Spina bifida comes with enough problems of its own.

I live life. I do my best.

I want as few problems as possible.

I think that's what most people want.

One friend says that I'm a sheep in a lion's den.

If I am out eating, I will not send anything back.

I've gotten the wrong meal before, and instead of telling the waitress I had ordered a steak and not the grilled chicken, I ate the chicken—and then left a thirty percent tip.

As I said, I was born with spina bifida.

I wore a diaper most of my life before getting a colostomy and urostomy (named "Lenny" and "Squiggy," respectively).

Unlike many others born with spina bifida, I can walk.

I'll admit that I am an amateur writer, which means you'll find grammatical errors.

I'll try to keep those to a minimum. I promise.

So, walk with me as I walk through life.

Walking with spina bifida.

Love you,

— Lynn

1: Frost Bite

There's no operator's manual for raising a kid born with Spina Bifida.

Mom didn't get a guidebook when I arrived. She just got me, with all my parts and missing pieces, and we had to figure things out together, one day at a time.

I've learned since then that moms have a special way of teaching lessons. They don't always use words or logic or even patience. Sometimes, they scare the fire out of you. And sometimes, that's exactly what's needed.

I was young. Real young. Maybe six or seven. Definitely before I hit double digits. Back then, I didn't understand how fragile my body was. With Spina Bifida, I couldn't feel much in my lower body. I would step on a sharp rock or drag my foot across something jagged and not feel a thing. But the blood trailing across the floor would always tell on me. Mom used to chase me around the house, hollering about shoes and socks.

"Lynn, you can't be running around barefoot! You don't know when you're hurt!"

And I didn't.

Then came the snow.

It was the first real snow I can remember. The kind that falls heavy and thick, covering everything like powdered sugar. I remember watching it come down, the whole world going quiet under it. That morning, we went outside and scooped big handfuls of snow into a pot. Mom made snow ice cream that day. Just snow, vanilla, sugar, and milk. Cold and sweet and perfect.

We also found an old sheet of tin roofing. In the South, we didn't have sleds. We had creativity. That piece of tin became our sleigh, and the hill in front of the house became a rollercoaster.

We played like kids who had never seen winter before. We screamed and laughed and flew down that hill over and over, not caring about wet gloves or numb fingers or, in my case, whether I could feel my feet.

I don't even remember what shoes I had on. Maybe old sneakers, maybe something thinner. But I know they weren't snow boots. I doubt I even owned snow boots.

By the time I came back inside, the house smelled like wood smoke and old quilts. The heater was rattling in the corner. I was dripping melting snow across the floor, and my socks squished when I walked.

Mom turned and saw me.

"Take those shoes off," she hollered, already halfway across the room.

I did.

She saw my wet socks.

That's when everything changed.

Mom's voice didn't get louder, but it got serious.

"Lynn, I told you to feel your feet with your hands."

She quickly pulled off my socks and touched my toes.

"Your feet are frozen, Lynn," she said, worried.

"We have to warm them up right now."

She pulled me into the bathroom and ran the water, checking it with her hand.

"It has to be lukewarm, not hot," she said. "If it's too hot, your feet could go into shock."

I sat on the edge of the tub, staring at my cold, pale feet under the water.

Mom looked at me.

"You better hope you don't have frostbite. They'd have to cut your feet off."

I stared back, scared.

"You think life's hard now? Try it without your feet."

She wasn't being mean. She was being a mom. She was scared. And she was trying to make sure I understood the cost of not listening.

Her voice softened.

"Son, I've told you over and over to watch your feet."

I whispered, "Are they gonna have to cut my feet off, Momma?"

She didn't say yes or no.

She just said, "We'll have to see. Maybe now you'll remember to check them."

And I did.

From that day on, I always paid attention to my feet. I still do.

Yes, moms can scare the fire out of their kids to get them to pay attention—and sometimes, it's one of the greatest tools they have.

Even now, when I sit down and pull on my socks, I remember that bathroom. The lukewarm water. The way she held my feet. The way fear can sometimes love you louder than comfort ever could.

And I am happy to report this.

I still have both my feet to this day.

2: First Memory

The very first memory I have of this life takes me back to a cool October afternoon in 1980. I even remember the exact day. October 7th.

Mom had just brought me home from daycare. I don't remember what I was wearing or what the sky looked like, but I remember the feeling. That calm, quiet comfort of being back home.

We pulled up the driveway, and there was my brother Tony, waiting for us like he had been standing there a while. He had that same spark in his eye that I'd seen a hundred times before I even knew how to name it. The spark of a plan.

He came right up to the car and said, "Come on, let's go to the dog pens."

Tony was one of my two older brothers. He was the middle child. Eight years old at the time, but to me, he already felt like a giant. The kind of giant who made everything seem a little more exciting.

To get to the dog pens, we had to walk across a little wooden bridge my dad had built. It stretched over a stream that ran right through our yard, and to this day, I remember the sound of that water—always moving, always talking.

As Tony and I stepped onto the bridge, I glanced down.

There, right in the middle of the walkway, was a nickel. Shiny. New. Sitting heads up like it had been placed there on purpose.

I bent down and picked it up.

Tony grinned. "That means you're gonna have a lucky day."

We didn't stay long at the dog pens. Just enough to say hello to the dogs, pat their heads, and laugh at whatever they were doing. Then we made our way back toward the house.

When we stepped inside, everything exploded.

"Surprise!"

My whole daycare group was there. Kids in party hats, cake on the table, chips and dip spread out across the counter. Streamers hung like magic from the ceiling.

I froze. Just stood there in the doorway, too shocked to speak.

Tony leaned in beside me and whispered, "You know what today is?"

I shook my head.

"It's your birthday. You're five years old today."

I stared around the room, trying to make sense of it. The hats, the voices, the colors. It felt too big for me to take in all at once.

We had cake. The kind of cake that sticks to the roof of your mouth. There were bowls of salty chips and a little container of dip I probably didn't touch, but I remember it being there. And everyone was laughing. Laughing like they were supposed to. Laughing like this was the best day of the year.

At one point, Tony nudged me again and said, "See, I told you a nickel on heads was good luck."

Many years later, I would realize what really happened.

Tony had put that nickel on the bridge. He had set it there for me to find, like a hidden treasure. He was only eight years old, but already he knew how to build a moment. How to make a small thing feel magical.

And that was just who he was.

If there was ever something I couldn't do because of my Spina Bifida, Tony would do it for me. Then he'd come back and describe the whole thing in perfect detail. Almost like he was talking to someone who couldn't see. He'd tell me what it looked like, how it felt, what it sounded like—all so I could feel like I had done it too.

He made me feel like I was part of everything.

He was amazing.

Tony passed away in 2010. He was just 38 years old. A brain hemorrhage took him, fast and without warning. He left behind three beautiful children.

And still, all these years later, I am glad—more than glad—that my first memory on this earth started with him.

This story, and all the others I'll tell, I dedicate to his memory.

3: ER Visit

It was 7 PM on a Thursday evening, at one of the many hospitals scattered across America.

My doctor had told me to go to the emergency room. My kidneys were hurting, and my fever had climbed too high. I wasn't in the kind of pain that makes you scream, but something wasn't right, and my body knew it.

When I arrived, the first thing I noticed was how full it was. Not just the emergency room, but the whole hospital. Filled to the brim with people — sick people, waiting people, tired people. There were no beds left anywhere. The place was holding on with both hands.

I sat down and thought to myself, What do you even do when a hospital runs out of room?

I didn't know the answer.

Part of me imagined a motel-style sign out front, blinking red: *No Vacancy*. But this was real. These were real people. Some of them dying.

To my left sat an older woman in a wheelchair. She had her knitting supplies folded neatly in her lap, like she had come prepared to wait all night. She looked like anyone's grandmother. Kind eyes. Tired hands. She was alone.

"Sir, can you help me take my blood sugar?" she asked me gently.

"Yes, ma'am," I said. "I'm diabetic too. I know how."

I took out my kit and checked it for her. The screen blinked a number that startled me. Her blood sugar was at 52.

If you don't know what that means, I'll tell you. Anything under 70 is trouble. 52 is an emergency.

"Do you have any tablets to bring it back up, ma'am?" I asked.

She shook her head slowly. "No."

I stood up and walked straight to the front desk.

"There's a woman in a wheelchair with a blood sugar of 52," I told them. "She needs help now."

The staff was running on fumes. I could tell. One woman behind the desk looked at me, her eyes wide and tired.

"Sir, every doctor and nurse in this hospital is with another patient," she said. "I've told them it's an emergency. I don't know what else to do."

So I did something I wasn't sure I should do. I got involved.

I walked over to the drink machine. I studied the options one by one, looking for something with enough sugar to give her a boost. I found a bottle of sweet tea, swiped my card, and pulled it out.

By the time I returned, another woman had arrived and was sitting beside the lady in the wheelchair.

"You know her?" I asked.

"Yes. I'm her friend," she said.

"Okay. Her blood sugar is 52. She needs sugar fast. Here's some sweet tea," I said, handing her the bottle.

"Thank you, sir," she replied.

"You're welcome," I said quietly and walked away.

A few minutes later, I looked up and saw a nurse rushing over with a medical kit in her hands. She knelt by the woman I had silently nicknamed *Granny*, and I felt a slow breath leave my chest.

I felt better.

Not long after, a teenage girl came in with her mother and sat close to me.

The girl was crying, shoulders shaking, head down.

Her mother got up to make a phone call, though she might as well have stayed seated. She was talking so loud the whole room could hear.

"This is me," she said into the phone. "Sissy is suicidal again."

She paused, then continued.

"Yeah! She went through her hissy fit, but this time she won't calm down. She's determined this time, so I brought her to the E.R. No! Don't come down. You know she hates you. I'll call you back when I hear something."

I know how this sounds. I'm not making it up. I'm just repeating what I heard.

"Sissy" sat quietly, close enough for me to see the pain in her eyes. She wasn't angry. She wasn't lashing out. She was just tired of it all. Her hands were trembling in her lap, and every breath she took seemed heavy.

I know too well that teenage suicide is real. When you're young and hurting, death can start to look like the only way to escape. Like the next thing has to be better than the pain of the thing you're living now.

I stood up and walked outside.

On the way, I passed a man in a wheelchair. His leg was swollen up, thick and tight, the size of a watermelon. His face was twisted in pain, and he was crying softly. His wife held his head against her shoulder, whispering something to him that only he could hear.

The place was full. Overflowing. And every face I passed carried the same weight.

It hit me then. The grief in this place was bigger than the walls could hold.

I kept walking.

Outside, the night air was cool and still. I heard sirens in the distance. Ambulances, one after another. At one point, I heard the medical helicopter flying overhead, blades chopping through the dark sky.

I stood there in the silence and felt my eyes start to water.

All of this pain. All in one place. And this was just one hospital. One town. One Thursday night. Multiply it across the country. Across the world.

It was too much.

I teared up again.

In that moment, I wished I still smoked. I really did. A cigarette might've calmed me. Instead, I popped a mint in my mouth and breathed in deep.

I knew how this worked.

They take the sickest first. I was ambulatory. I was walking around. I wasn't suicidal. I wasn't dying. I would be last.

It was 9 PM.

And I waited.

4: You Can Walk

By now, I've had more than thirty surgeries and procedures.

I lost count after a while, but I'd say the last ten were all done by the same surgical team. They knew me. I knew them. And by then, I knew how to be a terrible patient.

Most of the time, during those surgeries, there would be medical students sitting in. Not to operate. Just to observe. Silent eyes behind scrubs and masks.

One of them stood out to me. His name was Travis.

Travis had sat in on at least three of my surgeries. And he wasn't just some guy with a clipboard. He made the effort to learn about me. Really learn. Spina Bifida. Tethered spinal cord. Neurogenic bladder. Bad kidneys. The whole mess.

I knew he knew because he came to my room. He asked questions. He listened. That's why I remembered him.

Now, before I go on, let me be honest.

I used to be a terrible patient.

I'd sneak water when I wasn't supposed to. I'd wander out of my room. I smoked cigarettes back then, and I was ashamed of it. Still am. But at the time, I just wanted to feel normal. All the other kids smoked. So I did too. I've quit since. That wasn't easy. But I did it.

One of the last surgeries Travis observed was a minor one. The next day, I was out of bed. Not just walking around but outside — smoking.

That was me. Slipping out like a teenager sneaking into a movie. I disappeared often enough that nurses started calling codes when they couldn't find me. I think they called it a "Code White." Security would track me down and wheel me back to my room like I was a runaway.

One afternoon, Travis walked into my room. I could tell something was different. His face looked puzzled, like he had just seen something that didn't line up with everything he thought he knew.

He stood at the door for a second.

"Lynn… um, how you doing, sir?"

I smiled. "I'm doing great. Come on in. Sit awhile."

"Okay. Thank you. I have a question, sir…"

He looked hesitant. His words slowed down, cautious.

"I don't know how to ask this. I don't want to upset you. It's a sensitive topic."

"Go ahead and ask, Travis. You won't upset me. I'm an open book."

He cleared his throat, looked me in the eye, and said, "Okay, here she goes… I could've sworn that I saw you outside walking around. Smoking."

I laughed. "Oh yeah, I snuck out. The security guard caught me and brought me back."

He stared at me.

"Wait. You can walk?"

"Yep."

He blinked. "Don't you have Spina Bifida?"

"Oh yeah. But I can walk. Some people with Spina Bifida can."

"Oh my goodness. I thought this whole time you were paralyzed."

And then I lost it. I started laughing so hard my stomach hurt.

"This whole time, you thought I couldn't walk?"

He nodded, embarrassed. "Yeah. I feel like an idiot. And just to be sure, the doctor knows you can walk?"

"Yes sir. If you had asked him, he would've told you."

He looked like he'd learned something big.

"This is why I'm a student," he said. "I thought everyone with Spina Bifida was born paralyzed. I didn't know. I didn't even think to ask."

I shrugged. "Now you know to ask. You learned something."

We laughed about it together.

He told me later that he had looked up from his paperwork and saw me outside. There I was, walking around, pushing my IV pole, and smoking like I owned the place. He froze right there in the hallway.

That little moment sparked a big question in my mind, though.

Does my chart say I can walk? Does it say I'm ambulatory? What if something happened to me, and I came in unconscious? Would they know not to mess around with my spinal cord?

My Papa went straight to my doctor and asked. Thankfully, my file did note it. I was listed as ambulatory.

Travis is probably a full-fledged surgeon by now. Maybe he's teaching others, just like he was once taught. And I hope he remembers me — the guy who taught him that you can have Spina Bifida and still get caught smoking outside a hospital.

And I'm glad I could be a small part of his learning.

5: *Late Night Meal*

It was Friday night, and I had a craving.

I found myself behind the wheel, driving through the quiet dark, headed toward a little all-night diner that always had warm lights in the windows. The kind of place that smelled like bacon and old coffee, even from the parking lot.

It was late, and the place was packed. But since I was by myself, I didn't have to wait long. I grabbed a seat up front, slid into the booth, and looked around.

The air buzzed with energy. Four-tops waiting to be seated. People standing at the counter, hoping their call-in orders were ready. Everyone was talking at once, voices blending into that familiar late-night rhythm.

My waitress, Ms. Becky, was already running behind. I heard her talking to a coworker near the kitchen.

"I guess I ain't getting out anytime soon tonight."

She was supposed to be off at 9 PM. It was already 9:15.

She walked over to my table, pen and pad in hand, her hair a little frizzy from the rush.

"Honey, whatcha gone' have tonight?"

"Coffee and water. Cream for the coffee, please."

"That's easy 'nuff."

She smiled and dropped off the coffee a minute later.

"I'll get the water in just a sec," she said, already turning to take another table's order.

When she brought the water back, she asked, "You know whatcha want?"

"Yes ma'am. The 'All-Star' with hashbrowns instead of grits, eggs over easy, bacon, and a waffle."

She nodded. "Easy 'nuff."

She turned toward the kitchen and hollered out the order like a short-order poet.

"Pull one bacon, throw the hash through the shredder, make the eggs smile, and throw in a waffle."

At least that's what it sounded like.

I smiled.

"I hope you get to leave soon, ma'am," I said.

"Me too. I'm beat…"

"You're beat to the socks."

"Yep."

She laughed and kept moving.

Ms. Becky didn't stop. She was refilling coffees, clearing plates, juggling way more than any one person should be asked to juggle. I wanted to ask her about her life. About her story. But she was too busy. I didn't want to bother her.

My food arrived hot and perfect. Ms. Becky topped off my coffee without being asked.

"Thank you," I said. "I'm good. You don't have to worry about me anymore."

At 9:40, I paid the bill. As I stepped outside, Ms. Becky walked out with me.

"Thank you for coming tonight, sir," she said, genuine and kind.

"Thank you as well, Ms. Becky."

I climbed into my vehicle and pulled away.

Maybe next time, I'll get her story.

7: Best Western

I left the cabin early this morning, no real plan, just a direction. Somewhere along the way, I found myself pulling off in Chattanooga. I needed to stop for a telehealth appointment later in the day, and that felt like the right excuse to get a room for the night. Not that I needed much of an excuse. Sometimes you just need a little space with a door you can close and your name on the reservation.

I found a Best Western. Not a fancy hotel, just the kind I love. The old-school kind with drive-up rooms. You pull your car right up to the front door, step out, and your room is waiting. No elevators. No hallways. Just you and the quiet.

The room had everything I needed. A big bed. A fridge. A microwave. A TV. The usual. Nothing special, but I liked it. I always liked places like this. Comfortable in a way big places never were.

I set the A/C to 67 degrees. I always do. That's the sweet spot for me.

I had a telehealth appointment scheduled for 2 PM Central, and I wasn't sure where I'd be by then or if I'd even have a signal, so stopping here made sense. That's the thing about these kinds of road days. You never really know where you'll end up.

I laid down for a nap before the appointment. The air was cool, the bed soft, and for a little while, everything felt just right.

7: Chattanooga

The appointment went well. My doctor popped up on the screen, smiling, and we talked like old friends. Isn't telehealth amazing? I think it is. Especially for someone like me. With all my doctors and follow-ups, it's a blessing to knock out three or four appointments in one day, all from wherever I happen to be.

And if nothing's changed with my health, and I'm feeling good, then telehealth is perfect. No waiting rooms. No parking garages. Just a check-in and some peace of mind.

After the call, I walked across the lot to the "City Cafe." It's connected to the hotel and open 24 hours. I ordered country-fried steak smothered in gravy, with mashed potatoes and more gravy. Because, let's be honest, nothing tastes better after a doctor's appointment than gravy.

I sat there for a while, just eating and listening to the room hum. Laughter, forks on plates, waitresses calling out refills. It was busy, but peaceful in a way only diners can be.

I felt good. Good enough that I extended my stay until Saturday. No big plans. No tourist stops. Just rest.

8: June 30, 2021

Today was a good day. One of those slow, quiet days that sneak up on you with joy.

Yesterday, I drove over to the local Piggly Wiggly grocery store. Picked up everything I needed to make a batch of BBQ lil' smokies. It's a recipe I got from my aunt years ago, and it never misses.

I chopped up a sweet Vidalia onion, diced a bell pepper, and tossed them both into the crockpot with two packs of lil' smokie weenies. I'm sure there's a fancier name for them, but that's what I call them.

Then I poured in a whole bottle of my favorite barbecue sauce and let it all cook slow.

There's something about that smell — the way it fills the air and warms the corners of the room. You know it's going to be good long before it's done.

While the weenies cooked, I sank into the recliner, flipped on the TV, and visited Mayberry, North Carolina.

I'm a huge Andy Griffith fan. Always have been. Watching that show feels like visiting a place you forgot you missed.

And that was my day.

Just me, some BBQ in the crockpot, a visit with Andy and Barney, and a recliner room with the air set just right.

A great day indeed.

9: Heart Health Update

To all my family and friends who have kept up with me through the years, through surgeries, setbacks, and simple days filled with grace, here's the latest.

Lately, my heart's been racing more than usual. I've always had a fast heartbeat, hovering around 110 beats per minute. It's just how I've been wired, I guess. But recently, I noticed it rising higher.

At my last doctor's appointment, it hit 127.

The nurse raised an eyebrow. The doctor kept me a little longer than usual. I sat there in the exam room while they kept watch, quietly noting every beep, every number.

Since then, I've been monitoring it at home. Still high. Around 120 most days. Something's definitely going on. Maybe it's stress. Life has been heavy in its own quiet way. Or maybe it's just my heart asking for a little more attention.

The doctor referred me to a heart specialist. They called me today. I've got an appointment set for July.

In the meantime, I went on Amazon and bought myself a heart monitor. It's called the "Wellue." It connects to my phone with Bluetooth and runs like a little EKG right from my fingertips. I place my fingers on the sensor, and within seconds, the data shows up on my screen.

It's a strange comfort, being able to watch my heart like that. I'm hoping to have a month's worth of readings ready for the cardiologist when I walk into that appointment.

For now, that's all.

I'm doing alright. I just keep checking in with my heart, in more ways than one.

10: Chapters

I think life is made up of chapters.

Each one with its own setting, its own faces, its own version of me.

I've got a lot of chapters behind me now. Enough to know that when someone asks me about a memory, I have to first figure out where it belongs.

Was that before or after I lived in Virginia? Was that before 9/11? Was Nana still alive then? Was that before Tony died?

Time doesn't move in straight lines for me. It moves in chapters.

And when I look back at photos from those different seasons, I see how I tried to shape myself. My hair changed. My clothes changed. In every stage, I was trying to belong somewhere. Trying to blend in with the world, hoping it would see me and not just my Spina Bifida or my hospital records.

I remember one day in my late twenties, walking past a mirror and stopping cold.

Something had changed.

My face looked older.

Not just tired. Different. Like the first chapter of youth had quietly closed without asking me if I was ready.

I stared at myself for a while. That moment stayed with me for a whole week. It rattled me more than I expected. I wasn't the young man I thought I still was. That realization hit hard.

But the most recent time I passed by a mirror, it was different.

I saw the change again. My hair was greyer, not as soft as I remembered. My eyes had shifted too — not just older, but deeper somehow. Softer.

And this time, I didn't feel scared.

I smiled.

I thought about all the places I've been, all the people I've loved, all the days I thought would break me but didn't.

And I said to myself, quietly, "I look pretty good for a man who has written so many chapters."

11: Tommy the Dawg

We have a dog named Tommy.

He's a Black Lab mix, though we've never been quite sure what the mix is. It doesn't really matter. What matters is that he's ours.

I call him "Tommy the Dawg." You have to spell it that way. It just feels right.

This morning, Tommy discovered something brand new.

His reflection.

I sat with my coffee, watching as he stood in front of the window, barking like he'd just spotted an intruder. He barked, paused, tilted his head, then barked again, as if trying to convince the other dog to leave. But that dog wouldn't budge. Because it was him.

For ten whole minutes, he argued with himself. I didn't stop him right away. I sat there, watching, thinking. Wondering how I could make him understand.

Sometimes, when I don't know how to talk to an animal, I ask Jesus to do it for me. I know that sounds strange, but I believe He can speak to them when we can't.

After a while, I got up and walked over.

I stood beside Tommy and looked into the window with him. Then I lifted my hand and waved at our reflection. In the glass, he could see me waving.

Then, still in front of the window, I reached down and petted Tommy.

He watched as the man in the window reached down and petted his dog too.

"See, buddy," I said, smiling, "it's just our reflections."

We stayed like that a while. I patted his head. He stared quietly. No more barking. Just watching.

I think he figured it out.

Maybe next time, he'll recognize himself right away.

Or maybe not.

Time will tell.

12: My Baptism

Twenty-six years had passed since I got saved.

In that time, I had gone through a lot. I had finished college. Earned certifications in Microsoft, Novell, and CompTIA. I had built a career as an IT manager — and then left it when my doctor signed the papers that put me on disability.

I had buried people I loved.

Nana passed from brain cancer. My brother Tony died at just thirty-eight, taken by a brain hemorrhage. His loss still sits with me in quiet moments.

Eventually, I moved out of Huntsville and into the Birmingham area to live with family. It was what the doctor recommended, and I knew it was what God wanted too.

I rented out my house in Huntsville. Still do.

One afternoon, I was talking with my nephew and told him I was thinking about getting baptized.

His face lit up.

"You should let my preacher baptize you! Brother Steve would love to. He really would."

I told him I'd think about it.

I wanted the right person. Baptism meant something big to me. It wasn't just a ritual. It was a declaration.

I had already visited my nephew's church a couple of times. I liked it. I liked Brother Steve. It was early May 2015, and I felt like I was getting closer to the moment.

Then one night, I was reading my Bible, and I came to the part where Jesus Himself gets baptized by John.

I had read that passage a hundred times before.

But this time, it stopped me.

If Jesus — perfect, holy, blameless — chose to be baptized, then I knew it was time.

Not long after that, my nephew passed away. He was just sixteen.

It was sudden, and it was heartbreaking.

Brother Steve preached the funeral. I sat there in the church, listening to him talk about my nephew, and I felt the Spirit speak to me.

That's when I knew.

Brother Steve was the one who should baptize me.

We made plans, but there was a complication. I have a urostomy and colostomy. My stomach is heavily scarred from over thirty surgeries. I don't take baths. Just showers. Full submersion wasn't something I did.

Brother Steve listened. Then he came up with a plan.

"We'll wrap your stomach in Saran Wrap. Keep the water out," he said.

I agreed.

I invited everyone I could think of. Friends. Family. Even my oldest brother, who left his lake vacation early to come and record it.

July 11, 2015.

7-11-15.

Lucky numbers.

The church was full, just like a regular Sunday. Everyone I invited showed up. I wore one of my nephew's pairs of shorts under the robe.

Mom said she had never seen me look so calm.

And the Saran Wrap worked, by the way.

That day was the second-best day of my life.

The best?

The day I got saved.

I opened my eyes to cold, white fluorescent lights.

The room was still. Too still.

I was in a hospital bed.

I remembered I was supposed to have surgery. Normally, when I wake up from surgery, there's a nurse or someone nearby checking charts, and I'm in a room with other patients, all of us slowly blinking back into the world.

But something was wrong this time.

Beside me, a nurse leaned in, her voice calm but urgent. "Breathe in… breathe out… Mr. Thomas, I need you to breathe in."

For a moment, I wondered, had I been breathing for her this whole time? I took a breath in, and pain shot through my body. My brain was telling me to stop. It was telling me I didn't need oxygen. I forced the breath out.

The nurse's voice stayed steady. "Sir, do you remember what you're here for?"

I shook my head. "No."

She nodded gently. "You have to keep breathing. Your body is septic. You're very sick. You need to keep breathing."

"Breathe in… breathe out…"

She pointed to the monitor beside me. "Mr. Thomas, you see this number on the screen?"

I turned, slow and heavy, and saw it. The number: 18.

"We have to keep this number above 21, or else we will have to put you on a ventilator."

"Breathe in… breathe out…"

Somewhere in the corner of the room, two nurses entered, carrying bags of blood. They set them carefully on a table.

"Sir, your white blood cell count is very high," my breathing coach told me softly. "We're going to give you blood to help bring it down."

"Breathe in… breathe out…"

The two nurses began reading off numbers from the bags. One called out the numbers.

The other answered, "Check." Then they switched. Every number was double-checked, triple-checked.

They hooked the bags to my IV, then quietly left.

My breathing coach stayed beside me. "Your family is coming in to see you. You have to keep breathing."

I closed my eyes for a second.

When I opened them, my aunt was sitting next to me. She smiled gently and took the nurse's place.

"Do you see this number?" she asked.

I nodded.

"It has to get to 21 and stay there, or they'll put you on a breathing machine. And you don't want that tube down your throat."

I focused. Breathed in. Breathed out.

I watched the number climb.

21.

I looked up at the clock on the wall: 3:30. I pointed to my wrist, giving the universal sign for "What time is it?"

My aunt leaned in. "It's 3:30 AM."

If they were here at 3:30 in the morning, it wasn't good. People don't gather at a hospital in the middle of the night if things are fine.

"Breathe in... breathe out..."

Momma took my hand. I could barely speak.

I squeezed out the words, "It's bad, isn't it?"

She held my hand tighter. "It's going to be okay. Just keep breathing for now."

That's how we are in my family. We take care of the problem in front of us, one thing at a time. Right now, I just needed to breathe.

"Breathe in... breathe out..."

My family had to leave the room.

Each person came and kissed me — on the forehead, on the cheek — one by one.

Then my breathing coach came back in, settling into place beside me.

"Breathe in... breathe out..."

Hours passed.

"Breathe in... breathe out... breathe in... breathe out..."

At some point, I noticed something in the corner of my eye.

I turned my head, slow and heavy, and saw a man standing over me.

He was tall—towering, really—at least six foot five, maybe taller. Broad-shouldered, strong. He had the kind of presence that filled a room without saying a word. Not an ounce of fat on him. Just solid.

He spoke softly. "Mr. Thomas, I'm a chaplain here at the hospital."

I looked at him, eyes stinging with tears, and asked, "It's bad, isn't it?"

Unlike Mom, he didn't soften the truth. "Yes, sir. I'm afraid it is severe," he said quietly. Then he gave a faint smile and added, "They never call me in for the birth of a baby, sir."

"Breathe in… breathe out…"

The chaplain leaned in gently. "Sir, you may die tonight. Have you ever thought about the afterlife?"

I nodded. "Yes."

Tears rolled down

 my face.

"Breathe in… breathe out…"

Inside, I was desperate to tell him. I wanted to shout it, to make it clear. I'm saved. I'm saved! But I was too weak. My voice barely existed.

"Breathe in… breathe out…"

The chaplain asked, "Sir, are you a Christian?"

I nodded again. "Yes."

Suddenly, like a burst of light inside me, I found the energy.

I reached up, pulled the oxygen mask from my face, and gasped, "I got saved. I got saved at The Verdict at Gardendale First Baptist Church."

I caught my breath again, then added, "Jesus Christ is my Lord and Savior."

Then I put the mask back on.

"Breathe in… breathe out…"

The chaplain smiled. "You're doing good, Mr. Thomas. You have the number at 23 breaths per minute."

Then he reached out and took my hand.

I remember the way his hand felt. Smooth. Silky. Kind. That touch broke something open in me, and I cried harder.

"Sir, would you like for me to pray for you?"

I nodded. "Yes."

"Breathe in… breathe out…"

I don't remember all the words, but to this day, I believe he combined two prayers into one.

One prayer asking God to heal me. Another prayer asking God to accept my soul if He decided to bring me home that night.

When the chaplain finished, he began to pull his hand away.

But I didn't let go.

I couldn't.

I needed him there, just a little longer.

He leaned close. "Sir, do you want me to stay with you a bit longer?"

I nodded. "Yes."

"Breathe in… breathe out…"

Lying there, I thought about what he had said — about never being called for a birth.

"All he sees is bad stuff," I thought.

Then something stirred inside me.

I made a quiet promise, "I'm not dying. This chaplain is not seeing me die—not tonight. I'm not doing that to him. He's seen enough death."

And so I kept breathing.

Breathe in… breathe out…

14: Intussusception of the Bowel

I don't know if you've ever had a near-death experience, but in 1985, when I was ten years old, I faced death for the first time that I can remember.

It started like this.

My stomach hurt. Bad. Then I couldn't keep anything down. I was doubled over, vomiting, crying. Mom rushed me to the pediatrician.

When we got to the doctor's office, the waiting room was packed with other kids and their parents. I remember the noise—all the chatter, the movement—making me feel even sicker.

I told Mom I was going to lie down in the hallway.

My next memory was of the doctor examining me.

I loved that doctor. As much as a ten-year-old kid can love his pediatrician. He had taken care of me for years, and I saw him all the way up until I was eighteen, when he finally had to sit me down and say, "It's time to find a grown-up doctor."

He rubbed my stomach, gentle but focused. I think they took an X-ray too.

With my Spina Bifida, I lack feeling in many places, so by the time I sense something is wrong, it's usually already bad.

Then, suddenly, the doctor stopped.

He turned to my mom and said, "We don't have time to call an ambulance. Get him to the hospital now. I'll call ahead and meet you there. He's dying."

I don't know much about kids, but I do know you're not supposed to say "He's dying" in front of them. But in his defense, he was always honest. And to be fair, back then, not much was known about Spina Bifida. Doctors had told my family for years, "We don't know what's going to happen to Lynn."

But I hadn't really thought I could die—not until that moment.

In the car, as Mom drove faster than I'd ever seen her drive, I cried out, "I'm dying!"

Mom gripped the wheel and tried to reassure me. "No, you're not, baby."

When we reached the hospital, they weren't waiting with a wheelchair. They were waiting with a bed.

It was Carraway Hospital. It's closed now—just an old, abandoned building—but back then, I knew it well. I had been there so many times they always gave me the same room, the one right next to the kid's playroom. Even today, when I drive past that crumbling building, I can look up and see the window of my room.

My next memory is of being wheeled down the hallway.

I was holding Mom's hand, and she was running to keep up with the bed as the nurses rushed me toward surgery.

I looked at her and told her, "I love you."

The doctors said I was going into surgery right away. As they pushed me under the bright hospital lights, I remember thinking, "I don't want to go to Heaven yet."

I was just ten. Ten years old and facing death. And I was scared.

My next memory was waking up in my hospital room.

The pain was sharp, pulling. They had used staples, not stitches, to close me up, and they hurt. To this day, I always tell surgeons before any procedure, "Please, no staples."

I looked at Mom. "What happened?"

She told me, and her words have been etched into my mind ever since—and onto every medical form I've filled out since.

I had an intussusception of the bowel. A telescoping of the intestine.

When that happens, blood and fluids can't pass through, causing infection and even death to the tissue. That's what had happened to me. A large section of my bowel had died, and the surgeons had to remove it.

One of the good things about being a ten-year-old in the hospital was all the cards and flowers people sent. But honestly, a ten-year-old doesn't care about flowers.

What I did care about was the Mickey Mouse watch the guys from my dad's work gave me. They all pitched in and bought it for me.

I loved that watch.

I had it for years, until one day when we moved houses. I put it, along with other valuables, into a wooden box and buried it in the woods. I always told myself I'd go back one day and dig it up. But now, I wouldn't even know where to look. And honestly, I doubt that box—buried just a foot below the ground—survived this long.

When it came time to remove the staples from my stomach, one of them had bent inward. When the doctor tried to pull it out, it didn't come. Instead, he pulled my skin straight up.

It felt like it took him thirty minutes—at least in my ten-year-old mind—to straighten that staple enough to get it out.

And again, that's why I don't allow staples anymore.

These days, after any surgery, the first thing I do when I wake up is check to see what they used to close me up. Nowadays, they use thick surgical thread—it looks like deep-sea fishing line, at least to me—and I'm okay with that.

That one experience lit a fire inside me.

It started something that would shape the rest of my life.

My quest.

My quest to find out what happens after you die.

A quest that, eventually, would lead me to Jesus.

15: Spina Bifida Clinic

To everyone who keeps up with my health, I wanted to let you know:

Tomorrow, I have an all-day appointment at the Spina Bifida Clinic.

It's not something I ever look forward to.

Not because of the doctors or the staff. They're good people. But when I walk into that place, I see so many other patients worse off than me.

Some are in wheelchairs. Some are lying in beds.

And I feel it.

I feel the weight of walking into that room on my own two feet. I feel the guilt of it. I know I'm blessed, but some days, it's hard to carry that blessing when you see others struggling so much harder.

The appointment will last all day. I could be there until 6 PM.

I've been thinking about maybe getting a hotel room nearby, just for the day. Just somewhere to lie down between appointments.

Sometimes there's a long wait—hours, even—between seeing one doctor and the next. Having a quiet place to rest, even for a little while, would be nice.

But honestly, the hotels are probably full. Many patients come from out of town and stay overnight.

I'll be seeing, I think, four doctors tomorrow. There will be several tests, too.

It's going to be a long day.

That's all for now.

16: Spina Bifida Clinic Appointment

Today, I made it to my appointment at the Spina Bifida Clinic.

This clinic is a little different from most—it focuses specifically on adults living with Spina Bifida. That's rare. You might not know this, but there just isn't a lot of information out there about adults like me. Children with Spina Bifida? Sure. But adults? We're kind of a mystery. UAB Hospital in Birmingham is one of the few places that has a full program for us.

While I was waiting, I met a mother and son that reminded me a whole lot of my momma and me. The mother told me that her boy used to walk when he was little, up until around ten years old. He wasn't steady on his feet, but he got around. Now, at twenty-four, he's in a wheelchair full-time.

They had moved from Georgia to Alabama just to be closer to this clinic. Watching them laugh together all day… it did something to me. It felt like looking in a mirror, just a few years back. They were kind, and it was good to talk with them.

For lunch, I had planned on getting Chinese food.

But if you've ever been to downtown Birmingham, you know it doesn't work that way. You don't pick the restaurant—you park wherever you can find a spot and eat whatever is closest. I found a space near a Burger King. So that was lunch.

I did manage to drive the wrong way down a one-way street trying to get there. No cars were coming, thank God. Still, I'm pretty sure somebody's telling a story about me tonight at their dinner table.

They ran quite a few tests today—X-rays, ultrasounds, and the usual poking and prodding.

I already knew I had a kidney issue called hydronephrosis. My urologist has been keeping tabs on it for years. The scans today showed that it's gotten worse since my last visit. They let him know. That was the only change. Everything else was steady, and for me, that's good news.

Later, I sat down with Dr. Clayton, the neurosurgeon. He's sharp and kind, one of those doctors you feel lucky to talk to. I told him everything I've been dealing with from my tethered spinal cord. He really listened, and I left feeling heard.

At the end of the day, I joined a few research surveys. I always say yes when they ask. If my answers can help even one person in the future, then I'll keep showing up.

That's all for now.

17: Dentist Visit

Spent some time at the dentist's office today getting a temporary installed. I like saying it like that. Makes it sound mechanical.

I dread dental work. Honestly, I'd rather go through another surgery than sit in that chair for anything like this.

The dentist numbed my face so he could do what he needed to do. I don't mind shots—unless they're going into my mouth. Something about watching a needle come at your face and just letting it happen doesn't feel natural. It goes against every instinct.

They offered laughing gas. I declined.

I just gripped the armrests tight and let them go ahead with it. Face numb, jaw frozen, mouth full of tools.

When I got home, I waited for the numbness to wear off and had myself a mashed-up potato. That potato hit the spot.

That's all for today.

18: Restless Night

Last night, I couldn't sleep.

Not because of the bed—it's a great bed, comfortable in all the right ways. But my spinal cord had other plans.

With Spina Bifida comes something called a tethered spinal cord. And when it flares up, it feels like someone has a tight grip on the cord and is pulling it straight upward, slow and steady. The pain gets deep. Last night, it wouldn't let up.

When this happens, I know the routine. Staying still makes it worse. Moving around helps. So I moved.

I took a shower just to get through the ache and ended up going ahead and changing out my wafers and bags on my colostomy and urostomy. I was supposed to do it today anyway.

Then I slipped out and went next door to the 24-hour gas station. Got myself some snacks and walked around a bit. I knew sitting down in a restaurant wouldn't help. I'd have to stay still, and my body didn't want that.

The pain has calmed down now. I'm back home and thinking about crawling into bed again.

And when I wake up, I think I'll head over to Waffle House and treat myself to the steak and eggs.

That's all for now.

19: Evening Update 5/20/21

Most of the people staying at this motel work long days. They're blue-collar men—hard hats, work boots, lunchboxes packed in the early morning hours.

One group in particular stood out. Big guys with sun-leathered skin and strong backs. I overheard someone say they travel around the country laying pipe, job to job, town to town.

Starting around 5 a.m., one by one, they step out of their rooms and pack their trucks. The parking lot hums quietly with the sound of diesel engines and radio static. By 6:30, the lot is mostly empty.

Then, right around 4 in the afternoon, the trucks roll back in.

The men gather outside in folding chairs, talking about their day. Some light cigarettes. Some lean against their bumpers with a cold drink in hand. They laugh about work and talk softly about their wives, their kids, their lives back home.

By 8 p.m., most of them have gone back to their rooms. The whole rhythm resets again the next morning.

I overheard one of the bosses letting the guys know they'd be heading to a new job site by Wednesday. Seems like their lives are always in motion—new towns, new roads, always packing up, always moving forward.

After he walked away, I heard one of the men sigh and say, "I'll be glad when I can get back to my wife…"

Another nodded. "Yeah, I can't wait to see my kids."

They didn't know I was nearby, getting some of my medical supplies out of the truck. But I heard them, and I understood them. That ache for home.

Out on the road, you start noticing everything. I've seen more Amazon trailers pass this place than I can count. UPS trucks, too. Makes me wonder if there's a distribution center nearby. That or this is just a highway where the world moves through without stopping.

I think I'll shower and head to Waffle House for something warm.

That's all for now.

20: Morning Breakfast

It's 11:20 a.m. here in Chattanooga. I just got back to my room after having breakfast at the City Cafe downstairs.

It's a familiar place. We had one in Huntsville, too. When I worked there, I'd walk over from the office for breakfast or lunch. Same booths. Same menus. Same comfort.

This one's connected to the motel I'm staying at, and if I show my room key, I get a little discount. Nothing big, but it feels nice to be thought of.

Today I had a biscuit and gravy, bacon, and hashbrowns. Coffee and water to drink.

The City Cafe is famous for its desserts. The dessert menu alone is three or four pages long. They've got every kind of cake you can think of, along with pies, cookies, cannoli, and more.

I brought three cannoli and a slice of coconut pie back to my room. They're in the mini-fridge, waiting for me. I'll eat them later when my blood sugar comes back down a little.

For now, I'm going to put on a documentary and fall asleep.

That's all for now.

21: Friday Night in the City

The motel I'm staying in sits on one of Chattanooga's main roads.

All night long, I've been hearing emergency vehicles pass by—sirens from ambulances, fire trucks, and police cars echoing down the street. It's Friday night in the city.

Each time I hear a siren, I whisper a prayer for whoever they're rushing to help. I don't know their names, but God does.

There's a big gas station next door. Behind it, there's a large parking lot where the long-haul truckers park and sleep. Tonight, I counted over twenty diesel trucks lined up back there.

Out front, I stood for a little while. The air was humid, and the city never seemed to settle down. I could hear it all—the low rumble of traffic, the sharp honk of horns, the rise and fall of sirens, and, now and then, the burst of laughter.

A group of young adults, dressed in caps and gowns, filled the front of the City Cafe. Their parents were snapping pictures, hugging them tight. It must've been graduation night.

The kids looked full of joy, glowing like the world was finally theirs to hold.

I said a quiet prayer for them too.

22: Chattanooga

We had guests coming to stay at the cabin, so I needed to leave.

But on the drive back, something inside me said not yet. I wasn't ready to go home. So I stopped in Chattanooga and got myself a room at the Best Western.

I didn't go out to explore. Didn't see the river or the bridges or the museums.

Instead, I stayed in my room. Put on my laptop and spent the afternoon binge-watching old shows—Seinfeld, Andy Griffith, Friends. It was exactly what I needed.

I ordered a pizza from Papa John's, had it delivered right to the door. I changed my checkout to Sunday.

Sometimes, you don't need much. Just a soft bed, a quiet show, and a little time to breathe.

That's all from me.

23: Peein' Blood

Funny story.

Years ago, I had surgery to receive an artificial sphincter muscle. It was a big deal—life-changing, actually. The procedure went well, and everything looked good. After the operation, they sent me home with a Foley catheter. That's the kind that goes right into your urethra and connects to a nighttime urine bag.

That bag had a little hook on it so you could hang it on the side of the bed while you slept. I decided to hang mine on the handle of my chest of drawers, which sat just beside the bed.

One night, I was lying in bed watching TV, minding my own business, when I heard a noise at the window. A scratching sound. Then the window began to lift.

I looked over—and saw someone climbing in.

I panicked.

Didn't even think. I just jumped out of bed and took off running.

But I didn't get far.

Suddenly, my whole body jerked backward. I hit the floor, yanked hard by the Foley catheter, which had pulled tight. The urine bag was still hooked to the chest of drawers, and it had snatched me right back like a dog on a leash.

The pain was instant. Sharp. Like lightning up my spine.

Then I heard him.

"GOTCHA!"

It was my brother—coming through the window to scare me.

He succeeded.

I was peeing blood for two days.

It's tough growing up the youngest of three boys.

24: Naming My Ostomies

At this point in my life, I've had a colostomy and a urostomy. It's not unusual for people with disabilities to end up needing one—or both. I got both.

During one hospital stay, I was recovering from my urostomy surgery when a wound care nurse came into the room.

She asked me something I didn't expect.

"Have you named your newly installed urostomy yet?"

I looked at her, surprised.

"I didn't know I was supposed to."

She tilted her head. "You haven't named your colostomy either?"

"No, ma'am."

She smiled. "You need to name both of them. That's what the others do."

I didn't realize ostomy naming was a thing, but apparently it is.

So I thought about it.

If I'm going to give them names, I want the names to fit.

First off, they're close to each other, physically. So they're clearly friends.

I'm a guy, so they needed guy names.

They also get on my nerves. They never behave. They make noise at the worst times, and they've gotten me into more than a few awkward situations.

I sat there thinking about famous pairs who had those kinds of qualities—and then it came to me.

Lenny and Squiggy.

That was it.

My colostomy is "Lenny." My urostomy is "Squiggy."

They've been traveling with me ever since.

25: PCP Six-Month Check-Up

Today, I had my six-month check-up with my Primary Care Physician.

My heart rate has always been on the high side. Even when I was a teenager, it ran fast. Nothing new there. My doctor has kept a close eye on it over the years. I've even worn heart monitors to track it.

Whenever I've been in the hospital, lying down and resting, my heart rate usually stays around 90 beats per minute.

That's what we're used to seeing.

Lately, though, it's been climbing. On average, I've noticed it hovering around 110 bpm—and yes, I know that's fast.

But today, it went even higher.

At my appointment, the reading was 127 bpm. The doctor wasn't too happy about that. She kept me at the clinic for two hours, just monitoring it. The lowest it got was 120.

We went over everything. I told her how many caffeinated drinks I'd had that morning. She also reviewed every single medication I take. After going through them all, she didn't think the heart rate increase was medication-related.

As I sit here now, typing this, I checked it again. It's at 115 bpm—though to be fair, I was just up walking around.

My doctor said a cardiologist's office would be calling me soon to schedule an appointment. So that's next.

We'll see where it leads.

That's all for now.

26: A Frog Named Red

Watching someone you love fade from healthy to gone in six short months is something that stays with you.

My grandmother, who I always called "Nana," had been diagnosed with cancer. The doctors said six months. And they were right.

Every day during that time, Papa and I would drive down from Huntsville to see her. She and Pawpaw lived outside of town, and each visit felt both urgent and sacred. Then I'd drive home, park, and head inside to my little house in Huntsville.

And every night, sitting there on the back porch waiting for me, was a small red frog.

I'd pick him up, sit in the swing out back, and hold him for a while. Just me and the frog. I didn't know if it was a he or she, but something told me it was a he. So I guessed.

Every night I came back from seeing Nana, he was there.

After Nana's funeral, I came home and there he was again, just like always. This time, I named him. I called him "Red."

Red stayed for three more nights after the funeral. Then he disappeared.

Years passed. Then in 2010, I buried my brother.

Tony.

I came back to my house in Huntsville after the service. I walked up the steps, and there he was again. Red. I hadn't seen him in years. Not a glimpse.

But there he sat, on the back porch like he'd been waiting.

He came back for three nights. And then… he was gone again.

More time passed. My own health declined. I had to move back in with family, closer to Birmingham, and I rented out the house in Huntsville.

Then, not long ago, I had to attend the funeral of my nephew. A deep loss. One I still don't fully know how to speak about.

Driving back from that service, I wasn't sure what to feel. But I thought of Red. I wondered if he was back on that old porch in Huntsville, the house I couldn't go check on anymore. I wished I could drive up there just to look.

But when I pulled into the driveway of my current home, I didn't need to go to Huntsville.

Because there, sitting on the front porch, was a red frog.

No lie. I even took pictures.

I picked him up, just like I used to, and sat outside with him for a while. I knew it couldn't be the same frog. Different house. This one was fatter, rounder. But the color was the same. That deep red that doesn't belong in the usual southern frog catalog.

He made me feel better. In a way I can't explain.

It felt like God was sending me a message.

That my loved ones were okay. That I would be okay too.

That frog came back for the next few nights. Let me hold him. Let me sit in the quiet with him. And then he was gone.

Since then, we've lost two more people in the family, including Pawpaw.

And each time, a red frog showed up. Stayed a few days. Then disappeared, just like before.

I believe in God. So for me, it's not hard to understand.

God is using something as simple as a frog to say, "I see you. It's going to be okay."

27: May 30, 2021

Today was a good day. One of those days that starts early and leaves you full.

I got up before the sun and began moving around. My church had an outdoor service planned, and I wanted to get there early.

The weather was perfect—cool and overcast, like the kind of morning you'd find in the Smoky Mountains. Peaceful. Cloud-covered. The kind that makes you feel like you're inside a prayer.

I set up my chair and sat down to read the Scripture for the day, the one our preacher would be preaching from.

Even though we were outside, the service was streamed live, and the church made everything available digitally. We pulled up the hymns and bulletin on our phones. Technology can be a gift when it's used this way.

Brother Steve was on fire today. He preached from Daniel, 8, and it was one of those sermons that sticks with you long after the "Amen."

After the service, we gathered in a circle and prayed as a church family. Then we grilled hot dogs for whoever wanted one. Simple fellowship. Nothing fancy. But it filled a part of me that had been tired.

When I got back home, I did some cleaning in my room.

You might not know this, but ever since I had to move out of my house in Huntsville, I've been living with family. My room here is full of things from that old house. It's tight. Crowded. And since I have medical supplies to manage, it takes constant tidying to keep the clutter down.

I keep four tote bins full of supplies, all sealed and stacked. I restock them every month. It's just part of life now.

After the cleaning, I was wiped out. I went to bed around 3 p.m.

I woke up at 9 p.m. and sat down in my recliner, wide awake.

So I did what I often do on nights like this.

I started writing—first in my journal, then in my blog.

That's all for me today.

28: College Speech Class

I was born shy.

Not just quiet. Not just reserved. I mean shy. The kind of shy that feels like a weight on your chest every time a stranger says your name.

My brother Tony was the same way. Once, he needed to borrow our neighbors' encyclopedias for a school project. He couldn't do it. Too shy. So he sent me.

Me, the one who could barely look people in the eye.

I've learned how to talk a good game—on paper, in writing, maybe even online. But in person? That's a different story. It can take me years to feel comfortable enough to sit down and have a meal with someone. I'm getting better, sure, but it's been a slow climb.

So, naturally, the worst thing that could happen to a guy like me in college?

29: Speech Class

I avoided it for as long as I could. Signed up for every other credit, filled every other requirement. But I knew it was waiting for me. Eventually, I'd have to face it.

At the time, I was working as a server at a local restaurant, and one of our regulars was a college instructor. He knew my name. "Lynn," he'd say when he came in. I'd nod and say, "Mr. Wilson." He always left a good tip.

One day during lunch rush, I found the courage to ask him about his class.

"Mr. Wilson," I said, "you teach Speech, right?"

He smiled. "Sure do."

I leaned in. "Is it as bad as they say?"

He shook his head. "Not at all. I only give two grades—an A or a B. If you get up there and try, you'll get a B. If you do a good job, you'll get an A."

It sounded fair enough. But I still didn't trust myself.

So I did what I had done once before—I went to see my doctor.

"Doc," I said, "I can't give a speech. It just isn't possible. I need help. Can you write me a note or something?"

It had worked once for P.E., so I figured it was worth a shot.

No luck.

But the doctor did give me a suggestion.

"Go to the store," he said. "Get some over-the-counter sleeping pills. Thirty minutes before your speech, take half of one. It'll relax you."

(Side note: Don't try this. I'm not a doctor. This is not medical advice.)

Still, I was desperate. So I signed up for Mr. Wilson's class.

We had to give one five-minute speech every other week. I remember exactly where I sat—front row, fourth chair from the left. On speech days, I'd pull out a sleeping pill, break it in half, and take it about thirty minutes before the first person got up to speak.

Every time, I'd watch as each person went in turn—first, second, third—counting down until it was my turn.

Then I'd walk up to the podium, stare at the back wall, hold my note cards with trembling hands, and start every speech the same way:

"Oh, God…" (deep breath) "Thank you all for being here today…"

I can't tell you what any of those speeches were about. Not one.

But I got through them. And that half a sleeping pill? It helped. Maybe it was a placebo. Maybe it wasn't. All I know is that I survived.

Then came the final.

Ten minutes.

For a shy person like me, the final starts haunting you weeks in advance. I memorized where people sat in the classroom. I memorized where the clock was. I rehearsed how many steps it took to get to the podium. I didn't leave anything to chance.

This time, I figured I'd take a whole sleeping pill.

Five minutes = half a pill. Ten minutes = full pill. That was my logic.

I decided my topic would be Styrofoam.

Yes, Styrofoam.

I figured no one else would be covering it, and I could find enough material to stretch it into ten minutes.

The internet was still pretty new back then, but I used WebCrawler—the old search engine—to dig up facts and history, and some environmental stats. I was ready.

The day of the final, I took my pill thirty minutes before class started.

One student brought in a tent and demonstrated how to set it up.

Another gave an enthusiastic speech about the future of online banking. I still remember how excited she was, talking about all the possibilities of the internet.

The guy after her talked about fishing lures and the weather.

And then it was me.

I was still awake, in case you were wondering.

I stood up, walked to the podium, and looked out at the classroom.

Note cards in hand, hands still shaking.

"Oh, God…" I said, just like always. "Thank you all for being here today…"

And then I talked about Styrofoam.

Ten minutes.

And I got a B.

30: Mr. Darling

My Pawpaw's side of the family came from deep in West Virginia. Most of them are still there today.

(Hi, Aunt Nedra—I love you.)

If you go back even farther, I'm told we likely came from Great Britain. DNA tests say I'm about 75 percent British, which explains a few things. Probably my tea habit.

One summer, we had a family reunion in West Virginia. Pawpaw asked me to come along. He said he wanted to take me through his old stomping grounds—show me where he was born, where he went to school. He also wanted me to meet an old friend of his, someone named "Mr. Darling."

That was his nickname, of course. Pawpaw told me he earned it because he reminded everyone of the character Mr. Darling from *The Andy Griffith Show*. I didn't believe someone like that could exist in real life. I was curious.

To get to Mr. Darling's house, we had to drive long, winding dirt roads through thick woods and steep hills. The kind of backroads where the trees bend in toward the car and the sun gets caught in the branches. We kept driving deeper and deeper into the mountains.

At one point, I half expected to see the Robert E. Lee Natural Bridge—just like in *The Andy Griffith Show*. That's how far back we were going.

Eventually, we pulled up to a small weathered house tucked into the green. Pawpaw turned to us in the car and said, "Y'all stay here a second. Let me holler first so he knows it's me and not the revenue man."

He got out and waved toward the house.

"It's me! Claude!" he yelled.

A moment later, an old man stuck his head out the door, squinting into the daylight. Then his face lit up. He walked out slowly, holding a rifle in one hand and waving with the other.

"Come on out and meet my friend," Pawpaw called back to us.

Mr. Darling wore denim overalls and spoke with that same gentle, mountain rhythm you'd expect from the TV version. But this man wasn't acting. He was real. And I could feel right away that he had a good heart—warm and steady.

After we introduced ourselves, he took us over to a small lean-to style building beside the house. It looked like a carport, but it wasn't.

"This here," he said, patting the side, "this used to be our elementary school."

He and Pawpaw had both gone there as children.

"It even housed soldiers during the Civil War," he added, proud but quiet about it.

We stood inside the old building and talked about the history of that part of West Virginia. Then Mr. Darling turned to us and said something I'll never forget.

"You ever hear of that internet?"

We smiled and nodded.

"Well," he said, waving his hand around like the air itself was magical, "West Virginia is on that thing. I don't know how, but it is."

To him, the internet was almost witchcraft. The way he said it made it sound like we'd conjured it up out of smoke and wires.

While we were still standing in the schoolhouse, he reached up to a shelf and pulled down a tall Mason jar.

"Taste this stuff right'ch' here," he said, grinning.

We didn't taste it, as far as I remember, but we did open it and take a whiff.

It was clear, strong, and sharp as lightning.

Moonshine.

I hoped he might show us the still, but he didn't, and I didn't ask. Some things are best left unspoken.

Out in the yard, he showed us a large, flat rock. In it were round holes carved deep into the surface.

"See these?" he said. "That's where the Indians used to sit and grind with sticks. Used 'em for fire too."

He reached into his pocket and pulled out a few arrowheads.

"Sift through this dirt, and you'll find more," he said.

Pawpaw asked how he got the schoolhouse down into the yard.

He pointed up the hill. "That's where school got held. My son and I moved it ourselves. Rolled it on down here after I bought the land."

Mr. Darling had spent his life working in the coal mines. Hard work. Honest work. He did well for himself, and not just with money. Once a month, he'd head into town to buy groceries—not just for his house, but for anyone nearby who couldn't afford to buy their own. That's the kind of man he was.

He introduced us to his wife—a kind, lovely woman.

Pawpaw leaned in and asked, "Will you play your harmonica for us?"

His wife laughed gently. "It makes you run outta breath these days, hun."

Like most husbands, he didn't listen. He reached into his pocket and pulled out his harmonica.

And then, right there in the yard, he began to play mountain music. Real mountain music. Notes that twisted through the air like smoke from a chimney.

Then he danced.

And when I say danced, I mean danced like you'd see in an old movie—feet stomping, knees bouncing, full of life and rhythm. If Ernest T. Bass and the television Mr. Darling had been there, they would've joined in.

Pawpaw watched his friend with pride. Then they hugged.

Both of them knew—though no one said it—that this might be the last time they saw each other. Pawpaw lived in Alabama. Time wasn't on their side.

Years later, Mr. Darling passed away.

I never did learn his real name.

But I remember everything about him.

He didn't go to Yale or Harvard. He wasn't rich in dollars.

But he worked hard. Loved his family. Helped his neighbors. Danced when the music played. And made the best of what life gave him.

He had a wife who made their house a home.

He never met a stranger.

And he sure didn't care much for the revenue man.

He was one of the richest men I've ever known.

31: Outing with Momma

(Some stops have been left out for privacy, but the good parts are all here.)

"Where we gonna eat, Momma?"

"I don't know. Where you wanna eat?"

I leaned back in my seat and thought for a second.

"You remember when I was little, and we went to that real restaurant, and they asked me how I wanted my hamburger cooked? I didn't even know how to answer. I just said, 'It ain't a real burger if you gotta ask me how to cook it.'"

Momma chuckled.

"That's because we never asked you that at home, and McDonald's surely didn't ask."

"Yep..."

"So, where we gonna eat, Momma?"

She paused for a moment, then said, "Let's eat at Sneaky Pete's Hot Dogs."

"Okay."

We pulled in, ordered the special.

"We'll take the four hot dogs and get the fifth free. Give us a large fry and two large sodas."

We found a small table and unwrapped our hot dogs.

"I love their hot dogs," I said, biting in. "And these fries? They taste just like the ones they used to serve at the Fultondale Swimming Pool. Good stuff."

"Put some of this red pepper on your dog."

"Okay."

"That is good," I said, mouth full.

"It's a husband and wife who own this place now. I like it."

"Yeah, it is good."

We finished up, brushed the crumbs off our laps, and headed back to the car.

"Where we going next?"

"I need to stop by the Piggly Wiggly."

"Okay, let's head that way."

At the store, we wandered the aisles, each of us with our little missions.

"Hey, look, Mom, they got Banana Nut Bread in a box. Just add bananas, water, and eggs. They almost had me… but I'm not doing all that mixing. If it would've just said 'add water,' maybe…"

She smiled. "Son, go get the yogurt."

"Okay."

I came back with a pack in hand.

"What's the date on it?"

"Um… July 2nd."

"Okay, put that back and get some with a later date."

"Alright." I walked back and grabbed another.

"This one says July 17th."

"Okay, good."

"It's weird how my taste buds have changed. I never thought I'd grow up to like yogurt and cottage cheese."

She didn't even look up. "Yep."

We kept walking.

"Let's see… $3.28 for this oil. This one is $3.19. I'll get it."

"Every penny counts, don't it, Momma?"

"Yes, it does, son."

"Where we going next?"

"Home."

"Okay, good. One day they'll have Banana Nut Bread in a box, and all you gotta do is add water."

It was a good day.

32: Germs

Over the years, I've dealt with more infections than I can count. We finally decided it might be time to invest in one of those germ-killing lights.

You can look them up. They're supposed to sterilize entire rooms with ultraviolet rays.

And fewer germs in my life? That can only help.

So, I got one.

And I love it.

I don't know if it really kills germs, but my bathroom and bedroom sure smell a lot cleaner. That's good enough for me.

The way it works is simple. You turn it on with a remote and let it run for an hour—while you run for your life. Supposedly, it kills everything in the room while you're gone.

It worked so well in the house that I figured, why not try it in the truck?

Problem is, my truck's electrical system doesn't stay on unless the engine is running. So, I turned the key, left the engine on, turned on the germ-killing light, and headed back inside to relax.

I flopped down in my recliner and put something on the TV.

Next thing I know, the phone rings. I fumble through a pile of empty Diet Coke bottles on the side table and answer.

"Hello?"

It was Papa. "Hey, you know your truck is out here running?"

"Yeah," I said quickly. "I used that lamp to kill the germs."

There was a pause.

"Well, it was running last night too."

That's when it hit me.

It was morning.

"Oh, yeah," I replied, scrambling to recover. "I used it twice. Once last night and once this morning…"

Yeah. I lied. But I'm coming clean now.

I jumped up, grabbed a shirt, and walked through the house.

"I'm gonna, um, run to the gas station and get some stuff. I'll be back in time for church."

Outside, I found the truck still running—just a sliver above empty. Just enough to get to the gas station… maybe.

The air conditioner had stopped working.

"That's gonna cost about two thousand dollars," I thought.

I filled the tank with seventeen gallons and drove back home, windows down and sweat sticking to my shirt. No A/C.

So, what did I learn?

I now know how much gas gets used in twelve hours of idling—a quarter tank.

And I now know it'll burn up your air conditioner.

I have a cousin on Papa's side who owns a garage. I can already hear him shaking his head, saying, "Lynn, Lynn, Lynn…"

And my whole family will probably say the same.

So here it is:

Sorry, cousin Michael.

Sorry, Papa.

In my defense, I was just trying to stay healthy and fight off infections.

I just… fell asleep.

Next time, I'll set an alarm.

It was a costly lesson.

33: Health Update – June 28, 2021

To all the friends, family, and kind souls who keep up with my health—thank you.

You may already know, or maybe you don't, but I was diagnosed with Type II Diabetes back in 2019. Since then, I've been on medication and insulin, doing my best to keep it under control.

And for the most part, I have. My average blood sugar usually hovers between 105 and 110, which my doctor says is a pretty good range.

But this past weekend, something changed.

For reasons I couldn't explain, my blood sugar started spiking—high. Over 500 at times. I watch my carbs closely. I know I'm allowed around 45 carbs per meal, and I'm careful to stay within that limit. I've gotten good at reading labels and estimating counts. But this time, nothing made sense.

So today, my endocrinologist let me come in for blood and urine tests. I also handed over my blood sugar logs from the last seven days. He said he'd call as soon as the results came in.

I'm lucky. I really am. My medical team works closely with me, and they fit me in on a day like today without hesitation.

Now we wait.

As soon as I know more, I'll share it.

34: Spina Bifida and the Outhouse

Growing up with Spina Bifida meant a lot of things. One of those things was that I wore a diaper for much of my life. So when it came to using the bathroom, I didn't do it quite the same way as most folks.

I was born in the age of indoor plumbing—that's what I was trained to use. But that didn't mean everyone had made the switch.

My great-grandmother, Tot Tot, didn't upgrade to indoor plumbing until well into the 1980s. That meant if you needed to use the bathroom at her house, you used the outhouse. No questions asked.

I remember my first experience like it just happened.

I was probably eight or nine. We were visiting Tot Tot's house—me, Dad, and my brother Tony.

At some point during the day, I felt that familiar nudge.

"I need to go to the bathroom," I whispered to Tony.

Without even looking up, Tony said, "Go get yourself a new diaper and head to the outhouse."

Like it was no big deal.

So I grabbed a fresh diaper and walked outside. The outhouse stood just past the edge of the yard, back near the tree line. It looked like something from a different time. Weather-worn, leaning slightly to one side, with a rusty latch and wood that had gone soft with rain and age.

I stepped inside and pulled the door shut behind me. The air smelled like cedar, soil, and something older than memory.

And there it was.

The hole.

I just stood there, staring at it.

"That's a big hole," I thought.

I looked around, trying to figure out what exactly I was supposed to do with it.

Something didn't feel right.

"Tony!" I called out.

"What's wrong?" he shouted from the other side of the door.

"I think I'm in the wrong place. This can't be right."

"What do you mean?"

"I don't know what to do."

"You need to change your diaper, right? Just do what you always do."

"But where do I put the diaper?"

"Throw it in the hole."

"Won't that clog it up?"

"No, you're supposed to throw it in the hole."

"You sure?"

"Just throw it in the hole!"

His voice was growing more and more annoyed.

"Um, okay…"

It went against everything I'd been taught. The golden rule growing up was: do not throw your diaper in the toilet. And here I was, standing in a wooden shack, about to do just that.

But I did it.

I tossed the used diaper into the hole and walked out.

Part of me half expected Tony to jump out laughing, and yelling "Gotcha!" like he always did.

But he didn't.

He just nodded like it was any other Tuesday.

And I walked out of that outhouse a new person. A wiser person.

Not long after that, Tot Tot finally got indoor plumbing.

But I never forgot the lesson from that day—sometimes the hole is the right place, even if everything you've learned tells you otherwise.

35: July 4th, 2021

Happy Independence Day, 2021.

It was a better day—much better—than July 4th, 2020.

The morning started early. Like most mornings, my body felt like it had been through a long night of quiet battle. Spina bifida doesn't sleep, and neither does the pain it leaves behind. There were neuropathic twinges, deep muscle aches, and sharp bone pains that flared up when I moved just right—or wrong.

So I moved—slowly at first, stretching, shifting weight from one leg to the other, coaxing my body awake. Movement helps. It loosens the knots, quiets the nerves, and gives me a fighting chance at starting the day without being dragged down by discomfort.

I knew we were headed to my aunt and uncle's house in the afternoon, and I wanted to be in a decent place before we got there. Not pain-free—that is rare—but good enough. Good enough to sit, laugh, eat, and listen. And it worked.

When we arrived, the house was already alive with voices, laughter, and the smell of summer sunlight on grass, charcoal smoke, and food that only gets made once a year. There is something about family gatherings that feels like time travel. You walk in, and suddenly, everyone is younger, the air is lighter, and memories rise like steam from a plate of home-cooked food.

That is where I learned about the Colonel.

Turns out, I am related to a man who fought in the Revolutionary War. My great-grandmother's side—the Rogers family—has roots deeper than I ever imagined. A cousin dug through old records and traced our bloodline back to a Colonel who stood for independence when it cost people their lives.

Mom showed me the paperwork. She even went to a DAR meeting once with my cousin, thinking she might join. In the end, she decided not to. The process is strict, the documentation exacting. But now it sits with me—the idea, the possibility.

Maybe I will try to join. If they meet often enough, if I can get the papers in order, maybe I will take part in something bigger than myself—something that ties me to history in a way I never expected.

For lunch, I had:

Baked beans

Corn on the cob

Potato salad

Deviled eggs

Smoked BBQ

with banana pepper, onion, and tomato on the side

No dessert—not because I did not want any, but because the meal alone carried more carbs than I usually allow myself. Diabetes is always watching. Always calculating. Even on holidays.

36: Diabetes Health Update

To all who keep up with my health:

Last week, things got weird. Blood sugar spiked past 500, and nothing I did seemed to bring it down.

So I went to the doctor. My endocrinologist took blood work, looked at my logs, and gave me a plan.

He doubled my morning insulin dose.

Then, I take 14 units of fast-acting insulin—Humalog—before or after each meal. That part scares me a little. Confuses me, too.

The first time I took 14 units, my blood sugar dropped into the 60s fast. I remember the chill, the sweat, and the shaking hands. I had to scarf down juice, candy, or anything else to bring it back up. It left me rattled.

So now, I do things differently. I eat first, check my levels, and then give myself Humalog based on what the number says.

It is not a textbook. But it works—for now.

I am still learning. Still figuring out how to live with this. How to treat it, respect it, and not let it run my life.

But I will learn. And eventually, it will get easier.

That is all for now.

37: Space Shuttle Challenger

On January 28th, 1986, Mom, Nana, and I sat together in front of the TV. We were going to watch the launch of the space shuttle *Challenger*.

It was not how I imagined spending my day. I had broken my leg in two places while riding my BMX bike. A cast ran from my foot all the way up to my hip. I couldn't walk. I couldn't move fast. I had to be homeschooled for six weeks.

That morning, my tutor came and went. After he left, we got everything ready. Snacks, drinks, and the television were tuned in early. Mom said we'd watch the liftoff and then go out for Chinese food. That felt like a holiday.

Back then, everyone cared about space. Everyone watched. Schools wheeled TVs into classrooms so students could see history happening live. This was one of those moments.

I remember being in the restroom, trying to hurry, trying to get back on time. My cast made moving slow, making everything harder. Mom had to help me change my diaper. Spina bifida meant I always wore one. With the cast, it was a struggle. Every motion was awkward. Every second mattered.

From the other room, Nana called out, "Y'all are missing the launch! T-minus ten seconds!"

Mom and I moved as fast as we could. I washed my hands, grabbed my crutches, and made my way to the living room.

When I finally got there, all I saw on the screen was fire.

Just a ball of fire against the blue sky.

I didn't understand. I asked where the shuttle was.

Nana said, "I think it blew up. Something's not right."

Then she said again, "It blew up, I think."

The newscaster cut in. His voice was steady but serious. He told the world what we already feared: the space shuttle *Challenger* had exploded.

My heart sank.

I remember saying quietly, "That teacher was on board."

Christa McAuliffe. A real teacher. The first teacher in space. NASA had chosen her from more than eleven thousand applicants. She was supposed to inspire kids like me—to show us that anything was possible.

Mom and I sat still. Silent.

Nana kept repeating it over and over. "It just blew up."

We watched as boats and planes searched the ocean below. There was no debris field—just smoke and silence.

The newscaster tried to offer hope. He said the part of the shuttle where the crew was sitting might have survived. Maybe they were okay, maybe they were floating, and maybe someone would find them.

He was trying to give us something to hold onto.

Hours passed.

Finally, we got up, got dressed, and went out to eat. The only Chinese restaurant nearby was open. I ordered Beef with Broccoli. It was my favorite then—and still is—but I don't remember tasting it that night.

Not one of us said a word during dinner.

Later that evening, President Reagan spoke on television. His face was calm but heavy with grief.

He told us the truth. All seven crew members had died.

I remember tears coming when he said, "They slipped the surly bonds of earth to touch the face of God."

Even now, typing those words, I can feel my eyes well up.

Tony came home from school later that day. He had watched the explosion with his class. His eyes were red. His face was pale. He didn't say much. He didn't need to.

We all knew what we had seen.

All of America did.

Growing up, I didn't get to do many things that young kids get to do.

Things like Field Trips, Summer Camp, or even joining the Boy Scouts were out for me. It may have been my decision. But to tell you the truth, I don't remember. I do know that it would have meant me taking medical supplies with me, and I did not want to deal with that as a kid.

So, "Meet-Ups" and "Get-Togethers," other than our family reunion, were out for me.

Plus, I've never been a big fan of crowds.

That is all going to change this year, though. Yep. In the year 2021, Lynn is going to a "Meet-Up." Andy Griffith style.

Most people who know me know that I am a big fan of Andy Griffith. I'm an even bigger fan of *The Andy Griffith Show,* or TAGS for us Mayberrians.

A lot of people go to Star Trek conventions and other things, such as Comic-Con. Well, I'll be traveling to Mt. Airy, NC, for a "Mayberry Meet-Up."

Yes, for five days and four nights, I will be meeting up with a group of Mayberrians to hang out in Andy Griffith's hometown.

At night, hundreds of us will meet at a pavilion and watch *The Andy Griffith Show* on a big screen. I even have to bring a portable AM/FM radio to tune in to listen to the show. (Fancy.)

I won't be alone for the ride. I do have two family members going with me.

We will head out on the 14th of this month, drive for about five or six hours, and get a motel room off the interstate. Then, on the 15th, we will finish the rest of the drive into Mt. Airy, NC.

I'm super excited and have ordered extra medical supplies to carry with me.

I hope to have many stories to tell while on the trip. If all goes well, we will be gone from the 14th through the 19th and arrive back home on the 20th.

That is the latest on me.

39: Health Update 7/8/21

To all who keep up with my health:

I've always had a fast heartbeat.

However, on my last visit to my Primary Care Physician, my heart rate was in the 120s BPM, so I was referred to a heart doctor. I had that visit today.

I had an EKG done, and as usual, my heart rate hovered around 110 BPM.

The doctor thought I should wear a monitor for two weeks and have a stress test on my heart.

Heart monitors have come a long way. It's now a tiny device that tapes to your shoulder—nothing like those old ones with eight wires taped to your chest.

I'll wear this one for two weeks, then take it off, put it in the already addressed box, and mail it back. Simple.

I'll have the stress test in August. I'm not looking forward to that.

That's the latest on me.

40: 7/9/21 – Busy Day

I had a busy day today.

Let me start by saying that my bedroom is my living space. It has a recliner, a bed, a TV, and a handicapped bathroom.

It also holds many medical supplies, which are stored in clear, 64-quart storage boxes stacked on top of each other.

And there are things from my house in Huntsville, Ala., where I lived my bachelor's life—things I can't store anywhere else. Things I don't want to part with.

My mom says my room isn't "homie or welcoming" at all. And I agree.

To fix that, we had my cousin bring in a piece of furniture. We're not sure what it's called—we're going with "armoire," though.

So I spent the day clearing out four 64-quart storage boxes and putting my medical supplies inside the armoire. (If that's even what it is.)

I'll admit—it looks better now. Works better, too.

Before, I had to move boxes around just to find what I needed. Now, I open a door and grab what I need—easy.

After that, I took a shower and went to the dentist to get my permanent crown.

His office has a TV in every room, but they never turn them on. Today, though, the TV in my room was on and tuned to The Food Network.

The easiest part of the day was sitting there, relaxed, watching meals get cooked while getting my crown placed.

I was starving by the time they were done.

Of course, the dentist said, "Don't eat for several hours. That glue needs to dry…"

41: Urine Not Looking Good

First off, I feel fine.

I'm not running a fever either.

Today—this morning, really—my urine looked real bad. Like "Pet Milk."

It's normal for me to have pus or mucus in my urine. (At least, that's what it looks like.)

Today, though, my urostomy bag looked like a bag full of Pet Milk.

Since I started traveling, my urologist and I went over what to do if I ever got sick on the road.

I keep antibiotics on hand. I also have a way to get a message to him in an emergency. And I know to flush my kidneys and drink cranberry juice.

With today being Saturday and my doctor off for the weekend, I'm doing exactly what he and I discussed.

I sent him a message and started taking my antibiotics.

I'm also flushing my kidneys.

I hope I don't wind up in the hospital. That would mean canceling my trip to Mt. Airy, NC.

That's the last thing I want.

42: Trip Update 7/12/21

I'll be headed out on Wednesday, the 14th, for Mt. Airy, NC.

I've bought extra medical supplies.

Mom and Papa gave me an early birthday gift—some new, hard-shell rolling luggage. It's the perfect present.

The luggage should arrive tomorrow, Tuesday the 13th.

Earlier today, I posted that my urine was looking bad.

I've been taking my antibiotics, and my urologist knows about it.

My urine is looking normal again. (Normal for me is different than "normal" for most people.)

I'm not running a fever, and I feel fine.

Still, I'm nervous about the trip.

But knowing I'll be with two people who love and care for me helps a lot.

43: New Luggage For Trip

Happy early birthday to me.

The luggage Mom and Papa bought for my birthday arrived today.

I couldn't wait—I tore it open and immediately started packing the new suitcase.

I had some things in my old one that I needed to move over.

When I opened the old suitcase, a familiar pamphlet stared me in the face.

It was from our last trip to Mt. Airy—promoting something called "Miracle Salve." We'd bought several jars of it back then.

I smiled while reading it. It felt like a sign. A small one, sure—but maybe the trip was already starting off right.

The luggage came in three pieces.

One—the mid-sized one—went to my niece.

I kept the large and small ones for myself.

For the trip, I'll only need one suitcase.

Everything else will go in my medical box, packed with all my supplies.

I'll also bring my emergency hospital bag—just in case.

Thanks again, Mom and Papa. I love you both.

This trip really feels like it's coming together.

44: Countdown To Trip

—T-Minus 24:00—

In 24 hours, we should be on our way to Mt. Airy, NC.

I've double-checked—and triple-checked—my medical supplies. Just to be sure I have everything.

Still, I'm anxious.

Because I'm afraid I'll forget something.

Like every time before, I connect my urostomy bag to a nighttime urine bag before bed.

My urostomy bag only holds about 400cc of liquid.

But I put out over 2000cc at night.

So the nighttime bag is a must.

To hook them together, I use a tiny connector.

Without that little piece, I'm stuck.

I'll post a picture of it later.

Long story short—(too late for that)—if I forget anything, I'll have to turn around and come back to get it.

It's happened before.

So yeah, I worry.

I made a checklist. I packed everything on it.

Still, I worry.

We're checking into our room in Mt. Airy on the 15th.

So tomorrow, we'll drive about five hours and spend the night in a motel.

Then, on the 15th, we'll head into Mt. Airy.

I called ahead and confirmed our reservation is still good.

And yes, the room has two beds.

Overall, I'm super excited to hit the road.

I'd leave today if I didn't have a doctor's appointment.

It is now T-Minus 23:00.

45: T-Minus 13:00 HRS Till Trip

—Packing For Trip—

Since I have the most things to pack, my Aunt and Uncle came over so I could get my supplies together first.

I left out what I'll need for tonight and tomorrow morning.

I also kept my laptop close—it goes everywhere with me.

Plus, I have a backup in case something happens while we're on the road.

We're right at T-Minus 13:00 hours until we leave.

46: Mt. Airy Trip – Day 1

We made our way to Dandridge, TN today.

I know that's where we are because I asked my phone, "Okay Google, where am I?"

My smartphone said back, "You're in Dandridge, TN."

We left the house around 10 AM CST, heading as close to Mt. Airy, NC, as we could get before needing rest.

That place turned out to be Dandridge, TN.

We did lose an hour near Pigeon Forge, TN, thanks to traffic from either a wreck or roadwork. We never found out exactly why we kept stopping and starting again, over and over.

We stopped for lunch at The Cracker Barrel.

I always love shopping in their old "Pop" drinks section.

I bought three drinks—all alcohol-free.

I mention that because one was called "Butterscotch Beer."

I'm guessing it's like Root Beer.

When I showed them off to Aunt Claudine, she said, "Eww! Why did you buy 'Swamp Poop'?!"

"It's not 'Swamp Poop,' Aunt Claudine! It's called 'Swamp Pop.. ' POP! Like Mountain Dew, but Swamp Pop. Get it?"

At the Dandridge exit, there were four or five hotels and motels to choose from. So we got off the ramp and started looking for a room in our price range for tonight.

I had already decided $98 would be our budget for the night.

It's Wednesday, midweek, and from traveling, I've learned that's about how much a room with two beds should cost.

First, we checked into Holiday Inn Express.

They wanted $125 for what we needed.

Aunt Claudine gave the man her famous "Mean Stare" and said, "C'mon, let's go. We'll shop around..."

In that moment, I felt like Pawpaw was in the room with us.

Next, we went to Super 8.

The price was just right—$98 for one room with two beds for one night.

We paid, got our key, and headed to our room.

If we get hungry later, we have options—Shoney's, Wendy's, and Arby's are all nearby.

Right now, we're watching the news on TV.

Aunt Claudine and Shirley are already asleep.

I'm sitting at the little table provided, typing this post.

Soon, I'll get into bed and hit the sack.

We'll get up early and finish our drive into Mt. Airy, NC.

According to my map, we're about three hours away.

We can't check in until tomorrow evening, so we'll probably do a few things once we arrive in town before checking into the Mayberry Motor Inn.

That is all for now.

47: Dandridge, TN – Can't Sleep

It's 3:30 AM when I wake up.

My left arm is killing me, and I immediately feel the old, familiar hip pain, along with the spinal cord pain.

I try to get out of bed as quietly as I can.

The only thing that helps ease this pain is walking around or sitting in a hard chair. Driving around in a vehicle also helps, and Aunt Claudine told me I could use hers if I needed to ride around. But I don't want to drive around in a strange town.

By the time I put my shorts and shirt back on, it's clear I've woken everyone up. I quietly apologize and sneak out the door of our room to go down the hall and get a Diet Coke from the machine.

When I get back to the room and sit down, the alarm clock on my smartphone goes off.

See, it's now 4:00 AM CST—but I'm in the Eastern Time Zone, so it's 5:00 AM EST.

I had set my alarm to go off at 5:00 AM yesterday, and I forgot to turn the setting off.

It's now 5:10 AM. Everyone is either back asleep or trying to get back to sleep.

I've finished my Diet Coke, and I think I'll try to sneak out again to grab a coffee from the pot in the lobby. The receptionist said they keep the coffee fresh 24 hours a day.

48: Mt. Airy – Day 1

—The Mayberry Motor Inn – Day 1—

We've arrived at "The Mayberry Motor Inn" in Mt. Airy, North Carolina.

I went straight to the front desk, signed in, and backed our vehicle up to the door of our room for easy unloading.

Within 30 minutes, we were unpacked and felt right at home.

The people here are so friendly, and guests are already gathering at the Pavilion.

A big banner hangs over the entrance that reads, "Mayberry Meet-Up – 'Relax… What's Your Hurry?'"

I walked over to the Pavilion and casually introduced myself. I shouted, "I'm Lynn; nice to meet everyone! Are y'all here for the Meet-Up?"

Everyone said they were here for the "Meet-Up."

I was still sweaty from the drive, so I didn't feel quite ready to introduce myself properly.

I've organized my medical supplies and put away my clothes.

The room has two full beds, a TV, refrigerator, microwave, and enough space for bathing, showering, and getting dressed.

I brought the internet camera that I take with me on all of my trips and got it set up over the internet.

Because of my medical issues, I use that camera so my dear mother and Papa can check in on me. It has both audio and video.

Our host, Allan Newsome, hasn't arrived yet. I can't wait to meet him and his wife in person.

That is all for now.

49: Mt. Airy – Day 2 – Morning Update

I woke up this morning to sunlight peeking through the sides of the curtains and *The Andy Griffith Show* playing on the TV.

My Aunt Claudine and my step-grandmother, Shirley, are with me on this trip.

I remember once telling Papaw that Nana stepped ahead of us into Heaven, and Shirley stepped in to take care of me the rest of the way. He and Shirley both smiled when I said that. I love Shirley dearly. In fact, I've mailed her letters through the Post Office. You know I love you if I go through the trouble of sending a letter through the U.S. Mail.

But I digress.

We're hoping to schedule a Squad Car Tour today, though we may have to wait until tomorrow.

There are a lot of people here for the "Meet-Up," and the tours might already be booked.

During this trip, I plan to take Shirley and Aunt Claudine to eat at *The Loaded Goat.* Everyone I've spoken with—including "Ms. Betty Lynn"—has told me not to miss that restaurant.

There's also a popular Soda Fountain that serves malts, ice cream, sodas, and more that I want us to try.

Tonight, though, the real fun begins.

We'll gather around the Pavilion with many other folks and watch *The Andy Griffith Show* on a big screen.

We'll use a portable AM/FM radio to listen while we watch. I can't wait.

Everyone here has been so friendly.

I briefly spoke with Allan Newsome yesterday, but I had just arrived and was still sweaty from the drive, so I didn't officially introduce myself. I'll be sure to do that today.

I've already taken my shower, put on all of my Mayberry attire, and I'm ready to go out and explore "Mayberry."

That's all for now.

50: Mt. Airy – Day 2 – Midday Update

Mt. Airy is really hopping today.

Snappy Lunch had a line out the door, and people were strolling all up and down Main Street.

The Squad Car Tours also had a line, with about a one-hour wait. We gladly waited.

I love seeing a town like Mt. Airy, NC, thriving.

All the locals have been incredibly kind to us. And no, I don't mean "Gomer's" date "Mary Grace" kind of nice—they've been genuinely nice.

The Squad Car Tour is a must if you haven't done it yet.

It starts at the Rock Quarry, which plays an important role in the town's history, then takes you through Andy Griffith's life in Mt. Airy and highlights how the town influenced *The Andy Griffith Show.*

The tour takes you down the very streets mentioned in the show, past the funeral parlor referenced in an episode, Andy Griffith's childhood home, and more.

It lasts about 45 minutes and costs $40 per tour (not including a tip for the driver).

Afterward, we came back to our room to take a nap so we'd be rested for the "Meet-Up" tonight.

I can't wait.

51: Mt. Airy – Day 2 – The Meet-Up

It's a quarter past eleven, and I've just returned to my room from the "Mayberry Meet-Up" (Day 1).

Honestly, I don't have the vocabulary to properly describe the time I had tonight.

Around 6 PM, Aunt Claudine, Shirley, and I made our way to the Pavilion.

Many people were already gathered and chatting, so we jumped right in and introduced ourselves.

I finally got to meet Mr. Allan Newsome.

He's a "Tribute Artist" and does a fantastic impression of "Floyd the Barber."

Allan and his wife, Jan, are wonderful people.

I had Aunt Claudine take a picture of Allan and me together.

—I'll let you in on a little secret, though. I'm going to have to get another picture of Allan and me because, bless her heart, Aunt Claudine didn't actually take one. She thinks she did, but she didn't. (I guess she didn't know how to use the camera on my phone.)

And I don't want to tell her—that would break her heart.

So tomorrow, I'll have to ask someone else to take a picture of Allan and me, and I'll just pass it off as the one Aunt Claudine took. I digress.

I met so many wonderful people tonight and listened to several "Tribute Artists" share incredible stories—both about themselves and about the actors from *The Andy Griffith Show* (TAGS).

One man who spoke tonight once worked security detail for Don Knotts—Barney Fife himself!

Maggie Peterson (Charlene Darling) even called in on someone's cell phone. They put her on speaker so everyone could hear. She sounded like such a lovely person.

As night fell, everyone pulled out lawn chairs and found a place to sit and watch TAGS under the stars.

As the episode began to play, I looked around and saw people from all over the country sitting together, enjoying *The Andy Griffith Show*.

I wish I could adequately describe the feeling of excitement and love I felt tonight—but I can't.

It was something magical.

…And I don't think I'll ever be able to put it into words.

I can't wait for tomorrow night.

52: Mt. Airy – Day 3

I woke up around 6:30 AM, despite not getting to bed until after midnight. Normally, I hate when that happens—but this time was different. I'm in Mt. Airy, NC. Your location really does make a big difference in life.

My plans for the day included eating at *The Loaded Goat*, taking Shirley to Main Street to shop, and then heading to *The Andy Griffith Museum* to hear a professor speak about *The Andy Griffith Show* (TAGS).

After taking a shower, I got myself ready to see the sights of this beautiful town.

By 11:00 AM, we walked into *The Loaded Goat*.

I'd heard nothing but great things about this restaurant—even *Ms. Betty Lynn* said it was her favorite place in town.

Ol' Thelma Lou recommended it, so I had to try it.

The food was excellent.

They offer appetizers like *Fried Green Tomatoes*, *Nachos*, and *Wings*.

The menu includes burgers, sandwiches, hot dogs, and much more.

I ordered the Fried Green Tomatoes as an appetizer and the *Steakhouse Burger* for my meal. It came with French fries as well.

The burger was delicious—topped with A1 Steak Sauce, an onion ring, cheddar cheese, lettuce, tomato, and pickle.

It was so big I could barely fit it in my mouth, and it was a bit messy.

But I've found that most messy food is usually the most delicious—and this burger was no exception.

Delicious.

While we were eating, Mr. Allan Newsome and his wife, Ms. Jan Newsome, stopped by our table to talk—and I finally got a picture of me with Allan. That made my day.

After lunch, we went shopping on Main Street.

We spent about an hour and a half walking around, going in and out of stores.

I bought a TAGS shirt from *The Loaded Goat* episode.

Then we made our way to *The Andy Griffith Museum* to attend the lecture.

When we arrived, the line to pay for admission was stretched outside.

We'd already done a lot of walking, and I didn't want to make Aunt Claudine and Shirley stand out there—especially with rain in the forecast.

So we returned to our room to take a nap and rest up.

I'll post later tonight about the next "Meet-Up."

That is all for now.

That's all for now.

53: Mt. Airy – Day 4

After our church service this morning, many people packed up and headed home.

Aunt Claudine, Shirley, and I, however, are staying until Monday.

So off we went—into town, specifically Main Street.

Things were quiet today, being Sunday. Most people tend to leave on Sunday, which is exactly why I prefer to leave on Monday.

Our first stop was *Barney's Café* on Main Street.

The special today was the "Barney Burger" with fries and a drink for $8.50.

For just fifty cents more, you could swap out the fries for onion rings—which all three of us did.

The burgers were delicious, and the onion rings were just as good.

To drink, we each had sweet tea served in a souvenir cup.

After lunch, we walked down to *Walker's* for dessert.

I ordered a chocolate sundae with chocolate, caramel, and hot fudge syrup. They topped it off with whipped cream and a cherry.

(I figured I'd work it off later.)

Next, I split off from Aunt Claudine and my step-grandmother, Shirley, and headed to *Opie's Candy Store.*

I love *Opie's Candy Store* because they sell candy by the pound.

You grab a bag, a scoop, and just go for your favorites.

I got two bags of candy and had a pleasant conversation with the owner.

He told me that Mt. Airy, NC, is a great place to live. I believe him.

After that, I did a little window shopping while Aunt Claudine and Shirley browsed for souvenirs to take home.

We all met back up at the vehicle and returned to our room here at *The Mayberry Motor Inn.*

Tonight, I'll go ahead and pack up the vehicle so I don't have to worry about it in the morning.

I've learned I can't pack very well when I'm half-asleep—so best to do it before bed.

Tomorrow morning, we'll head back to Alabama.

This has been one of the most memorable trips I've ever taken, and I'll admit—it's going to be hard leaving in the morning.

I'm already looking into booking a room for *Mayberry Days* in September.

Unfortunately, *Mayberry Motor Inn* is already full that week.

Once I get home, I'll start calling around to try and find a room somewhere nearby.

But I will be back—you always come back to Mt. Airy.

So, hopefully, I'll return this September.

That is all for now.

54: Mt. Airy – Goodbye

—Saying Goodbye—

We gathered at the Pavilion this morning for a final church service.

The lesson came from an episode of *The Andy Griffith Show*—specifically, the famous one titled *"The Case of a Punch in the Nose."*

I walked away from that service feeling wiser.

Most everyone had to leave and head back home today.

We all said our goodbyes with hugs or handshakes.

But it didn't feel like strangers parting ways. No—it felt more like family saying goodbye after a reunion.

That's the feeling I had throughout my entire time here—like family gathering together at a family reunion.

It's truly amazing that two people—Andy Griffith and Don Knotts—found each other.

Even more amazing that they created one of the most significant pieces of American television ever made.

And if it weren't for them finding each other, I wouldn't have found this whole new family of mine.

I know one thing: I'm going to try to make it to more of these events from now on.

That is all for now.

55: *Nite Under The Pavilion*

I'm a bit late sharing the story from night two of the "Mayberry Meet-Up," and for that, I apologize.

In my defense, it was a special night—and I needed some time to reflect on it.

Night two of the Meet-Up was met with rain. Lots of rain. Torrential rain.

Many of us grabbed umbrellas and ponchos and returned to our chairs, patiently waiting to see if our "Nite Under the Stars" would be called off.

Slowly, we each came to realize—the rain was here to stay.

One by one, fellow "Mayberrians" stood up and headed back to their rooms, until finally, I was the only one still sitting in the field. I had my aunt's umbrella and was wearing a poncho.

Sitting there alone, I felt like "Mr. Schwump."

Some people waved as they passed, and I smiled and nodded in return.

Eventually, even I gave in and returned to my room. It looked like our night had been ruined.

But then, something happened.

Mr. Newsome had prepared for just such an event.

He instructed everyone to get out their portable radios and tune them to FM Station 93.7.

You see, he had set up his equipment to broadcast the sound directly to that frequency.

People began pulling their vehicles up in front of the screen and tuning their car radios to 93.7—just like a drive-in movie.

Others sat outside their motel rooms, tuned in on portable radios, and watched the screen from their doorsteps.

I went to sit under the Pavilion with twenty-four others. (Yes, I counted.)

Together, from our own little viewing spot, we watched *The Andy Griffith Show*.

The rain didn't win. It didn't stop us Mayberrians from coming together.

As we sat under the Pavilion, people passed around snacks—bags of chips, popcorn, even a box of peaches. Someone else brought peanuts.

Laughter rang out from cars, motel rooms, and our small crowd beneath the Pavilion.

We laughed together as we watched *The Andy Griffith Show*.

It was a beautiful thing.

Yes, it was a special night, and I'll never forget my *Nite Under the Pavilion*.

Thank you to everyone who made the "Mayberry Meet-Up" such a success.

56: A Good Day

Yesterday, I had lunch at one of our local Mexican restaurants.

As I sat enjoying my steak fajitas, I looked out the window and noticed a surprise—a Shaved Ice Stand.

"Mmm-mmm," I thought to myself as I scarfed down my food.

"Miss, I need a to-go box, please," I said to my friendly waitress.

Now, if you know me, you know about my diabetes. And yes, I was aware of it too.

I drank water with lunch and ate the steak fajitas without the tortilla. Steak is mostly protein, so I did the math and figured I had room for about 35 more carbohydrates and still be in the safe zone.

I paid my bill, grabbed my to-go box, and headed straight for the Shaved Ice Stand.

When I walked up, the cutest little kid—maybe five years old—poked his head out the window and asked, "How are you doing today?"

"I'm doing just fine, sir. How are you?" I replied.

"Good."

His grandmother, who stood nearby, smiled and said, "He loves talking to people."

I said, "You've got a cute son, ma'am."

"Oh, he's my grandson," she replied.

"You don't look old enough to be a grandmother."

"Well, thank you," she said with a laugh.

"It's hot today," the little boy added.

"It sure is," I said, smiling at him.

I asked the grandmother, "How long have y'all been here?"

"We just got here this week. We'll be here until the end of summer."

"Well, I'll be coming here as much as I can. I love shaved ice."

"Which flavor do you want today?" the little man asked.

"You know, I love the Pina Colada," I told him.

"Large or small?"

"I'd love a large, but I better stick with a small."

I handed over my money along with a tip, and the grandmother passed me my shaved ice.

"You come back," the little salesman said sweetly.

"Oh, I will. I'll be back."

"Thank you, and please come back and see us again," the grandmother added.

"Thank you. I hope y'all do well here. I know I'm glad you're here," I said, turning to head back to my vehicle.

And it was a good day.

57: School Skipper

I hated school.

When I was in the 7th grade, I skipped school a lot.

Believe it or not, getting in trouble for skipping sounded better than actually going.

It was easy for me to skip, too.

We walked a quarter mile to the bus stop. ("Uphill both ways," if this were my Pawpaw's story.)

The bus stop was right next to a bridge that ran over Black Creek.

I would walk there with my brothers, then hide under the bridge and wait for the bus to pass.

The day before, I'd already prepared my survival kit.

It had cans of soup, a handheld can opener, a canteen filled with water, peanut butter and jelly sandwiches, a mess kit for cooking, and things like matches, etc.

After the bus passed, I'd crawl out from under the bridge and head back home.

By that time, Mom and Dad would've already gone to work.

I'd gather my survival kit and either my .22 rifle or a rod and reel for fishing—but not both. It was always one or the other.

I hated school mostly because of my medical issues.

It was tough being a kid with Spina Bifida.

Kids can be cruel. And back in the '80s, there were no "anti-bullying" campaigns—not where I lived, anyway.

My survival kit was packed in an army backpack from the surplus store.

Wearing it freed up my hands for my rifle or fishing rod.

Then I'd head down the train tracks and play all day.

Now, this is the part where some of you may ask, *"Didn't the school call your parents to say you were absent?"*

No. The school knew I had Spina Bifida and had been told by my parents that I might miss school often.

And I knew they knew that. And I knew they wouldn't call... I digress.

Down the train tracks I'd go.

To the deep hole for fishing.

Or to the woods for squirrel or dove hunting.

The world was my oyster.

I felt like Tom Sawyer or Huck Finn.

I just had to be back home by 3:45 to answer the phone when Mom called to check in.

One time, though, I took it too far.

I skipped Monday. Then Tuesday. Then Wednesday and Thursday.

I remember my brothers telling me I'd pushed it too far.

They said the teachers were asking about me.

But I thought, *"Who misses Monday through Thursday and then shows up on Friday?"*

To me, it was a no-brainer.

So, I skipped Friday too.

That day, I didn't go far. I figured I should play it safe and stay close to home.

Around 11 a.m., I went up into the woods to hide because Dad often came home for lunch between 11 and 12.

This day was no different.

At about 11:15, I saw Dad's truck coming down the road toward our house.

But what happened next *was* different.

Dad got out of the truck and walked over to the bottom of the hill—right where I was hiding.

He hollered, "Lynn! Lynn! Get down here! I know you're up there! Get down here now!"

The jig was up. I was caught.

The school had called Mom. Mom had called Dad at work.

Plenty of phone calls had been made that day trying to find me.

Dad knew exactly where I was.

I came trotting down the hill and asked,

"Dad! What are you doing home?"

I don't remember what he said to me. I don't remember what kind of trouble I got in.

I guess my mind has blocked that part out. The mind tends to do that.

But I do remember showing up to school that next Monday.

Every kid knew I had skipped a whole week.

I was a regular *Ferris Bueller.*

And if I had it to do over, I think I'd do it again.

I hated 7th grade.

Still, I went on to graduate college. Everything worked out.

But 7th grade…

I hated 7th grade.

Sometimes, a kid just needs to grab his rod and reel—or rifle—and go be Tom Sawyer.

58: 7/28/2021

This morning, I got up, got dressed, and drove to Jack's for a sausage biscuit.

Afterward, I headed back home and took a quick shower. Yes, I went to Jack's before showering—it was just the drive-thru.

We've got a new storage building now. Originally, the Chapel was supposed to serve that purpose, but Momma put a stop to it.

To be fair, we all love the Prayer Chapel. It holds a special place in our hearts.

I've been slowly moving items into the new storage building—emphasis on slowly.

Papa and I aren't in any rush. We're both taking our time, doing things at our own pace.

Honestly, we prefer it that way, and it's working out nicely.

Later, I drove over to CVS and ran into a childhood friend I hadn't seen in years.

And that's when I messed up.

I was excited to see him, and when he asked how I was doing, I overshared.

Everything you know about me through my stories—I told him in about one minute.

I led with details about my colostomy and urostomy. I have no idea why. Definitely too much information for two friends just catching up.

Why didn't I just say, "I'm doing good, man. You?" Geeze.

I did give him my email address, though. Maybe we'll go fishing sometime.

Later in the day, I stopped by one of our local spots, The White House Restaurant. It's a favorite in our community.

I ordered the smoked sausage and onions. It was delicious.

I got to sit quietly and think, free from distractions.

When I got up to pay, the waitress told me someone had already covered my bill.

Thank you, and God bless whoever did that for me. I did pay it forward.

All in all, it was a good day.

That's all for now.

59: 7/30/2021 – Health Update

To those who keep up with my health:

COVID has made its way into our family.

(Mom, Papa, and I have all been vaccinated.)

Mom, Papa, and two of my nieces have tested positive for COVID-19.

Thankfully, I've been tested three times and all have come back negative—one test was even sent off for confirmation.

Still, because of my health conditions, my doctor put me on medication as a precaution. I'm also taking all the vitamins recommended for COVID, just like the others.

I'll be quarantined in my bedroom until everyone recovers, but I am allowed to get in my vehicle and ride around, which I'll probably do often.

So far, they're doing fine.

No one has a fever, everyone's oxygen levels are normal, and we're all on some form of medication.

That's the latest on me and the family.

60: 7/31/2021 – Health Update

Since we already knew Mom had COVID-19 and I had tested negative, I took the opportunity to head to the pharmacy and stock up on things I thought we might need.

One of the items I bought was a pack of five COVID home tests—one for each family member.

When I got home, I discovered that each box actually contains two tests.

Now that the other four have already tested positive at the doctor's office, I've been using the home tests daily to monitor myself.

Before using them, I showed one to the nurse to get her opinion.

She said they looked identical to the ones they use at the clinic and added that if the result shows positive, the person is very likely positive.

She did caution that false negatives are possible.

I tested again this morning and am still showing "Negative."

I went out for a little drive earlier and listened to some good ol' '80s and '90s "Classic" rock.

Hard to believe the music I grew up with is now considered classic.

Does that mean the heavy metal from that era is now "Classic Metal?"

That's all for now.

61: The Night the Lights Went Out At...

I've been holding onto this story for a while.

I didn't want to share it in a way that makes any business look bad—that's not who I am.

If I have a problem with a place, I take it to management, not social media.

...But this story is just too good not to tell. At least I think so. Maybe you had to be there...

It's 9:10 pm.

I pull into a fast food restaurant and ease into the drive-thru lane.

There's one car ahead of me placing its order, so I wait patiently behind it.

At 9:13 pm, they finish ordering and pull up to the window.

I move forward to the speaker and wait for someone to ask for my order.

At 9:15 pm, the car in front of me drives off with its food.

Suddenly, still 9:15 pm, the lights go out.

I glance over at the dining room, and the interior lights are off too.

At first, I think maybe there's a power outage. But then I spot the employee at the drive-thru window counting money in the register— and that area still has lights.

It hits me. They've closed. And no one is even going to come on the speaker to tell me.

In that moment, I think to myself, "This is my entire 45 years of life summed up at 9:15 pm on a Thursday..." and I start laughing.

I laugh all the way as I drive off.

Then I went to Jack's. They're open late.

PS: I've eaten at that place since. They really do have good food.

62: COVID Update – 8/1/2021

As many of you know, five people live in this house.

Four have tested positive for COVID—two elderly and two young ones.

I tested negative at the doctor's office and continue to test negative with the at-home COVID test kits.

One of my tests was even sent off to the lab, and it came back negative as well.

I know the home test kits are working because they detected COVID in the others who tested positive here at home.

Due to my health being compromised by Spina Bifida, the doctor started me on Ivermectin and a regimen of daily vitamins.

The others are also taking vitamins, along with the medications prescribed by their doctor.

I wear a mask whenever I move around the house.

I'm also keeping a log of everyone's vitals—well, their COVID vitals.

Every two hours, I check and record their temperature and oxygen levels.

So far, only once did Mom and Papa run a temperature.

It was 99-something for both of them.

Two hours later, their temperatures returned to normal.

Oxygen levels have mostly stayed above 95, which is within the normal range.

Mom and Papa have lost some of their sense of taste.

The girls haven't reported any loss of taste so far.

I'm doing fine. I feel fine.

I monitor my own vitals, and everything has remained normal.

Throughout the day, I've been praying for everyone here.

I pray out loud and call each person by name.

That is all for now.

63: COVID Update – 8/2/2021

Maybe you had to be there…

It's 9:10 pm.

Went to Jack's. They're open late.

So far, only once did Mom and Papa run a temperature. I'm doing fine. I feel fine. I got up early this morning to make my rounds… I sound like a medical professional.

If I'm not careful, I might let it go to my head.

Anyway—

I checked the vitals of "Patient Zero," one elderly female, at 0800 hours.

Her oxygen level was 97, which is within the average range.

Her temperature was 98.1—also normal.

Seriously though,

I've been checking vitals every two hours.

At noon, Mom's temperature was 99.3, and her oxygen level was 98.

I expect her temperature will be back in the 98-ish range by my 2 p.m. check.

Papa's vitals have been normal throughout the day.

I retested myself for COVID again, and it was still negative.

Overall, we're all doing well.

Mom is resting in bed today.

She told me she isn't sick—just tired.

I wake her every two hours to take her vitals.

Same with Papa. If he's napping in his recliner, I still wake him up.

Everyone here gets checked—myself included.

As for me, I was supposed to see my heart doctor today for a test.

I think they mentioned an "echo" test, though I'm not completely sure.

They ended up rescheduling all three of my appointments to one all-day visit in September.

That actually works out better. Instead of three separate trips, I'll just go once.

Ironically—or maybe oddly enough; I need to look up the word "ironically" again—my heart has been fluttering today.

I've been monitoring it using my device, which can detect AFib and other irregularities.

Right now, it's beating at 127 bpm, which is the same rate it was at during my last visit with my primary care doctor.

I'll post another update tonight before bed.

That's all for now.

64: COVID Night Update – 8/2/2021

A short update:

Everyone is doing fine tonight, and everyone's numbers are stable.

A few people have asked what I'm doing to protect myself from getting COVID, so I thought I'd explain.

When four out of the five people in your house have COVID, there's not a lot you can do—except leave.

Leaving, however, wasn't a road I wanted to go down, even though my Aunt kindly offered her cabin.

My doctor, who confirmed I was negative and understands my health issues, started me on Ivermectin.

He felt it might help keep me from getting infected.

A couple of my family members were relieved to hear I was on it.

I'm also taking vitamins daily. My regimen includes:

Vitamin C

- Vitamin D3
- Zinc
- Pepcid
- Baby Aspirin

Our local pharmacy sells a "COVID kit" that contains all the essential vitamins, along with instructions. It costs about $24.

To minimize exposure, I mostly stay in my bedroom.

No one with COVID has stepped inside.

I spray disinfectants in there multiple times a day and also use a "germ-killing light."

I only leave my room to take vitals and go to the kitchen.

Every two hours, I put on my mask, enter each room, scan their forehead for temperature, and they read their own oxygen level to me.

I log the results and head back to my room.

I also take frequent showers—around five a day—just during this COVID situation.

I eat when others are not in the kitchen.

Once everyone is done, I mask up, go in, fix my plate, and eat alone in my recliner.

Each morning, I test myself with the at-home COVID kit.

It's easy now that I've learned how to use it.

It caught COVID in those who tested positive here, and it's continued to show me as negative—which the doctor confirmed.

I pray throughout the day—out loud—and I say each person's name as I pray for them.

I also ask God specifically to protect me from catching the virus.

And that's pretty much my daily routine.

Mom and Papa did ask me to consider staying somewhere else until this was over.

But I chose not to. You do for family.

That's all for now.

65: COVID Update – 8/3/2021

I've made my rounds today, and everyone's temperatures and oxygen levels are normal.

I tested myself this morning, and I'm still negative.

In earlier updates, I forgot to mention that I've been getting in my vehicle and driving around—a lot.

I figure if I'm quarantining, I might as well do it with the windows down and some good tunes playing.

I've also spent a lot of time in the garage.

I'm slowly moving items to the storage building.

When I say "slowly," I mean it—one day I moved two things, another day I managed five.

I know my limits and follow the doctor's restrictions closely.

This afternoon, I'll be using Wal-Mart's "Contactless" pickup. Mom and Papa placed the order, paid for everything, and listed me as the pickup person.

The employees are supposed to load it into my truck without me getting out or coming into contact with anyone.

Honestly, I'm looking forward to it.

That's all for now.

66: COVID Night Update – 8/3/2021

Everyone is still doing well here—including me.

Mom placed an order with Wal-Mart Pickup, and I went to get it.

It was my first time using the service, and I'll do better next time.

Mom told me to take a cooler for the refrigerated items, which I did—but it wasn't big enough.

Then I realized, if I'd gone inside to shop, I wouldn't have used a cooler anyway—I would've just driven home.

The employee who loaded my truck wouldn't accept a tip.

She said it was against the "No Contact" policy.

She was right.

Honestly, it's a convenient way to shop.

You just go online, fill your virtual cart, check out, schedule a time, and show up.

When you arrive, you call and give them your parking spot number, and they bring your order right to the car.

Simple.

Still, I miss shopping at the good ol' "Pig" (Piggly Wiggly).

After that, I went through the Arby's drive-thru, got food for everyone, and brought it home.

I love their Curly Fries. I ate all of them on the drive back.

On the way home, I listened to "Africa" by Toto.

I've never actually learned the lyrics.

Truthfully, I sing a lot of songs I don't know the words to. Doesn't bother me.

I pretty much sing it like this:

"It's gonna take a lot to DA-DE-DAAAAH from you

There's nothing that a hundred men ON MARS could ever do

I DA-DE-DA-DA-down in Africa

Gonna take some time to do the things we never DAAAAH."

Good times.

That's all for now.

67: COVID Update – 8/4/2021

I tested negative again today.

Well, it took a while, but they've finally learned to take their own vitals.

All you need is your temperature, oxygen level, and heart rate.

(The heart rate monitor is built right into the oximeter.)

I'm glad they've got the hang of it, because I just couldn't get going today.

I moved three things from the garage to the storage building and then went back to my room to watch TV. That was around 11 a.m.

When I woke up, it was after 2 p.m.—I had fallen asleep while watching TV.

I feel fine. I'm just tired—busier than usual this past week.

I need to figure out when I should test everyone again. If anyone has suggestions, I'd appreciate it.

Might be an early bedtime for me tonight.

That's all for now.

68: The Legend of Birdie Franklin

There's always that *one* guy in high school who can do anything he sets his mind to.

For us, that guy was "Birdie Franklin."

Birdie was about five years older than me and a good friend of my brother Tony—so that made him my friend too. Whether they wanted me around or not, Tony's friends were my friends.

To me, Birdie was the most athletic person in school.

He could play anything—baseball, basketball, football. You name it.

I once saw Birdie hit a tennis ball over seven apartment buildings with a tennis racket.

In his defense, he told the guys that day, *"I want to play baseball, not tennis."*

And tough—*Whew!* Birdie was the toughest guy I knew.

We only owned one pair of boxing gloves growing up. Yes, one.

So, when we wanted to box, each person got one glove, and the other arm had to go behind the back.

It looked ridiculous, but it worked.

When Birdie landed a punch, the match was over.

I was glad he was my—well, Tony's—friend.

I remember one time we had a pillow fight in the basement while we were living in Virginia.

I accidentally took a cheap shot and hit Birdie pretty hard with my pillow. Yes, it was accidental.

We had a rule: *no cheap shots.*

Birdie shouted, "Stand up and take your lick, 'Lynn.'"

See, if you took a cheap shot, the other guy got a free one—no dodging.

I remember standing there, eyes closed (which I don't recommend), bracing for Birdie's shot.

It was a Thursday afternoon when he took it.

By Wednesday, when I *finally* woke up, my head still hurt.

I never took a cheap shot at Birdie again.

When Birdie lived with us in Virginia, he and Tony were both out of high school and over 21.

They did everything together—golfing, snow skiing, and most of all, clubbing.

Mostly they chased ladies at the clubs.

I remember one time I had to go back to Alabama for some doctor appointments.

When you're born with a disability, you stick with the doctors who know your history.

I knew many people who traveled from out of state to see the doctors at UAB, and I was no different—traveling from Virginia to Alabama for care.

I was supposed to take the Amtrak train, and Birdie said he'd ride with me.

That made Mom feel better, knowing Birdie would be with me.

We lived in Harrisonburg, VA, and the Amtrak left from Charlottesville.
The train ride to Birmingham took over two days.

It first went to Atlanta, then you'd switch trains there to get to Birmingham.

(You thought *only* planes made you change in Atlanta? Nope—*everybody* changes in Atlanta.)

I was excited to ride the rails with ol' Birdie.

He was "Tough Guy Birdie" to me.

The train ride was amazing.

If you haven't seen the countryside by train, I highly recommend it.

Beautiful. *Beau-ti-ful.*

We played cards—Five Card Draw, maybe some Rummy.

We ate in the dining car and spent hours just watching the scenery.

But the moment that sticks with me most was when the train pulled into Birmingham.

We stopped right beside the Ringling Brothers and Barnum & Bailey Circus train.

I didn't even know they had a train until that moment.

Clowns waved at us from their cars.

You could see animals in the animal cars.

Some of the clowns even performed little tricks while we watched from our seats.

I remember it like it was yesterday.

Birdie sat next to me and, almost to himself, said, "Awe... the circus. The circus is in town..."

Then he started pointing at the clowns:

"Look at that one over there."

"Hey, look at that one."

Then he muttered, "I guess they're gonna be in Birmingham at the BJCC..."

I was stunned.

This was *Tough Guy Birdie*—sounding like a little kid.

He kept watching the clowns and, after a moment, said, *"...I wonder if they sell beer at the circus..."*

Birdie eventually had a big family.

All his kids look just like him.

I saw him not too long ago. He still looks the same.

Only Birdie could raise a family, get older, and still look exactly the same.

I often think about the good times Tony, Birdie, and I had growing up.

And when I do, I smile.

Birdie is still a tough guy.

He works out at the gym regularly.

But I know—deep down—he's still a kid at heart.

I love you, Birdie.

69: COVID Update – 8/6/2021

Finally.

Everyone here tested negative for COVID.

Even me.

Papa can start his 73rd year off COVID-free.

...And that makes for a great birthday gift.

That's all for now.

70: A Good Day?

The day started like usual.

Painfully, I got out of bed to begin the day.

Riding around in my truck in the morning helps with my pain. I usually swing through a drive-thru and get a steak biscuit, tater tots, and a large Diet Coke.

Today was no different.

When I got to the fast-food joint, there were twelve cars ahead of me.

It's usually like that on Saturdays.

So I waited in line, listening to some *Classic Rock.*

(Still hard to believe my music is now labeled *"Classic."*)

I placed my order and inched forward to the window.

Once there, I paid and got my food.

I noticed some local kids raising money for the schools, so I quickly grabbed some cash to drop in their bucket.

Back on the road, I reached into the bag to grab a tater tot—my favorite thing to eat while cruising around.

Instead of grabbing a tater tot, I pulled out… a bowl of grits.

Panicked, I rooted around the bag again.

Nothing but a spoon and a bowl of grits.

They'd given me the wrong order.

And I wasn't exactly dressed to go inside and fix the issue.

See, I had on a pair of shorts, a white undershirt, some suspenders, and shoes.

No socks.

Now, for most folks that might be fine.

But for me? Not quite.

My two ostomy bags—*Lenny and Squiggy*—hang out the bottom of my undershirt.

They're not shy, and they sure weren't hidden.

So I pulled off the road and ate my grits.

I *hate* plain grits.

This may offend a few of you, but I usually put sugar in my grits.

(Yeah, I said it.)

But today I had no choice:

Wait again in a now 15-car-long line, place a brand-new order, or eat the plain grits.

Naturally, I ate the plain grits.

You might've handled it differently—I don't know.

On the way back home, I put on some more *Classic Rock,* rolled down the windows, and sang out loud.

Try it sometime.

Roll the windows down, crank up a good song, and sing your heart out.

Nothing gets your day back on track quicker than that.

It's going to be a great day.

That's all for now.

71: A Day in the Life – Ostomy Care

When I started *Walking with Spina Bifida*, I wanted to share the real, day-to-day experience of living with a disability. The good, the bad, and the ugly.

This one falls into the "ugly" category.

So, fair warning—if you've got a weak stomach, maybe skip this one. I'll try to keep it clean, but "poop" is going to come up more than once. Literally and figuratively.

Every three to four days, I have to change both of my ostomy systems—Lenny (urostomy) and Squiggy (colostomy). I use Hollister for the urostomy, ConvaTec for the colostomy.

Now, in order to put on the new bags, you've got to remove the old ones. That means for a short time, you're fully exposed and vulnerable. And when you've got no control over either system, that vulnerability can become... messy.

Yesterday, I did a full system change, so today should've been an off-day. But sometimes, the adhesive wafers don't stick right. When that happens, you've got to change early. Today is one of those days.

Morning is usually the best time for a change—your body tends to be less "active." Not always, though. And not today.

Here's my step-by-step routine:

1. **Prep the Supplies**:
   I get the wafers out and cut the openings to match my stomas.
   After years of doing this, I've got it down to a science.

2. **Shower and Strip**:

I hop in a hot shower, let the water warm my stomach, then rip the old appliances off and toss them in a ziplock bag. Now I'm exposed, so I say a quick prayer. You never know when something might suddenly… shoot out.

3. **Clean-Up**:

I use hot water to clean off the leftover adhesive. Then I shave the area—glue doesn't like hair. I wash everything down with a non-oily soap so the next set of wafers will stick properly.

4. **Drying Off**:

After drying off with a towel, I place it across the sink as a "catch-all"—because, again, you never know.

5. **Hairdryer Time**:

I use the hairdryer on high heat to dry my skin. That's usually when pee shoots out of my stoma and hits the mirror. I quickly grab the towel to catch it. (Pro tip: always move the hairdryer away before this step. You do *not* want electricity and pee mixing.)

6. **Round Two**:

Clean up, sanitize, grab a new towel, and repeat if needed. Some days, this takes more than one round.

7. **Apply the Skin Barrier**:

This protects my actual skin from irritation. Some people skip it, but I've learned the hard way—my skin turns red and irritated without it.

8. **Warm and Apply the Wafer**:

I use the hairdryer again—first on the wafer, then on my skin. The warmth activates the adhesive. I press the wafer on, firmly. Lenny goes first. Then I repeat the process for Squiggy.

9. **Snap on the Bags**:

I use a two-piece system—think Tupperware for your body. The wafer sticks to my stomach, and the bag "snaps" into place.

And that's it. If all goes well, I'm good for another three or four days.

This version is the *best case* scenario. Some days require multiple showers and clean-ups. But once everything's back in place, I get dressed, go out, and live my life.

I think I managed to keep this version pretty clean. At least, I tried.

72: Memories

As I sit here in my recliner, trying to think of what to write, I reflect on the past few weeks. At first, I thought—*nothing much has happened.* But then I remembered Uncle Bubba's storage shed.

When I moved down here from Huntsville, Alabama, I had no space for most of my stuff. Uncle Bubba let me use his shed to store it all. Recently, I went over to collect what was mine.

As I opened the boxes, I realized—this was a time capsule from my "Bachelor Pad" days.

One of the first things I pulled out was a picture frame filled with ticket stubs from concerts I'd been to:

* Pink Floyd
* Lynyrd Skynyrd
* Aerosmith
* An unused front-row Creed ticket
* Hank Jr.
* Motley Crue
* Poison
* Molly Hatchet

...and many more.

About 25 stubs in total. I didn't always keep them, but that unused Creed ticket? That one made the cut.

Then I found my vinyl records:

* *The Wall*
* *Dark Side of the Moon*

...and a bunch of others I still know by heart.

I set those back down and kept digging.

I got a little sad. Not in a bad way—just nostalgic. Every object had a memory attached. A time, a feeling, a younger version of myself. That twenty-something-year-old kid is now forty-five. That's just life. But those memories—they hit you.

Then I found my CDs. Four full tote bins of them. And now, all of that music fits into my phone. Go figure.

Then, the jackpot: a disposable camera that hadn't been developed. And a separate roll of film.

I took them to CVS. They said it'll take three weeks to get the photos back.

Now, I feel like a kid waiting for Christmas.

Two weeks, six days, and counting…

So, I guess I did have a story to tell after all.

73: Defibrillator

With our health being what it is in this house, we decided it was time to get a defibrillator in case of an emergency.

Defibrillators are devices that restore a normal heartbeat by sending an electric pulse or shock to the heart. They are used to prevent or correct an arrhythmia—a heartbeat that is uneven, too slow, or too fast. Defibrillators can also restore the heart's rhythm if it suddenly stops.

That is copied straight from the National Heart, Lung, and Blood Institute:

https://www.nhlbi.nih.gov/health-topics/defibrillators

I researched other defibrillators, and I felt the "Philips HeartStart" was the best option for us.

In case of an emergency, we open it up and begin following the voice prompts.

The unit should walk us through every step.

It will even tell you if an electric shock is **not needed.**

It comes with scissors (in case we need to cut off clothing), a razor (in case we need to shave hair), gloves, a CPR mask, and a few other items.

My Philips saleswoman was very easy to deal with, and the unit was delivered within three days of placing the order.

I pray to God that we never need it—but I'd rather have it and not need it than need it and not have it.

My next step is finding a central location to store it.

That's all for now.

74: Ridin' A Horse

When I became an older teenager, I received an artificial sphincter muscle.

That artificial sphincter muscle was a game-changer for me and my life.

It works like this:

It "crimps" the urethra shut, much like crimping a garden hose to stop the water from coming out.

With the urethra crimped, I don't pee on myself.

To pee, I press a button located in my scrotum, which "opens" or "un-crimps" the artificial sphincter muscle.

Pee then exits my body freely.

I also catheterize myself to make sure I get all the urine out of my system.

After about three minutes, the artificial sphincter closes back.

That's a very basic version of how it works.

I tell you that story, to tell you this story:

When I was a teenager, my dad had two horses.

He kept them in a good-sized field, and each horse had its own stall in the barn.

My brothers and I even helped fence the field in, making sure the horses couldn't get out.

I lived with Mom and Papa at the time and would come over on weekends or weekday afternoons to help put up the fence and take care of "Smoke" and "TJ."

Dad would give us $20 a week for our help, which was good money to a kid back then.

Dad had found a vast, open field to ride the horses.

It was several football fields in size.

To get there, we had to ride through the woods on a trail next to the famous "Turkey Creek."

The last time I rode a horse, I rode "Smoke," and my brother rode "TJ."

We were taking them to the field, and Dad would meet us there by car.

We had gotten close to the end of the trail when Smoke and I came upon a log.

To get past the log, Smoke would have to jump over it.

It was nothing new and not concerning at all—just a small log.

When he jumped, I got "bucked" a little, which pushed the button on my sphincter muscle and "opened" it.

I know this because I began peeing all over myself and all over "Smoke."

I guess Smoke realized I was peeing on him, because he bolted— and I got bucked up and down even more.

In no time, we were on the field, and Smoke was running at full speed.

As he ran, I kept getting bucked, which caused every muscle in my body to tighten—including my stomach muscles.

As my muscles tightened, I would pee.

The more I peed, the faster Smoke ran.

The faster Smoke ran, the more he bucked me.

And the more he bucked, the more I peed on him.

It was a vicious cycle, and I knew I was going to die that day.

We were quickly halfway across the field, and I was holding on for dear life.

"Stop!"

"Whoa, boy!"

"Smoke!"

"I'm sorry for pee'in on ya!"

"Smoke, no!"

"Whoa!"

Smoke was no longer listening to me.

He was in charge.

I was peeing on him, and he didn't like it.

I just knew I was about to get bucked off.

I didn't want to get dragged on the ground if my feet got caught in the stirrups, so I took both feet out of them.

I had my arms wrapped around Smoke's neck, holding on as best I could.

The end of the field was getting closer, and after that was a trailer park.

"Smoke!"

"Dear God!"

"Stop!"

I had forgotten every command that Smoke knew.

"Whoa" was the only one I could remember—and it wasn't working.

I knew I was going to be peeing for about three minutes.

I also knew I should've peed before getting on the dang horse. After all, I had drunk several Mt. Dews before we started.

My bladder had a lot of pee, and it wasn't going to stop until the sphincter muscle closed back up.

My brother Tony and his horse were way behind me at this point, but Tony knew something was wrong and was trying to catch up.

I was within fifty yards of the end of the field, and I knew this horse was not stopping.

He was getting peed on, and he wasn't having any of it.

I knew I was going to have to jump off.

I began counting down for my jump.

"10, 9, 8…"

Tony and TJ passed by and got in front of Smoke and me.

Tony then stopped TJ in front of Smoke, which made Smoke come to a halt.

"What happened?" Tony asked.

"I'm covered in pee!"

"What happened?"

"I'm covered in pee!"

"Why?"

"Somebody's gotta give 'Smoke' a bath. I peed all over him."

My brother's famous grin now grew on his face.

"You peed on him, and he bolted?"

"I guess he could smell it. I don't know. I know I can…"

I began hopping off Smoke.

Dad came over. "You tired of riding already?"

"You gotta take me to my car… now, please…"

"What happened?"

"Somebody's gotta ride 'Smoke' back to the barn and wash him," I said.

"I'm covered in pee… and so is your horse, Dad."

And that is the last time I ever rode a horse.

75: *Purple Hearts*

In 2021, for Mother's Day, I purchased several plants for the front yard.

Among the plants I bought were three "Purple Heart" plants.

I've also heard them called "Wandering Jews," and to tell you the truth, I don't know which name is correct. Maybe both are.

Maybe you can tell me.

I hung the "Purple Heart" plants up because they came in hanging planters.

Mother's Day came and went. Mom loved all the plants I bought and had planted in the front yard.

Now, we have three dogs:

Tommy, Jett, and Cooper.

Tommy is part Black Lab, Jett is an Australian Shepherd, and Cooper is a mini Australian Shepherd.

All three are best friends—and all three love one thing… destroying the yard.

We had the dogs on a wireless "invisible" fence to keep them contained, but between the mail carrier refusing to deliver packages because of them, and the dogs tearing up the yard, we decided to fence in the backyard.

However, before the backyard got fenced, the dogs found the Purple Hearts and destroyed the planter they were hanging in— leaving the Purple Hearts lying on the ground.

When Mom found the Purple Hearts on the ground, she decided to leave them where they lay and water them daily, hoping they'd take root and grow right there.

It worked.

The dogs didn't win.

We now have Purple Hearts—or Wandering Jews, whichever name is correct—growing in three different spots in the front yard.

And we've got a pretty neat story to go with them.

76: Old Newspapers—August 1977

News of Elvis Presley's death has just hit the world.

My mother recalls that only the Memphis reporters had the exclusive.

The Birmingham, Alabama newspaper didn't have as many pictures or as much detail.

(Remember—no internet back then.)

I was just one year old—my birthday wasn't until October.

Mom hears that one of the local malls has copies of the Memphis newspapers and they're selling them—first come, first served.

At the time, Mom was not only watching my brothers and me, but also two of my first cousins. All of us were under nine years old.

She decides she wants a Memphis newspaper.

Remember, this is 1977. Car seats existed but weren't mandatory—not much was "mandatory" back then.

So, Mom loads up five kids—all under nine—and drives to the local mall to buy a Memphis newspaper.

It's something I've inherited from her—newspaper collecting. I have a collection of my own now.

I also inherited the need to write from her.

She's written many things over the years. So did her mother—my Nana.

All writers.

I guess they were "amateur" writers like me, but I love reading their words.

I digress.

Mom arrives at the mall, dragging all five kids in with her—me in her arms.

She thinks the name of the business selling the papers was L & S Electronics, though she's not completely sure.

To her surprise, she's the first one there.

The papers weren't available yet because the guys hadn't made it back from Memphis.

A line begins forming behind Mom.

Businesses had sent their employees out to buy copies. Mom talked with a few of them while they all waited.

Eventually, the guys arrived with stacks of Memphis newspapers.

Mom bought three.

One of those copies is now in my personal collection of old newspapers.

I didn't dig it out tonight for a photo—it's packed away. Out of sight, out of mind.

But I do have this framed photo that sits on top of my armoire.

Papa gave it to me.

I love it.

77: Morning Drives

My mornings are all the same.

I get up, get dressed, and take a drive. No real destination—just me, the road, and this mountain we live on.

The older folks still call it "Rattlesnake Mountain." But somewhere along the line, someone must've realized folks don't exactly line up to buy property on a place named after venomous reptiles. So now, officially, it's got a nicer name. A friendlier name – It's still full of Rattle Snakes, though.

Recently, I've spotted more deer and fawns than usual while riding around on the mountain.

There's a stretch of road where a doe and four fawns have made their home. Same spot every time. Right there near the bend. I slow down when I pass, just in case they decide to leap out.

Every once in a while, they do jump out and cross the street in front of me.

This morning, though, it wasn't the fawns that got me. It was a big four-point buck. He stepped right out in front of my truck. I stopped, waited. But instead of moving along, he turned and walked right up to my window. Just stood there, staring at me like he expected me to say something. I just nodded and drove on.

I always feel better after taking a drive. These drives really help me.

It's how I wake up, not just physically, but spiritually. A few miles of road, some good air, and the quiet kind of peace that only comes when you're not trying too hard.

It helps with my pain.

And now that I've sat here and typed all this out, I think I understand it even better.

That drive each morning; it's how I remind myself that I'm still here. Still moving. Still breathing.

78: Morning Drive 8/23/21

I went for my morning drive today.

As I've said before, it helps to get my day started.

Sitting in my driver's seat and cruising around really helps ease my pain and puts my mind in a positive space. It's a wonderful way to kick off my day!

Today I saw two deer and a family of ducks.

As I stumbled upon the ducks, I initially thought they were black buzzards and assumed they would take off as I got closer. To my surprise, I discovered it was a sweet family of ducks, and I knew I had to stop to avoid flattening them. So, I came to a halt.

"Quack, quack, quack, quack, quack!" the mother duck—or father duck–hollered at me. I could tell I had upset it.

I was in a quiet little neighborhood, around 6:30 in the morning. I figured if I lay on the horn, I'd wake up half the block. So I just sat there and let the duck fuss at me.

"Quack, quack, quack, quack, quack!"

"You're gonna wake people up with all that quacking," I called out the window.

Eventually, they made their way across the road, still quacking, mind you—and then flew off toward the pond like it was the plan all along.

A few minutes later, I rolled up on two deer standing by the road. They looked at me. Looked at the other side of the road. Then looked back at me. I stopped, just in case.

You never know with deer—they can be standing there one second and dart out the next.

After some thinking, they walked on across. I gave them their space and moved on.

I pulled into the local fast-food joint to grab a biscuit. While I waited in line, I had my SiriusXM set to Channel 148—Radio Classics. They were playing the old shows this morning. *Johnny Dollar, Gunsmoke,* a couple others.

When I got to the window, the woman leaned out and said, "The car in front of you paid for your meal."

Now, I don't know who that was—but if you're reading this, thank you.

I paid it forward by covering the order for the guy behind me.

After that, I rode around for a little while longer, listening to the radio and eating my tater tots with a cold Diet Coke in hand.

Now I'm back home. The sky's clear, the air's good, and I'm ready to start the day.

It's gonna be a great one.

That's all for now.

79: Last Day with Tony

I remember it as if it were yesterday.

I was living the bachelor life in my cozy home in Huntsville, Alabama.

It was a beautiful Sunday, and I had risen pretty early. But this day held something special.

I suddenly found myself with a strong craving—a craving for a delightful Banana Split! I thought to myself, "Why am I craving ice cream so badly this morning?" It felt like I should be craving eggs, bacon, flapjacks, or at least something more traditional for breakfast.

Despite that, I couldn't resist the urge. So, I slipped on my shorts and happily drove over to Walmart to satisfy my sweet tooth.

At Walmart, I picked up some delightful vanilla ice cream, fresh bananas, chocolate, caramel topping, cherry toppings, and those fun little sprinkles that are perfect for adding a pop of color to the ice cream.

As much as it pains me to say it, I ended up spending $60 on this banana split adventure.

On my drive home, I couldn't help but think, "I need to call 'Tony' and share my tasty plans with him." Tony absolutely adored banana splits. Honestly, he had a sweet tooth for everything, but banana splits held a special place in his heart.

Tony wasn't just my brother; he was truly like a best friend to me. He was my biggest supporter, and I genuinely believe that.

"With all these toppings I bought, I can just imagine Tony driving up to Huntsville to indulge in a banana split with me!" I excitedly pondered.

Then I remembered that Tony wasn't feeling well. I had talked to him the night before, and he was dealing with a migraine. He sounded so uncomfortable.

I realized I had forgotten to tell him, "I love you," before we hung up. It really made me feel upset that I didn't say, "I love you, brother."

Once I got home, I quickly unpacked everything, feeling a little rushed. Then, I took out my bowl and decided to make the biggest banana split I had ever attempted. It turned out to be absolutely delicious, though my mouth was a bit sticky from the sweet mess!

After finishing one banana split, I couldn't help but make another.

"I know Tony would love this! I'll give him a call this afternoon to share all about it. By then, he should be feeling better."

But here I was at 9:30 in the morning, and I had ruined my breakfast!

I was feeling a bit under the weather from indulging a little too much, so I decided to lay back down. Being a bachelor definitely has its perks!

I turned on the History channel and snuggled back into bed for a nap.

Around 12:30, my phone rang, but I let it ring for a bit. I was still feeling a bit off from my earlier binge. Eventually, the call went to voicemail.

Then the phone rang again right away; this time, I picked it up. It was Papa, and he shared, "An ambulance is taking Tony to the hospital. I'm at his house, and I found him unresponsive".

I replied, "I'm getting in the truck now and heading that way!" The moment I hung up, a heavy thought crossed my mind: "What if Tony's gone?"

The day had been quite strange, and there was this gut feeling that something was off with Tony.

Before I headed out, I sent a quick message to a friend, letting him know I needed to go to Birmingham. I also asked if he could keep an eye on 'Max,' my beloved dog. He was concerned and asked what had happened, so I shared that I thought my brother might have passed away; at the very least, I knew he was at the hospital.

I arrived at the hospital at around 2:00 p.m., and I found out that Tony had, in fact, died. He had a massive brain hemorrhage and died instantly.

I won't dive into all the details of what happened at the hospital.

To this day, though, I wonder if Tony was somehow enjoying that banana split with me.

Maybe vicariously.

80: Gatlinburg – First Night

It was a bit unexpected, but we had some cancellations at our cabin that we rent out. I saw this as a wonderful opportunity to drive up, check on things, and enjoy a little "Mental Vacation." —That's what I've decided to call it!

My uncle mentioned that the interstate can get tricky around Chattanooga, TN, and he was absolutely right! It took about an hour to get through Chattanooga, but after that, it was smooth sailing all the way.

I'm planning to avoid any crowded places since I want to steer clear of the latest COVID variant. Staying away from crowds feels like the best approach for now!

I'm excited to enjoy a delicious Reuben Sandwich at "The Hofbrauhaus and Cheese Cupboard" in Gatlinburg without the hassle of crowds. I'll definitely be visiting that spot!

I've unpacked my bags, set up the cameras so Momma and Papa can check in on me, and I've had a refreshing shower.

Right now, I'm enjoying some TV and plan to hit the sack soon.

We have a visitor coming in on the 15th, and I'm aiming to be out by the 12th.

That's all for now!

81: Gatlinburg Day 1 – Crockett's Breakfast Camp

I woke up bright and early this morning to head over to "Crockett's Breakfast Camp" for a delightful breakfast.

"Crockett's" opens at 7 a.m., but I got there around 6:30 a.m. and happily claimed my spot in line—I was the second person in!

I was hoping it wouldn't be too crowded this morning, and I was half right. A friendly line of about fifteen people formed, and at 7 a.m., we were all welcomed in and seated. They made sure to place us a reasonable distance apart for everyone's comfort.

Crockett's is famous, at least in my circle, for their mouthwatering "Skillet" breakfasts.

They serve up several delicious dishes that arrive sizzling in a big ol' skillet!

I got their:
Black Bear Camp Skillet.
Sugar Cured Ham
Pecan Smoked Bacon
Sausage
2 Eggs Any Style
Hashbrowns
Biscuit
Gravy
Grits

When the Cook brought my food out of the kitchen, men from across the room said to their wives, "That's what you wouldn't let me get!"

I ate like a king that day.

—The pictures do not do it justice.

Now it's time to go back to bed.

That is all for now.

82: Gatlinburg Day 2

I woke up this morning at 8:00 a.m. EST.

It's Sunday, and I plan to watch my Church at 10 EST. Besides that, I don't have any specific plans, but I might still head out for a little adventure!

I've been keeping an eye on the weather lately. Lots of my family and friends live near where Hurricane Ida is expected to make landfall, so I'm hoping they'll stay safe. My waitress at "Crockett's" shared that local businesses are gearing up for many evacuees coming to Gatlinburg, which shows how kind the community is.

I also have a small "Bucket List" of things I'd like to do while I'm here. It's not too long, mostly filled with outside activities or places where I can enjoy some peace without large crowds.

I'm excited to get this day started and see where it takes me!

That's all for now!

83: Big Lots

I took a drive to "Big Lots" today, and wow, I've been really missing out!

It was my first visit to a "Big Lots" store, and I was pleasantly surprised by what I found.

With limited counter space in my kitchen, I was looking for a small toaster oven that wouldn't take up too much room, and I also needed a fan. Luckily, Big Lots had both!

After my shopping trip, I planned to stop by the grocery store, but I didn't have to because I discovered they have a grocery section right there at Big Lots.

I may not be sharing anything new, but I was amazed by the variety of "things" you can find at Big Lots—including furniture!

On my way home, I noticed a few attractions I haven't visited yet, and I plan to check one out tomorrow. I have a feeling it won't be too crowded.

Now, I'm back at the cabin, relaxing and watching some TV.

That's all for now!

84: Gatlinburg Day 3 8/30/21

I woke up this morning around 7:30 a.m. EST.

I brewed up a pot of coffee and used the brand-new toaster oven to make some delicious cheese toast—four pieces, to be exact!

I haven't had a chance to take my shower yet, but I plan to do that right after I finish posting this. For me, my day doesn't really kick off until I've enjoyed my refreshing shower!

There are two lovely places I'm considering visiting today, and I need to choose just one.

Don't worry, the other one will definitely be on my list for tomorrow!

That's all for now, and I'm looking forward to seeing where the day takes me!

85: Hillbilly Golf

I had a blast playing Putt-Putt tonight at "Hillbilly Golf." It's such a charming place located in Gatlinburg, right at the end of the strip leading to "Pigeon Forge." They've been delighting visitors for over fifty years now, which is pretty impressive!

As a child, my brothers, cousins, and I would eagerly play Hillbilly Golf every time we visited Gatlinburg, and those memories always bring a smile to my face.

This evening, I pulled into the Public Pay Parking Lot, and to my delight, the friendly manager of Hillbilly Golf came over to me with a warm smile.

"You here to play Putt-Putt?" he asked.

"Yes, Sir," I replied, feeling excited.

He kindly said, "Use our parking lot. It's free."

I thanked the man as I pulled into their parking lot, which can easily be missed if you're not paying attention!

"Hillbilly Golf" is Putt-Putt on the side of a mountain. Yes, you heard that right! Putt-Putt, on the side of a mountain—how cool is that?

To reach the top of the mountain, you ride on an incline rail. The top is an impressive 310 feet high!

Once we were all settled in the rail car, an employee warmly explained what we should expect:

"Welcome to 'Hillbilly Golf' everyone! This car will take you up 310 feet to the top of the mountain. When you get to the top, there are two 18-hole courses—one to your left and one to your right. One is called 'Thick Brush,' and the other is called 'Thin Brush.' Any questions so far?"

Since no one had a question, he continued:

"Now, we've posted our phone number at every hole for two important reasons: First, if you accidentally knock your ball off the side of the mountain, just give us a call, and we'll be happy to bring you a new one. Second, if you happen to spot a bear, please call us right away, and we'll come to help; we had two cubs appear just last night."

I raise my hand…

"Yes, sir?"

"Um, did you say last night?"

"Yep."

"Cubs?"

"Yep."

"Where was the momma?"

"Good question."

"Crap… It'll be me who gets eaten…"

"Better you than me…"

"Thanks…"

"Any other questions?"

Everyone seemed to be enjoying the moment, and soon the incline rail whisked us up to the mountaintop.

The holes are quite manageable and designed for a fun experience with low scores in mind. Each one is either a Par 3 or a Par 2, and I even managed to score a couple of hole-in-ones!

While I was playing one of the holes, I noticed nutshells gently falling from a tree onto both me and the course. It took a moment for me to connect the dots and realize that if the shells were dropping down, there must be something up in the tree munching on nuts…

I slowly turned my head up to see what was in the tree above and spotted a little squirrel curiously watching me as he stuffed his cheeks full of nuts. I couldn't help but let out a relieved sigh.

The heat was quite intense up the mountain today. Thankfully, there are coolers set up along the course with water bottles available for just a dollar, and they operate on the honor system.

The entrance fee is $12.99 for adults, while children pay a lower price.

One thing to note is that there aren't any restrooms on the course; however, you can easily find them at the Public Pay Parking Lot right next door.

Also, be prepared for a workout, as there are quite a few steps, especially when enjoying the game while walking down the mountain.

The course itself is beautiful and well-maintained. It's clear that the employees take great pride in their work and truly love what they do.

I had such a great time playing "Hillbilly Golf" tonight, and I can't wait to come back for another round!

That's all for now.

86: 8/31/2021- I slept like a baby last night.

I don't know why people say they "slept like a baby." I'm told that Babies wake up at all hours of the night.

I slept well last night.

It's raining outside since morning.

It would be a great day to stay in and nap. I can't do that, though.

I have a reservation at one of the attractions here for 2 p.m.

I hope to write about it when I return home.

So, my plans today are to take a shower and make my 2 p.m. reservation.

Then, hopefully, find a place to eat.

I think that is enough on my plate for one day.

I am looking forward to seeing how this day plays out.

I'll write more later.

That's all for now.

87: Titanic Museum

On April 10th, 1912, the Titanic embarked on its maiden voyage from Southampton, England. At that time, it was celebrated as the largest and most advanced ship ever built.

And, on April 15th, 1912, at 2:20 a.m., the Titanic sank.

Fast forward to August 31st, 2021, and here I am, visiting the "Titanic Museum" in "Pigeon Forge, Tennessee." I had to make a reservation to visit.

I'm not sure if that's the usual practice or just a precaution due to COVID.

I booked my reservation for 2 p.m., thinking it wouldn't be too crowded then, and it turned out to be a pleasant time! They only allow a limited number of guests inside the museum at once, which adds to the experience.

Like many other people, I wore a mask while exploring the exhibits.

The employees are all dressed as Crew Members and embrace that title throughout the museum, which adds a special touch to the visit.

I have to admit, I won't be able to do justice to describing the museum, and they do not allow for pictures to be taken while inside.

However, I will do my best to describe it using the notes I took.

Yes, I took notes. If I can't take pictures, I'll take notes.

I opened Microsoft Word on my smartphone and began typing away.

The museum is divided into several sections.

Many sections are an exact replica of a Room or Hallway on the "Titanic."

Inside, they have some incredible items that were recovered from the Titanic. Some of these treasures were found floating during the initial recovery efforts when the Titanic sank, while others were recovered many years later during Research and Recovery Expeditions.

I discovered so many fascinating facts about the Titanic that I didn't know until today!

For instance, the Titanic boasted two luxurious Millionaire Suites.

Each Suite featured two spacious Bedrooms, a private Kitchen, a cozy Living Room, and a Bathroom. They even had an electric fireplace and electricity throughout!

Can you believe that, in today's money, a one-way ticket for the Millionaire Suite would cost a staggering 125,000.00 dollars?

They also have an exact replica of the famous "Grand Staircase."

It was so intriguing to learn that the flooring used in the Grand Staircase is known as "Millionaire Flooring." It got this fancy name due to its versatility, although nowadays, we simply call it linoleum.

Yep.

One section is shaped like the "Wheelhouse," which is where the Captain steered the ship. Just in front of the wheelhouse, there's a fascinating section with seawater kept at a chilly 28 degrees—the very temperature of the sea the night the Titanic sank. Visitors are warmly encouraged to dip their hands into the seawater to see just how cold it was that fateful night. It was absolutely freezing! Seawater actually freezes at 28.4 degrees, which explains why those waters felt so icy.

As I toured around the museum, delightful music played overhead. While it wasn't "My Heart Will Go On," it certainly had a similar feel. Entering one section, I stumbled upon a beautiful 115-year-old piano right in the middle of the room, with a crew member playing the music from 1912.

I paused by the piano and enjoyed the lovely tunes. Eventually, he did play "My Heart Will Go On," and it sounded just as beautiful on the piano.

Another section features a replica of a standard "Third Class Cabin." Honestly, I thought the Third Class Cabin looked quite charming—good enough for me, but I also enjoy staying at cheap motels.

It is an audio-guided tour.

They have one audio experience for adults and a separate, engaging audio tour for children.

I wholeheartedly recommend visiting the "Titanic Museum" if you find yourself in "Pigeon Forge, TN."

Plan on staying for two hours.

Oh, and bring your children, too.

That's all for now.

88: Cherokee Grill

After finishing my time at the "Titanic Museum," I found myself craving a hearty meal—nothing beats a big steak and a baked potato!

I made my way to "Cherokee Grill," nestled in Gatlinburg.

The atmosphere was calm, and I was quickly seated at a cozy table.

As I browsed the menu, I felt inspired to treat myself and order only the finest tonight. Yes, indeed, only the finest tonight.

When my waitress brought my water, I eagerly ordered a Shrimp Cocktail to start. Really, just the best tonight!

For my main course, I chose a 14-ounce Prime Grade New York Strip with a loaded baked potato and a fresh salad. Absolutely the best tonight!

I mentioned to my waitress that I might not be able to finish it all, but to my surprise, I polished off every last bite.

The steak was truly one of the best I've ever had. And shame on anyone who would dare dip this steak into sauce. Shame, shame, shame on them!

The salad was so fresh that I couldn't help but ask my waitress if they sourced their vegetables locally.

She happily confirmed, "Yes, everything that we can get local, we get local, and that includes all the vegetables and the trout."

My waitress was an absolute delight. She and her husband both work at Cherokee Grill—he in the kitchen and she as a waitress. They have two lovely children: a seven-year-old and a nine-year-old. She shared that it's truly a joy to work at a restaurant that serves great food, and she's spot on; the food is fantastic!

So yes, nothing but the best tonight!

89: 9/1/2021 – Night Update

As I mentioned in my morning post, I woke up feeling quite a bit of pain today. The rain outside created the perfect cozy atmosphere for a nap while I waited to feel better.

By the afternoon, I was happy to say I felt much better.

I got myself a shower and began cleaning up around the Cabin. I also took care of a load of laundry and washed the dishes in the dishwasher.

Afterward, I went to "Food City" to grab some frozen Pizzas. While I was there, I bought a Flag for the Cabin! I also spotted some Single Pizzas I hadn't noticed before and decided to buy two of them. They're called "Screamin' Sicilian Pizza."

Then, I popped into "Dollar General" and picked up a few other things for the Cabin.

Once back, I hung our new Flag, finished cleaning up, and cooked the "Screamin' Sicilian Pizza." It turned out to be pretty tasty! I'd definitely buy it again.

Now, I'm getting ready to hit the sack.

That's all for now!

90: Music Outlet

Today was quite a busy day for me!

I made my way over to "Music Outlet" in Sevierville, Tennessee. It's amazing to think they've been in business for 45 years!

As I chatted with my salesman, he shared that his father and uncle started this wonderful shop all those years ago. I truly enjoy purchasing my musical instruments from family-owned and operated businesses. But today, I wasn't shopping for myself; I was on a mission for my dad.

A few years back, I surprised him with a Gibson Les Paul Epiphone guitar and amp. He loved it, though he often finds dragging out the amp a bit of a hassle. Recently, he asked me if I could help him find a nice acoustic guitar at a reasonable price.

He mentioned this while I was relaxing at the cabin in Gatlinburg, TN. I remembered wanting to check out "Music Outlet," and today, I finally got the chance to see it in person for the first time!

The moment I opened the door and stepped inside; I was struck speechless— "WOW!" doesn't even begin to capture how incredible it felt.

It was like a book lover entering an enchanting old bookstore for the first time; the sight and scent combined created a magical atmosphere.

They have a wide array of stringed instruments—everything from acoustic guitars to bass fiddles and so much more. Their inventory is massive! I was even lucky enough to play "Stairway" while testing out the guitar I had my eye on. It's funny how "Stairway to Heaven" is often frowned upon in music stores these days...

Many recording and touring artists also get their instruments from this fantastic place.

When I explained what I was looking for, my salesman eagerly began showing me all the options. I could really tell he wanted to make me a happy customer.

After sharing my budget with him, I was thrilled to find out that with his help, I ended up spending less than I had originally planned.

I know this sounds like an advertisement, but I genuinely love wandering through a music store—it's an even better when I get to buy something.

And now, I have this lovely Fender Acoustic Guitar to keep me company for the rest of my trip! I might even come up with a name for her before I gift her to dad.

Back at the cabin and getting this guitar setup.

I'd say it was a pretty good day.

That's all for now.

91: A/C Out In Vehicle

My vehicle's A/C kept acting up today—sometimes it would go out and then come back on, only to go out again. When it stopped working, there was no sound or air at all.

After I returned to the cabin and turned off the vehicle, I decided to see if it would start working again when I cranked it up. Unfortunately, it didn't.

Many kind friends from my Facebook friends tried to help out, and I really appreciate all their support.

A family member who owns a garage suggested I try replacing the "AC Clutch Relay," so I headed to Pigeon Forge to get a new one.

The trip to Auto Zone was a bit slow because it was the weekend and a holiday, and unfortunately, they didn't have the relay in stock.

Luckily, O'Reilly's Auto Parts was right next door. They only had one left for $7.99, so I grabbed it.

I replaced the relay and started the truck again to check if the A/C was working now… but it was still not blowing cool air.

I went inside to ask if they could test the relays, and they did. Both the old relay and the new one worked fine, so the issue was likely something else—and that means I'll need to wait until I get home to figure it out.

On the way back to the cabin, I kept the windows down and was sweating a bit, but I managed to get home.

Just hoping it will be working tomorrow!

92: Backroads

Gatlinburg and Pigeon Forge are both bustling with visitors, so there's no room for more. Instead, I took a relaxing drive along some backroads today, intentionally getting a bit lost to enjoy the adventure.

I made turns left and right, traversed dirt and gravel roads.

Along the way, I watched horses playing and cows lying peacefully, which made me think that the fish must be biting.

The weather was pleasantly in the '70s, with a beautiful sky and clouds that looked just like marshmallows.

After a couple of hours, I decided it was time to head back to the cabin. I used "Google" with a voice command to take me back. Since I have the cabin's address saved as "Cabin" in my maps, I simply said, "Ok Google, take me to the cabin," and the friendly female voice responded, "Sure, setting your destination."

At that moment, I realized I was a bit lost myself, relying on the cheerful voice to guide me in the right direction.

I continued driving through gravel and dirt roads, making turns as I went. Pretty soon, I started wondering if Google was really taking me home, or maybe still taking me farther away.

I pulled over to check the map closer and discovered it was leading me to a place called "The Cabin" in Georgia, far from where I wanted to be!

So, I reset my destination to our actual cabin's address and headed back on the right track.

Throughout the day, my vehicle's A/C kept running perfectly, despite driving over potholes and bumps—it didn't turn off once!

Oh, and I've also changed the name of the "Cabin" in my Google Maps to make things even clearer.

All in all, it was a fantastic day full of little adventures.

That's all for now.

93: Gladys And The Cubs

I managed to get a lot of chores done at the Cabin today.

Yes, Sir, I bought 64 Dollars' worth of shelves and cleared out the "Owner's Closet," which was a real mess, piled up five feet high.

I took everything out, installed the new shelves, and by the end, everything was neatly on the shelves or hanging on the wall instead of on the floor.

While I was changing the outside floodlights, I heard footsteps in the woods. Looking down from the porch, I saw a Momma Bear, whom I've named "Gladys," along with her three adorable Cubs.

I always name the Momma bears "Gladys," you know! Gladys has that orange tag on her ear, so she's easy to spot.

The Cubs were so playful—wrestling, licking, jumping around.

I didn't bother them, just enjoyed the moment. After that, I finished swapping out the floodlights and headed back inside.

Now, I'm relaxing and watching "The Andy Griffith Show."

It's been a wonderful day!

94: Grady The Bear

I woke up this morning at 8 a.m., which seems to be my usual schedule these days. I noticed it had rained overnight, and I wanted to check if the sealant around the lamps I installed yesterday was still doing its job.

So, I headed outside to see if the lights were still working. The lights have a handy 'Test" switch that lets me check if they're functioning properly.

I pressed the switch, and the light came on. I took a quick look, and it seemed like the sealant had kept the rain out, which was a relief.

While I was at it, I sensed something watching me. I turned around, and there it was. A bear, less than six feet away. My colostomy, "Lenny," started making noises, followed by my urostomy, "Squiggy." Honestly, if I ever need to hide quietly, I think "Lenny and Squiggy" might just give away my hiding spot! So, note to self: don't hide with me.

This bear wasn't "Gladys the bear" either. This one wasn't tagged, and I have a feeling it was a male. So, I decided to call him "Grady." Since "Gladys" starts with a "G," I figured Grady should too. Just a little fun aside.

Once I regained my composure, I walked back to the cabin, opened the door, and headed inside. I made sure to visit the restroom before settling down.

That's all for now.

95: Gatlinburg Bypass

Today, I visited Pigeon Forge, and I might write about it, or maybe not. On my way back, I took the scenic 'Gatlinburg Bypass,' which I highly recommend if you're ever nearby.

The views are absolutely breathtaking, so much so that the city has even set up several pull-off spots where you can stop, step out, and snap some photos.

As I was driving, I noticed a couple in a truck just ahead of me. I could tell they were a couple from the way they interacted. I even caught some of their conversation through their gestures. The woman kept holding her camera up in front of his face, trying to take pictures of the scenery out his side window, while he was trying to focus on the road.

It looked like he was asking, "Hun, do you want me to pull over so you can get a better shot?" and she responded, "No, I'm fine just taking pictures through your window."

He then offered again, "We can pull over right here if you want to get some good pictures." She replied, "No, we'll be late getting to Donna and Jerry's, so I'll just hold my camera here and take some shots out your window."

He kindly suggested, "We won't be late; I can pull over quickly, and you can grab a few pictures." But she was content, saying, "No, you're doing great. Just keep driving, and I'll keep capturing those beautiful views through your window with my camera right in front of your face."

At that point, I found myself speeding up just to see what was happening in their truck and to keep an eye on if anything went wrong. I decided to slow down and fall back about a hundred yards to keep a safe distance.

96: 9/9/2021 Cabin Updates

Not much to report today.

I drove by the "Sky Bridge" and 'Anakeesta,' and both were bustling with visitors.

I took a moment to reflect on everything happening in our lives right now. Sadly, we lost another family friend to COVID. He was a dear friend of Papa's. Currently, two other family friends are in the hospital with COVID as well. They're from my hometown and are around the same age as my oldest brother.

Because of that, I decided to stay in today instead of joining the crowds.

Last night, a storm swept through here, and unfortunately, the base of the new American Flag I hung was twisted in the wind and broke off. Luckily, I had another base on hand. I drilled an extra hole and added an extra screw this time, hoping it will hold up better during future storms.

I also took some time to pack away a few things I won't need anymore.

Plus, I stopped at the bottom of the hill and picked up two small 12-ounce bottles of 2% milk. Just perfect for my midnight cereal. That should keep me comfortable through Saturday night.

That's all for now.

97: 9/11/2001 – It Was Hell

NOTE: In short, this is my recollection of 9/11/2001

It was Tuesday, September 11, 2001

The day started just like any other day. I woke up at 7 AM, ready to start my day and head to work.

At that time, I was living with my parents in Alabama and was considering buying my own home in Huntsville. I was 25 now, optimistic about overcoming my Spina Bifida, and thinking about making a fresh start in Huntsville.

My dad, mom, and I all worked for the same company. Dad was the President of the Huntsville branch, Mom was the Vice President of her department, and I served as the I.T. Administrator.

On this particular morning, I carpooled to work with Dad, little did I know how the day would unfold.

Mom stayed at a nearby hotel the night before, as she and the other department heads were preparing for a trip to Mississippi from Birmingham. Papa and I met at the car, eager to head towards Huntsville, chatting about work and lunch plans, something we often enjoyed doing together.

Suddenly, Mom called, voice tense, telling Papa about a small plane hitting one of the World Trade Center Towers. She wondered if she should return home, sensing something was wrong. I can still hear her asking, "How can a plane not see that huge building?" Despite her worries, Papa advised her to continue to Mississippi.

On our ride, we usually listened to talk radio. That day, it was the "Rick and Bubba morning show." That's when we learned it wasn't a small plane but a large commercial jet that hit the first tower. I started to feel that Mom might be right. I remember asking Papa if he thought it had happened on purpose.

We were on I-565 heading toward Huntsville when we heard the news that another commercial aircraft had hit the second World Trade

Center tower. In that moment, we realized we were under attack, and everyone in America, and indeed the world, knew it too.

I remember vividly telling Papa, "We gotta pray now!" He turned down the radio, and together, we prayed.

Soon after, we learned that yet another plane had been hijacked and flown into the Pentagon.

Out loud, I said, "They need to land the planes!"

Just as we were about to pass in front of Huntsville International Airport, the radio announced, "The FAA has ordered all aircraft to land immediately." I looked out the passenger window, hoping to see some planes.

Papa, who had been silent all the way, softly said, "It's going to be a bad day today, son."

Huntsville, Alabama, is actually a high-tech hub, something not many people realize.

We arrived at work a little late that day. As I walked in, I heard someone say, "We're at DEFCON 3!" I wasn't sure if that was good or bad, so I guessed it was probably serious.

Because of Redstone Arsenal, the whole area of Huntsville was in chaos. Many people living in Huntsville have family members in the military, and they either work at Redstone Arsenal or have relatives in New York and all over the world.

I remember one coworker, who is also a good friend of mine, praying out loud in her office. Her husband was in the military and was in New York that morning. She was trying to reach him, but couldn't get hold of him.

She was on the floor of her office, arms raised to Heaven, crying out to God, "God, Please! God Please! Oh, God, don't let him get on that plane!"

Many of us prayed for her husband that day, and I was one of them.

In my office, alone, I also said many prayers.

Then, we saw the South Tower fall. Everyone just…stopped. …They paused what they were doing and simply sat down…

I sat quietly, saying nothing.

We all just sat in silence…

Someone kindly mentioned that each tower could hold over 30,000 people.

I stepped outside.

Once outside, I saw a man standing, with a Bible in his hand, hollering to people, "Repent! For the Kingdom of God is at hand!"

He caught me staring at him, and he said, "Hey!" Then, he ran over to me with his Bible opened up and said, "Read this!"

I read the Book and Verses that he asked me to read.

I won't say which Book of the Bible or which verses it was. But, know this, on 9/11 2001, if you read that story of the Bible, it might scare you as much as it did me.

I walked away while he continued, "Repent, the Kingdom of God is at hand!"

I think in his mind, the rapture was going to happen within the hour. And I'll admit, I, too, felt the rapture might happen that day as well.

I went to my office and got my Bible.

I went to my friend's office and showed her the Book and the verses in the Bible.

She was knowledgeable about the Bible and a Christian. So I trusted her on this.

She said, "No, that's not what's happening." I felt a little better.

Going back to the TV, I learned that Flight 93 had crashed in a field.

Though I was many miles away from everything happening, I felt as though I was right in the middle of it all. We all shared that feeling.

I was 25, soon to be 26, and among the many tragedies I've experienced, the Challenger disaster was the first national tragedy I remember. I recall overhearing people at the Arsenal discussing the DEFCON level, but to this day,

I don't know what level we reached on 9/11/2001. My co-worker mentioned he suspected Bin Laden was involved. That was the first time I heard that name, and I asked him who he was.

He responded, "Don't you keep up with the news?"

I didn't at that time in my life.

He then asked, "Where is our President?" That question suddenly made me think for the first time. Yes! Where was our President? Had he been harmed? Where exactly was he? Later on, we learned that he was on Air Force One, the only plane flying in the sky except for the fighter jets escorting him.

Then, I watched as the second tower collapsed.

I wasn't even close to where everything was happening. But I felt like I was right there with it all.

We all shared that feeling. We felt like we were right in the middle of it all.

Because we are all Americans, this was an attack on each of us.

We are brothers and sisters. We all bleed the same blood. We are in this together.

It was our buildings that fell.

It was our Pentagon that was attacked.

Those planes carried our brothers and sisters, and those buildings housed our fellow Americans.

We're all in this together.

It wasn't even noon yet, and so much had already happened.

September 11, 2001—It was a day of hell.

Since then, our lives have never been the same.

But the very next day, September 12, 2001, is a day I will remember forever.

On that day, most Americans were out buying American flags for their homes.

98: *Old Memories*

It might be surprising, but there was a time when cell phones didn't have cameras. Actually, there was also a time when people didn't have Mobile Phones at all. We used to just call them "Mobile" when we wanted to sound cool. For example, I might ask, "You got your mobile on you?" but I often had to borrow someone else's since I didn't own one myself. And back then, it was pronounced "Mo-Bile." When I was younger, I didn't usually have a camera to snap photos of my friends and me—unless it was a special occasion, like a concert, then it was a different story.

For such a special occasion, I'd head to the local "Mart" store and pick up a disposable camera or maybe buy a camera, keep the receipt, and then return it after the "Event" to get my money back. I know... I was just a kid back then...

The date was November 29th, 1997.

The place was the Birmingham Jefferson Civic Center.

The event was the Aerosmith Nine Lives Tour.

I was super excited because I was finally going to see Aerosmith live! I was so stoked!

I managed to get a camera to take some photos at the concert. I knew security might check at the entrance, and if they found the camera… well, I wasn't quite sure what would happen.

At that time, I was wearing a diaper, and I knew I'd need an extra one to change in case I went to the restroom.

I had to hide it because my friends didn't know about my Spina Bifida yet. I didn't hide my condition when I was younger, but I didn't really talk about it either. And people often assume you're not wearing a diaper, which can make things tricky to bring up.

Usually, I'd wear a jacket and hide the extra diapers in the sleeve. It's a good hiding spot—who's going to feel your arms?

Anyway, I just have to share this incredible experience. Two of my friends and I got into the concert, and while I'd love to say we were right on the fifth row, it was probably a little further back, but definitely on the floor and close to the front. I was so thrilled! I've already seen Pink Floyd back in '94, and now I was lucky enough to see another one of my favorite bands live.

One of the first songs I learned to play on the guitar was Aerosmith's "Dream On." I loved Old Aerosmith—they were way better than some of their recent stuff. Their classic songs were so good that I could forgive them for their newer material. My main reason for going was just to hear those old hits.

Towards the end of the concert, more and more people moved closer to the front, and we managed to get pretty close, too. I was determined to watch Joe Perry play his guitar—and I did! Near the end, Steven Tyler started taking song requests from the crowd.

I yelled as loudly as I could, "Kings And Queens!" To my surprise, Joe Perry pointed at me, looked over at Steven Tyler, and echoed my request, "Kings And Queens." Steven Tyler then cheered, "Do it!" and they launched into "Kings And Queens." That moment truly made me feel on top of the world.

Twenty-three years later, I came across a roll of film. I also wrote about discovering it. Not knowing what was on it but feeling excited, I hurriedly took it to CVS to have it developed. Today, I finally received the film back. I was a little nervous as I carefully opened it. Once I got it open, the memory I just shared with you flooded back as I looked through the pictures from the "Aerosmith Nine Lives" concert of '97.

99: Health Update

To my dear family and friends who stay updated on my health:

I've mentioned my fast heart rate before.

My heart usually beats around 110 bpm, and it's been that way for as long as I can remember. My Primary Care Physician (PCP) wants me to get it checked out since I'm now 45 and will soon turn 46.

I've already had one appointment with him, and I even wore a Heart Monitor for two weeks.

Tomorrow, I'm heading in for my Nuclear Stress Test, which is an all-day event with several tests scheduled.

At 3 PM, I'll meet with my heart doctor to discuss the results of the stress test and the heart monitor.

I promise to keep you all updated on what I learn.

That's all for now.

100: Dragging

I woke up at 6 AM CST this morning, feeling a bit stiff but hopeful for the day.

I sleep with a nighttime urine bag that holds 4000cc of output, connected to my Urostomy, lovingly called "Squiggy," through a 6-foot hose.

I slowly get out of bed, saying "Ouch" a few times as I rise, and head into the kitchen. My bag gently drags behind me, making a little noise on the floor, while my curious cats try to chase it playfully.

I plug in the coffee percolator, which contains yesterday's brew—still flavorful and extra strong, just how I like it.

Today, I need to be at the doctor's office by 10 AM, so I'm taking my time to loosen up before my shower and leaving. I've already had three cups of coffee, which is helping me feel more awake, and soon I'll hop into the shower to start my day.

Though I'm feeling a bit sluggish, I remind myself that I'm taking it one step at a time… even with my pee bag trailing behind me.

101: Health Update

To everyone keeping an eye on my health, I wanted to share a little update.

I arrived at the heart doctor's office at 9:45 AM. Even though it was busy, everything moved smoothly, and I was called back right at 10:00 AM.

My nurse asked if I had any caffeine this morning. I admitted, "Um, yeah. Lots. I've had plenty of caffeine. First some day-old coffee, then I brewed a new pot and drank that too."

She then asked if I had taken my diabetes medication. I assured her I had taken all my medicines. When she inquired if I had read the instructions they sent in the mail, I explained

I had just gotten back from a fifteen-day trip to Gatlinburg and hadn't gone through my mail yet, they mostly look like bills to me.

Turns out, I wasn't supposed to take my diabetes medicine or consume caffeine this morning. My appointment has been rescheduled for October 12th.

I asked if I could try the treadmill, but she wanted me to walk while she watched. I did, and she said that because of my gait, she couldn't allow it, which led to the doctor ordering some nuclear tests.

I apologized repeatedly for missing the mail instructions. They told me it's common, and I'm the third person this week to have their appointment rescheduled because of this. That's all for now, but I appreciate your support!

102: Diabetes Update

I prick my fingers to draw blood and monitor my blood-sugar levels throughout each day. My fingertips are raw and hurt all the time because of all the "Pricking."

Seriously, I check my blood sugar around six times, if not more, each day.

When I returned home from Gatlinburg the other day, Papa had picked up my Prescriptions from the Pharmacy.

Unbeknownst to me, my diabetes doctor had sent a prescription for me to start using the "FreeStyle Libre" system. I was so happy.

With the "FreeStyle Libre" system, I attach a device to the back of my arm and scan it using the handheld reader to get my blood-sugar numbers.

The reader keeps track of everything.

I can now scan myself all I want without having to prick my fingers.

If it's high, I can make a note on the handheld device that I've given myself some fast-acting insulin.

If it's low, I can make a note to eat some food or drink something to bring my blood sugar back up.

My doctor will be able to see all of this when I go back to see him.

In return, he'll be able to better care for me. It's a win-win.

Both my fingers and I are a lot happier.

103: Bears, Bears, Bears

On 9/13/2021, I had quite an exciting visit to The Cabin in Gatlinburg!

Early in the morning, I spotted a bear at the bottom of the driveway, and across the street, I saw a curious cub perched atop the cabin's roof. The little one had happily climbed the tree next to the cabin and then hopped right onto the roof! I wished I could have snapped a photo, but I didn't have my camera handy.

I also thought about letting the neighbors know, but since it's a rental cabin, I wasn't sure how to get in touch with anyone. Plus, I wasn't about to walk over and knock on the door, especially with Mama Bear hanging around.

Soon, the cub scurried over to the tree, hopped back up, and slid down with so much ease.

Curious to see more, I decided to hop into my truck and drive down to the bottom of the driveway for a closer look. That turned out to be a great idea! I ended up seeing a total of seven bears.

I was able to take pictures of one mama bear, whom I've now named Gladys, along with her three adorable cubs. Gladys was quite clever—she got into the neighbor's trash bin, pulled out the can, and placed it in the middle of the road for her little ones. They ate like kings, and I watched happily until they wandered off with full tummies.

I then drove around the can and was delighted to come across another mama bear, "Gladys #2," along with her four adorable cubs.

They all sprinted away before I could even stop for a quick photo, but luckily, my dashcam captured some fantastic footage. I have a feeling it's pretty good!

I've also heard that the bear population is larger than usual this year, and it definitely seems true. Here are the pictures I managed to take.

104: 9/22/2021

Today was a bit busy, but also quite relaxing.

I really enjoyed getting outside and soaking in the beautiful weather. Nothing beats blue skies and white clouds.

I had to drive to school to drop off two Ibuprofen tablets for my niece since schools no longer give out medicine like Ibuprofen or Tylenol anymore.

Afterwards, I went to Hobby Lobby to get some pictures framed, hoping to hang one at the cabin. I also picked up a shelf for my room.

While I was in Gardendale, Alabama, I stopped by "Milos" for a tasty burger. If you ever visit Alabama, I highly recommend trying Milo's, especially their hamburger with that amazing Greek sauce.

It's so delicious! When I got home, I set up the shelf. That's about it for today. It was pretty simple, but I really enjoyed it.

105: Morning Coffee

I woke up today and decided to go for my usual drive, feeling a little hungry. I thought I'd stop at a local fast-food place for a biscuit, but the line at the drive-thru was so long it went out onto the street. Instead, I chose to go inside a nearby, fairly new gas station—only about three years old. Inside, they had all kinds of treats, from Donut Holes to Bear Claws. I decided to grab a cup of Donut Holes, a Bear Claw, and some coffee.

As I got back into my truck and took a Donut Hole, I couldn't resist popping another and then another, before driving off. While on the road, the cup of Donut Holes slipped between my legs and fell onto the truck's floor. I pulled over to pick them up. That's when I noticed "it." "It" was a dark green film on every Donut Hole. I looked closer and realized it was mold. All of them had mold. Can you believe it? I had already popped at least three into my mouth!

Not wanting to risk it, I threw everything, including the Bear Claw, into a bag and tossed it into the back seat of my truck.

I tuned my radio to Sirius XM Channel 148, "Radio Classics," and enjoyed listening to "The Affairs Of Anatol" featuring Orson Wells.

I started driving again, savoring my morning coffee.

At least my coffee was good.

106: Evening Update 9/24/2021

Today was a wonderful day! I had the pleasure of sharing lunch with my beloved Aunt Ann and Uncle Jim. We dined at The White House Restaurant in Warrior, Alabama, a place I always enjoy visiting. Interestingly, I was there yesterday too!

Yesterday, I indulged in liver and onions. I'm a true Southerner. All true Southerners eat Liver and Onions. Today, I opted for a delicious vegetable plate.

This afternoon, I visited the local Dollar General to hunt for tiny treasures to put inside a snow globe. I love searching for small items that fit perfectly inside, but today, I didn't find anything special.

For dinner, I treated myself to a tasty Pickle Loaf Sandwich.

Now, I think I'll curl up and find a wonderful Christmas movie to enjoy tonight.

Here's a cozy thought: something fun to listen to while drifting off to sleep.

Or maybe I should go for a thrilling scare and watch a good scary movie instead. I might start with "Halloween" parts 1 and 2. That's all for now!

107: Diabetes Hiccup 9/27/2021

I've been working on something pretty exciting for me. I don't want to go into it here, right now, but I'm praying something good comes of it.

So, with that in mind, I was pretty busy during the first part of today.

So much so, I think I might've ignored my diabetes a little.

I'm still fairly new to diabetes. I believe I've had it for three years now. The pandemic has thrown me off. I keep forgetting about the year 2020. It feels like that year didn't even happen. So, sometimes it feels like I've only had diabetes for two years. But if I count 2020, then yeah, it's been three.

What I do know is that I got up around 5 AM this morning and took my meds, which include my diabetes medications and insulin.

Before leaving the house, I had a sweet tooth. That should've been a red flag. I don't usually get a sweet tooth in the morning.

I ate some donuts.

Around 8 AM, I left the house.

I think I was back in my truck heading home by around 11:30 AM.

I checked my blood sugar, and it was in the 70s. That's not normal for me. I usually stay around 105.

When that happens, I get a sweet tooth. It's my body's way of saying it needs sugar. So I drove through a fast-food place, got a drink and a bite to eat, and felt fine again.

I remember having a snack between lunch and dinner, too.

Around 5:00 PM, dinner was ready. Mom called out, "Dinner's ready!" and we all came out of our rooms to sit down at the table.

Papa said the blessing.

Right about then, I started shaking. I checked my blood sugar, and it was 66.

I piled some potatoes on my plate and started shoving them in my mouth. Potatoes are carbs, good for bringing sugar up.

A few minutes later, I scanned the chip on my arm to check my sugar level again. It was 59.

I asked Mom for some of her "Sweet Tea." Her secret? 400 cups of sugar and a little bit of tea.

I drank a glass.

Still shaking, and now with cold sweats, I drank a glass of lemonade, too.

I scanned again—57.

Anything under 70 is low. Too low.

I knew I had taken in enough sugar and carbs to raise my blood sugar above 300. I figured it just needed a little more time to kick in.

The shaking started to ease, so I finished my meal.

I told Papa we might need to call 911 or head to the hospital if I couldn't get things under control.

Thirty minutes later, my sugar was up to 186.

It should've been around 300, considering everything I'd eaten: Mom's super sweet tea, lemonade, potatoes, bread, you name it.

But forty-five minutes later, it had already dropped to 165. That's about a point a minute.

I decided not to take my nighttime diabetes medications. I want to talk to my doctor first. I'll call him tomorrow.

Now, don't think all I did was scan the chip in my arm.

I also did finger pricks and checked my blood that way. It was still all over the place.

I knew it was messed up because I was feeling sick, cold sweats, shaking.

As I'm typing this, it's at 150.

It's not dropping a point a minute anymore, but I also didn't take my diabetic meds.

Still, I had a great day. It really was a great day.

Just a minor hiccup.

I'll check it again in the morning and call my doctor.

That's all for now.

108: Disabled Fighting

Twice in my life, I've seen a man beating up on his girlfriend or wife.

Both times were at concerts, and both times, I had a friend with me.

Also, both times, I started walking over to step in.

Each time, my friend pulled me back and went instead.

Later I'd hear them say, "You can't get involved in something like that! You'll get killed, you dang fool!"

Now, twice in my life, I've met someone with one arm.

Both times, it was a man, and both were mad at the world and mean.

I'm not saying all one-armed people are angry or mean, I'm just saying the two I met were.

I tell you that, to tell you this:

I had to drive up to the cabin today. I'll go into why in another post.

In another state, I made a pit stop to stretch my legs and grab a drink.

When I travel, I hook my 2000cc urine bag up to my Urostomy. That way, I don't have to stop every thirty minutes to empty the smaller bag.

At the gas station, I unhooked myself from the travel pee bag and got out.

As I walked in, I heard a guy yelling at his girlfriend. (We'll say girlfriend for this story.)

Inside, I bought some Diet Cokes for the cabin, some chips, and a lottery ticket.

Then I headed back to the vehicle.

Outside, the guy was still going off, calling his girlfriend all sorts of names.

I noticed he only had one good arm. The other stopped at the elbow; a nub.

"Angry at the world," I thought.

As I got to my vehicle, I heard a "Pop" sound…

I knew right away that he'd hit her.

"Crap… I'm gonna get hit in the face with that nub…" I thought.

I opened the car door, took a deep breath, and dropped everything into the driver's seat.

Then I leaned in, grabbed my pee bag, and hooked it back up to myself.

I knew what I was about to do.

I leaned against the car and stared at the guy.

He looked about 28. Not skinny, not fat, just a thick build.

He had her by the arm with his one hand. His other arm, the nub, was swinging wildly.

I lifted my shirt and left it up, showing my colostomy and urostomy. I wanted him to see I was disabled too—and that I cared about his disability just as much as he cared about mine.

I started walking over.

I was thinking, "I'm gonna get hit with that nub, and I'm gonna hit him with my poop bag."

Then I thought, "Great. The news is gonna be all over this… If this is how I die, my nieces and nephews will talk about it for the next hundred years… And not in the way I'd want to be remembered."

I had my pee bag hooked to my belt loop. It had about 1500 cc's of urine in it. I figured I could swing it like a weapon if needed.

Our eyes met.

I saw his eyes move from my face down to my exposed stomach; Lenny and Squiggy.

His eyes widened.

We were about ten feet apart. I kept walking toward him with confidence.

That's when two police cars pulled up, lights flashing, and parked behind the couple's vehicle.

I immediately turned around, pulled my shirt down over Lenny and Squiggy, and walked back to my truck.

In my family, that's the protocol. If the police show up, turn the other way. Act like you were minding your own business.

I got in my truck and saw the police walk up to the one-armed man to talk to him.

"Saved by a friend, again," I thought.

And I drove away.

109: The Police and The Donut Friar

I got up at 7 AM EST this morning.

I'm expecting Mom and an Aunt, and an Uncle to show up while I'm here, so I needed to get some food for us.

The first thing I wanted was some donuts from "The Donut Friar."

They are excellent.

Their donuts rank right up there with "The Fultondale Bakery," located in Fultondale, Alabama.

They must both use the same recipes and ovens.

By 8 AM, I got in the car and headed out to get some fresh donuts.

Gatlinburg has a great parking rule on certain days of the week.

You can park on the street, right next to the sidewalks, up until 9 AM.

After 9 AM, though, you need to be gone.

I found a spot to park on the side of the road. I was in a row of about 20 cars.

I headed into "The Village" and went straight to "The Donut Friar."

"What can I get for you, sir?"

"You got any crème-filled? I don't see any."

"We've got Eclairs coming out in fifteen minutes."

"Oh, Bavarian Crème?"

"Yep. It's worth the wait."

"I'll wait. Let me get a coffee while I wait, please."

"Sure thing."

While waiting, I struck up a nice conversation with an older lady who was also waiting for the Bavarian Crème-filled Eclairs.

An employee came out carrying a tray of freshly made Cinnamon Bread.

Steam rose off the bread.

I almost let out an "Eeeee" screech as I saw her holding the tray.

I could immediately smell the sweet aroma of the hot bread; it was a sweet, sweet smell.

Next, another employee brought out a tray of cinnamon twists.

More steam rising.

"Eeeeecce…"

Then came the Eclairs.

Chocolate on top, sweet Bavarian Crème in the center.

The owner motioned for me to come to the counter, and I walked over.

"You want anything else with your Eclairs?"

"Uh, yeah. Yeah, I do. I'll take a loaf of the piping hot Cinnamon Bread, two Cinnamon Twists, and two Bavarian Crème-filled Eclairs. Thank you."

"It's hard to pass up the bread. Especially when it's fresh out of the oven."

"Yes. And just so you know, it's not all for me. I can only have a little because of my diabetes. There'll be others back at the cabin eventually."

I got my order and headed back out to the car.

As I walked through The Village, I could see the road, and I noticed that all the cars that had been parked on the side were now gone.

"Oh, dang. I forgot the time."

I pulled out my phone to check, and it was 9:04 AM.

"I didn't realize how long I'd been in there," I thought to myself.

As I turned the corner, I saw blue lights flashing and a police cruiser parked behind my vehicle.

"Darn it," I thought.

Embarrassed, I walked up to the passenger side of the cruiser and kindly waved to the officer.

His window was down, and I said, "It's me, sir. That's mine. I am so sorry, sir."

"Oh, it's okay. I figured you were just running a little behind, and I parked here to keep your vehicle safe. You're fine."

Relieved, I said, "Thank you. Thank you so much, sir. I apologize again."

"It's fine. You have a great day, sir."

Now, I had this freshly made loaf of Cinnamon Bread and some fresh donuts, and I thought I'd be polite and offer a box to the friendly officer.

"Do you want some donuts?"

As soon as the words left my mouth, I realized I just offered a police officer some donuts…

"Wait, I don't mean it like that, sir. You've been nice, and you have a hard job, and I have freshly made bread and donuts I'd share with you if you'd like."

"That's okay, sir, but thank you."

"Okay, sir. Thank you, too, and again, I'm sorry."

I got in my car, buckled up, and headed back to the cabin.

I'll go shopping at the grocery store later.

110: Elk Burger

I met up with my Aunt and Uncle yesterday to have lunch.

We ate at "The Diner" in Pigeon Forge, Tennessee.

I ordered an "Elk Burger." My Uncle ordered one of the other burgers on the menu.

I'd never had elk before, and the menu said it was sweet-tasting, so I figured I'd give it a try.

We sat outside under an umbrella table while my Uncle went inside to place the order.

When he brought the food out, both burgers looked the same— same toppings on the side: lettuce, tomato, onion, and a pickle spear.

Both had American cheese, too.

So, we weren't sure which one was the Elk Burger.

Mine tasted like a regular hamburger, and my Uncle said his did too.

Now, I don't want you to think the burgers weren't great; because they were.

Big, juicy burgers with tons of flavor.

We just didn't know which one was the "Elk Burger."

Honestly, it didn't matter to me which one I was eating.

It was just nice sitting outside on a cool, sunny day, enjoying lunch with family.

In the end, though, we still don't know which one of us ate the Elk Burger.

Thanks for buying my lunch, Uncle. I love you.

111: Cabin Update 10/4/2021

I woke up this morning at 6 AM EST.

I haven't talked much about why I had to make a quick trip up here, and that's been on purpose.

See, I want to post pictures when I finally share the reason behind this trip.

I should be able to do that by tonight.

I'm making a pot of coffee.

As I type, I can hear it dripping into the pot.

I can already smell the aroma. Mmm-mmm.

My Aunt and her friend will be here today to help me out, and I'm really looking forward to that.

I haven't eaten out much at all.

I've spent $87.00 on food, and I plan on making that last.

Here's what I got:

- Thin Sliced Ham
- Thin Sliced Salami
- Potted Meat
- Bread
- Onions
- Pickles
- Chips
- Mustard
- Mayo
- Milk
- Cercal
- Diet Cokes

And I've really been enjoying the Potted Meat sandwiches.

I add onion and mayo to them. They're good.

That's all for now.

112: Christmas in the Mountains

Today, my Aunt, her friend, and I decorated the Cabin for Christmas.

That's the whole reason for the trip up here.

When Mom and Papa began renting out the Cabin, we didn't think about setting aside time for us to come up and decorate.

And the place is rented from now through the New Year.

I brought decorations from home, and we set everything up.

But honestly, the place didn't feel Christmassy enough.

The family renting the Cabin for Thanksgiving and Christmas also rented it last year during the same time.

So, I decided that my Christmas gift to Momma and Papa would be more decorations for the Cabin.

I figure the family staying here will enjoy it, and it'll be a nice help to Momma and Papa, and to the Cabin.

My Aunt and her friend both said I needed to go to "Old Time Pottery" for all my Christmas needs.

I'll admit that I didn't believe them at first...

But right after walking through the door, I turned into a bit of a kid.

Some might say, "Like a kid in a candy store."

The employees had put out aisle after aisle of Christmas stock. They had Christmas items I'd never even seen before—all for pretty cheap.

A lot of workers and shoppers stopped what they were doing just to watch me.

I went through the store, grabbing things off the shelf and tossing them into my buggy.

"Oh wow! Look at this! We've gotta have this at the ol' Cabin."

"Oh wow! Look at this church!"

"A Santa boot!"

I'm big on buying things that don't require any assembly.

Everything I bought could go straight from the buggy to the Cabin—"set it and forget it!"

I got six Nutcracker statues, present boxes to go under the tree, and mini-Christmas trees for each bedroom.

As employees added more items to the shelves, I kept tossing them into the buggy.

I was on a full-on Christmas shopping high.

I got a little church for the living room table, and it even lights up.

A Santa boot for the dining room table, it has a floral arrangement coming out of the top. (I think that's what you'd call it.)

Everything I picked up was between $2.99 and $14.99, just so you know.

It'll all be easy to store in a tote box, and again, no assembly required.

My Aunt and her friend said the real treat for them was just watching me.

The best part for me was buying things that'll be a part of this Cabin's story for years to come, even after I'm gone.

And the Cabin looks all Christmassy now.

Allow me to be the first to wish you a Merry Christmas.

That's all for now.

113: The Local Guy

I ran down to the bottom of the mountain tonight to grab some Diet Cokes and see the fellas.

Over the years, I've become friends with a few of the guys who work at the store down there.

"Steve" was working tonight along with one of the newer guys.

As I walked in, I was met with the sweet aroma of some great-smelling food.

"Luke," the new guy, had brought in some of his homemade cooking and was sharing it with Steve.

They were laughing, cutting up, and enjoying dinner together.

"That smells great!" I said. "I had a potted meat sandwich for dinner…"

"Well, I'm sorry you had to come in here and smell this then," Steve joked.

We laughed.

"Luke cooks all the time," Steve said. "He's pure Italian and an incredible cook."

"Oh, I've got a couple of Italian friends who love to cook too."

"Yeah," Luke said. "It's in our blood. My Grandma cooked, my Ma cooked, and now I cook."

He went on, "Grandma only cooked Italian. Ma cooked Italian, and she'd cook other stuff now and then. I cook everything, though."

"We eat like this all the time," Steve added. "But it's more than just the food. It's the talking and the bonding."

I chimed in, "The breaking of bread with your friends. The socializing."

"Yes!" they both agreed.

I added, "If you're laughing, talking, and cutting up, even if the food's not that great—it's still a great meal."

"Exactly."

I asked Luke, "Hey, is 'Best Italian' in Elks Plaza actually the best Italian around here?"

"It's good. It really is. But there's also 'Taste of Italy' across from Food City, next to the liquor store—that place is great. An Italian family from Brooklyn owns it. Great food."

"They're my people. I'm from Brooklyn," he smiled.

Then Luke asked, "You're local, right?"

Steve laughed, "He's actually from Alabama, but he's up here more than he's down there. You'd think he was local. He'll say he's heading home, and then the next week, he's back!"

I laughed.

Luke said, "I see you so much, I figured you lived around here."

I think I'm going to try "Taste of Italy" tomorrow.

I've also decided to get them both a gift certificate to "Taste of Italy" since I now know they like it.

The Cabin's rented out through the New Year, so I won't be back until 2022.

That means I won't get to see them at Christmas, or any time soon.

And I think the fellas would appreciate it.

That's all for now.

114: The Fellas

I wrote in a previous post that I found out about "Taste of Italy" from the fellas at the store at the bottom of the mountain, and that I was going to take them a gift certificate as a "Thank You."

I did that tonight.

"Steve" and "Luke" were both working when I walked in.

"How was 'Taste of Italy'?"

"The best. That other place is now ranked second."

"I knew you'd love it. I was thinking about you earlier and wondering if you'd gone."

"Yep. The owner, Geraldine, said for you to come and see her."

"Oh yeah? She and my Pop are friends."

"Well, I got y'all a little something for being so nice to me every time I come up here, and for turning me on to that restaurant." I then handed them the gift certificates.

We all shook hands, and we each said "Thank you" a couple of times.

"Luke" used to be a commodities dealer on Wall Street in the '80s.

During that time, he purchased 60 acres with two cabins here in the mountains.

He's now retired and living on that property in one of the cabins. His parents live in the other.

Like a lot of folks with a busy career, he put off marriage and kids until later in life.

He got married around the age of 40.

They had a child, who's now in their first semester of college.

Luke retired from his company on Wall Street and then moved to Gatlinburg.

He now works part-time just to stay active.

I got the chance to pick his brain about what I should do if I ever make it to New York.

I've always wanted to go but have been too nervous to try.

Luke made it seem doable; he made it feel less scary than I'd built it up to be in my head.

I told them I wouldn't be back until after the New Year.

We exchanged contact info, and I added them both to my phone.

We're going to try to grab lunch one day when I make it back up here.

Before I left, we shook hands again, and they wished me safe travels.

I'm going to miss seeing them, but it's time to head back home and let the renters enjoy "Christmas in the Mountains."

I head home in the morning.

That's all from "Grand View Mountain Chalet."

115: Taste of Italy

I made my way over to "Taste of Italy" today.

They've been voted "Best Italian" in the county, and I'll say that title is well deserved.

"Taste of Italy" will now be my first choice for Italian food whenever I'm up in Gatlinburg.

I know that might be surprising to some, but it's true.

That "other" place is now in second place.

"Taste of Italy" is a well-hidden gem here in Gatlinburg.

A gas station actually blocks the building and the sign, so it's easy to miss.

I met the owners.

Geraldine (or "Jerry") is from Brooklyn, New York, and has that thick Brooklyn accent you can't help but fall in love with.

She told me she's about to be 80 years young.

My jaw dropped. She looked much younger. At least 20 years younger.

She said she and her husband couldn't sit around in retirement, so they opened a restaurant.

I got to hear the whole story of how she went from working at IBM in New York to owning a top-notch restaurant in Gatlinburg, Tennessee.

If you want to hear it for yourself, just ask for "Jerry" when you visit, because now, I have to talk about the food.

Everything on the menu is made in-house from family recipes.

I imagine that if I visited Jerry's home, she'd serve me the exact same food.

I also imagine she'd hug me, kiss me, and pinch my cheeks before I left; she's that kind of Italian.

She told me all of their ingredients are top of the line.

"The veal is real veal, not that stuff they serve at other places," she said.

They bring garlic knots to your table as soon as you sit down. They come with a house-made marinara.

For an appetizer, I ordered the Caprese.

Slices of fresh mozzarella and basil on top of fresh tomato, all drizzled with olive oil and balsamic vinaigrette.

For my main course, I got the homemade lasagna. It's their most-ordered dish. The chicken parmesan is the second most popular.

It came with a side salad. I went with Italian dressing.

My Aunt ordered the "Taste of Italy" sampler. It included:

- Homemade Lasagna
- Chicken Parmesan
- Manicotti
- Pasta

My Aunt's friend, and my new friend, Linda, ordered the Philly Steak Salad.

They actually have a fantastic salad section on their menu.

I have to say, we each loved every bite of our meals.

We sampled from each other's plates, and everything was delicious.

It was more food than we could finish.

We each took home a to-go box.

We sat around enjoying each other's company and enjoying the same kinds of meals Ms. Geraldine grew up eating. It was a beautiful thing.

Linda said it was the best time she's had out in a long while. Aunt Claudine and I agreed—it was one of our best times out, too.

When the bill came, my Aunt grabbed it and paid.

"Happy Birthday to you!"

"That's right! Tomorrow's my birthday! I forgot…"

I thanked my Aunt for picking up the bill.

I also picked up two gift certificates for the fellas at the store down at the bottom of the mountain.

It's the least I could do for them turning me on to "Taste of Italy."

Taste of Italy, one of Gatlinburg's hidden gems.

116: Broken Wing

The drive home from Gatlinburg, Tennessee, to my home in Alabama is about six hours.

About four of those are on the interstate.

While on my way home, I noticed a car pulled over on the side of the interstate.

The driver was standing beside the car with both hands on his head, watching something in the road.

As I got closer, I could see the back spoiler of his car lying in the middle of the interstate.

I call them "wings," but they're actually called "spoilers."

It had apparently fallen off, and the driver was praying that nobody would run over it before he could get out there to retrieve it.

It reminded me of the '94 Camaro I had as a teenager.

Growing up, the guys either had a truck, a Mustang, or a Camaro.

I had the Camaro with T-tops.

I don't think they make cars with T-tops anymore. I sure don't see them.

One time, I was about to get on the interstate, so I took my T-tops out of the back storage compartment and locked them back onto the roof.

I got up to about 40 miles per hour when my driver-side T-top flew off the roof and shot straight into the air.

I pulled over immediately and jumped out of the car.

The top was still in the air. That's how fast I pulled over and got out.

Apparently, when they designed the T-tops, they expected this sort of thing.

I watched the top spin like a helicopter blade and gently float back to the ground.

It landed softly in the grass on the side of the interstate.

I ran over, picked it up, and put it back in place.

Turns out, I hadn't locked it correctly.

I made sure to do it right that time, and it never happened again.

Anyway, back to the wing in the road.

The spoiler was lying between the two lanes, half in the fast lane, half in the slow lane.

The driver was now squatting down, still with both hands on his head.

You could tell he was praying no one would hit it.

I made sure to avoid it as I drove past.

Then I checked my rearview mirror to see how the cars behind me were handling it.

That's when I saw two semi-trucks coming, one in each lane.

That spoiler didn't stand a chance.

I watched as both trucks ran right over it.

I couldn't see the driver anymore.

But in my mind, I imagine he fell to his knees, hit the ground with his fists, and screamed, "Noooooooooooo!"

That's how I picture it.

117: Stress Test 10/12/2021

I had my stress test done on my heart yesterday.

I also had an echocardiogram performed.

I was at the doctor's office from 10:15 AM until about 1:30 PM.

I was able to go to the cafeteria between tests and my appointment to grab something to eat.

When I got my results back from the doctor, he said he didn't see anything concerning.

I asked about my fast heart rate, and again, he said, "I didn't see anything concerning."

He asked how I felt overall.

I said, "I feel like I have Spina Bifida… but outside of that, I feel fine."

He asked a few more questions.

In the end, he told me he wasn't concerned and that he'd send the results to my Primary Care Physician.

He said if I start experiencing any other symptoms, I should come back right away, and they'll perform an arteriogram.

That's all for now.

118: Sick 10/13/2021

I became sick today.

My stomach was torn up, and I was cold and shaky.

When this happens, my output, both numbers 1 and 2, becomes very acidic.

The acid tries to eat through the wafer that holds my bags.

Much like a river forging a new path, the output tries to come out of the side of the wafer instead of going into the bag.

So, I put on new wafers and bags before going to bed.

I also straightened the pad I lay on at night. It's there in case something bursts while I sleep.

I went to bed.

At 6 PM, I woke up.

I was shaking, had cold sweats, and needed more blankets.

That's when I realized the acid had won.

My bag had burst open while I slept.

Even though I had put on new wafers and bags, the acid had forced its way out the side of the wafer.

I hope that makes sense.

So now, I'm cold, sweaty, sick, and shaking.

And no matter how bad I feel, I know I have to get into the shower.

I whispered, "Father God, give me the strength."

My Momma is an angel.

When I call for Momma, I call her in two different ways:

"Momma, could you help me?"

and

"Momma, I need some help."

She knows the difference.

It's one of the special features of a Momma.

I've had dreams where my momma is the biggest angel in Heaven.

I digress.

"Momma, I need some help," I said out loud.

I heard her stop what she was doing and walk toward me.

"What is it, baby? Oh my. Okay, it's no big deal. We've done this before. Let me get a towel."

Believe it or not, Mom and I have this down pat.

I have to get from my bed to my walk-in handicapped shower without making a bigger mess.

We wrapped me in towels.

Mom led my shaking, weak body to the shower.

The water felt like needles as it hit me.

It was hot, but not hot enough. I was still cold.

I turned it hotter.

I washed my body with a soap that also kills germs.

Afterward, Mom took everything outside.

She probably burned it all.

At least, in my mind, that's what happens.

Now, my right kidney is hurting, and it's all starting to make sense: an infection.

I took an antibiotic.

My temperature is normal.

I also gave myself a COVID test, just to be sure. It came back negative.

Now I'm in bed.

Fresh sheets. Clean pad.

But I've got my "hospital bag" ready, just in case.

I knew that if I waited to journal this tomorrow, I wouldn't do it.

That's all for now.

119: Ridin' Around

I got up around 2:30 PM today and got dressed to head to one of our local fast-food chains.

I had to hurry because the place gets slammed after school lets out, and it was already 2:30.

I ordered a "Twisted Pretzel" and a "Diet Coke."

When I got to the window, the employee, who sees me all the time in the drive-thru, said, "You just get up?"

"Yep."

"Got up and thought you'd get a pretzel and a Coke, huh?"

"Pretty much," I smiled.

I took the long way home so I could listen to "Jimmy Stewart" on an old-timey radio show, *The Six-Shooter.*

I think Jimmy Stewart did some of his best acting on the radio, back when families gathered around the radio to listen to shows instead of watching them on TV.

I promise, listening to ol' Jimmy eat while he talks about "the situation" will make you hungry for whatever it is he's eating.

(Read this in Jimmy Stewart's voice)

"Mmm-mmm, no one makes better cornbread than you, Maud."

"Tom, try a piece of Maud's cornbread. It's pipin' hot."

"Now, what we need to do is… mmm, that's good… I think… these molasses are delicious… I think… we need to go down to the saloon… mmm… and talk to the fella. Hear his side of the story before we go off half-cocked."

"Well, let's go, then!"

"But not until I finish eatin' Maud's pipin' hot cornbread. Mmm."

When I got home, I heated up a piece of Mom's cornbread and ate it with some molasses.

I'm feeling much better today and have gotten my appetite back. That's all for now.

120: Sniped

2:00 AM

I'm walking through a cemetery.

This particular cemetery is located inside "Disney World."

Yeah. I didn't know Disney World had a cemetery either, until I walked up on it while touring through the park.

I see my best friend about 50 yards away.

I notice a red laser light on his chest.

The laser moves from his chest up to his forehead.

I look around to see where the laser is coming from, and I see a sniper in a nearby window, aiming his rifle at my friend.

I take off running, trying to tackle my friend and save him from getting shot.

Bam!
My elbow hits the wooden floor of my bedroom.

My hospital tray, which stays beside my bed, turns over and spills everything on me.

A cup of water splashes me in the face.

The tray, along with everything on it, crashes down on me.

The bell I keep on the tray for emergencies hits the floor and rings as it lands.

Mom hears the noise and comes into my room.

"Oh, dear. Another bad dream? Let me help you."

"Yeah. Just another typical dream."

"What was it this time?"

"I was walking through a cemetery in Disney World, and a sniper was trying to shoot my best friend. You know, the one who died 25 years ago."

"I'm sorry."

"Look at my elbow and see if it looks bad, please."

"It's just really red and skinned up."

"Okay. It'll be stiff in the morning."

"Yeah. You're going to be stiff for a few days, I'm afraid."

I'm now sitting in my recliner watching TV.

The time is now 3:00 AM.

121: The Teen Years

My niece, whom I live with, turned thirteen.

We celebrated her birthday today by having five of her best friends over and going out to eat at Olive Garden.

After that, we went to Urban Air, which is one of those trampoline places for kids.

Mom paid for Olive Garden, so I figured I'd pay for Urban Air.

"Yes, five tickets for these teenagers, and it looks like I'll need five pairs of Urban Air socks as well, please."

"Yes, sir, that'll be $98.50. Cash or credit card?"

I stared at the young employee in a daze.

"You say $98.50?"

"Yes, sir."

I mumbled to myself, "I knew I should've paid for Olive Garden..." Then I handed her my debit card.

I looked at my niece and said, "This is my birthday gift to you. Happy Birthday."

She smiled, and that was all the thanks I needed.

The kids ran off and started jumping on the trampolines. Mom and I watched.

I drove us back home after we finished at Urban Air.

On the way home, the girls were acting just like thirteen-year-old boys, really. I guess at that age, kids are just kids.

"That wasn't me!"

"Ew. Who did that?"

"Someone cut the cheese!"

"Roll the windows down, please!"

"I'm not rolling the windows down until the person who did that confesses."

"Oh, please. It's killing me!"

"Whoever did it, 'fess up, and I'll roll the window down."

"Okay, okay, it was me! Roll 'em down!"

"Okay, I'll roll 'em down."

We made a quick stop because one of the girls had forgotten her bag of clothes. Of course, all the girls got out and went inside with her.

As I watched them run inside their friend's home, I thought to myself, "It was just yesterday that I was that age."

I don't think I ever really believed I would get old. Yet, here I am.

We finally arrived back home.

The girls ran through the house. It sounded like they were going to fall through the upstairs floor and land on my bed. But they were having the time of their lives tonight.

In just a few more years, they won't dare 'fess up to doing anything like cutting the cheese.

No, because they will become ladies.

They'll wear nail polish and lipstick and dresses.

Or maybe they won't wear any of that.

They'll still become ladies. It's inevitable.

But not tonight.

Tonight, they're still kids. Playing chase, hide-and-go-seek, eating Doritos, and saying things like, "Pull my finger."

I think she had an excellent thirteenth birthday.

122: Lynn Meets Thelma Lou

Ms. Betty Lynn, remembered fondly as "Thelma Lou" on *The Andy Griffith Show,* has passed away.

I got to meet her once. Yes, and I even wrote about it. This is that journal entry.

Mount Airy, North Carolina

Lynn meets Betty Lynn

After visiting Main Street in Mount Airy, I made my way to The Andy Griffith Museum.

I didn't get any pictures of the museum because I got straight in line to meet Thelma Lou.

I got in line around 11:15, and she was scheduled to arrive at 1 PM. I was sixth in line.

As I waited, the line got longer and longer. I counted over 150 people waiting to meet her and get an autograph from sweet Thelma Lou.

Her assistant came out and gave us the rules:

- No kissing on the mouth. (I guess someone had tried that before)
- Keep the autographs short.

I had no problem with those rules.

I had paid for several autographs, though, and I felt bad having her sign so many pictures.

I asked the assistant if it was okay, and she said, "Yes, just keep it at 'Betty Lynn.'"

I was fine with that.

Betty took her time with each person, which meant I had to wait another thirty minutes before it was my turn, and I was only sixth in line.

There were still over a hundred people behind me.

But I didn't mind waiting.

Finally, it was my turn.

I walked around the corner, and there she was. Thelma Lou. Barney's girl. Good ol' Thel.

I forgot everything I was going to say. I couldn't remember my name.

I couldn't remember *her* name.

You remember in *A Christmas Story* when Ralphie finally gets to sit on Santa's lap and forgets everything?

Yep. That was me.

She motioned for me to come over.

I tripped over my feet walking to her.

She had the biggest grin.

She reached out her hand to shake, and I shook it.

She asked, "What's your name?"

I had forgotten to even introduce myself!

I said, "Lynn! Like your name! Lynn! Even spelled the same! L-Y-N-N! My name is Lynn! You're Betty Lynn, and I'm Lynn!"

I finally calmed down and shook off the jitters.

I said, "Miss Betty Lynn, I drove all the way from Alabama to see you."

(Actually, I drove from Alabama to Gatlinburg, Tennessee, for vacation and decided to drive over to Mount Airy for a mini vacation, but I didn't want to explain all that to her.)

She told me that Goober and Gomer were from Alabama too. I agreed.

There was a bit of a pause. It wasn't going well.

I pulled out the pictures and said, "Ma'am, I was going to give some of these out for Christmas gifts, so I bought a lot of pictures. If you don't want to sign them all, you don't have to. I apologize."

She said she would sign all of them.

I told her she could just sign her name.

She signed one of them "To Lynn."

The rest she signed "Betty Lynn, 'Thelma Lou,'" with the date.

I felt I needed to say something kind before I left, so I said, "You are one of the greats. You're up there with Lucille Ball."

She thanked me for the kind words.

For some reason, as I was leaving, I blurted, "I love you!"

Then I quickly followed it up with, "I meant, God bless!"

Then I tripped over my feet again and rushed out, embarrassed, without looking back.

Well, I wanted her to remember me, and I think she will…

RIP, Ms. Betty Lynn. You will always be the Cats.

123: Latest Update 10/22/2021

Hi all,

I haven't posted lately. My mind has been elsewhere, I guess.

I did get to visit my Aunt and Uncle earlier this week.

We sat on the porch and counted cars while talking about life.

It's always good to sit and talk with them. They are both fountains of knowledge.

I had made plans for the weekend, but all that changed. I got the news that a dear friend's husband passed away from COVID pneumonia.

So, I will be attending the viewing and then the service afterward.

Her husband was 83, and I'm guessing she was close to that age as well.

They came into my life when I was just twenty years old.

You may or may not have guessed it by now, but I have a lot of friends who are much older than me.

She came into my life at a critical time. In fact, I had been begging God to send Jesus down to talk to me face-to-face.

He sent me her.

So yes, I have to attend her husband's funeral.

I have to see my friend.

124: Baseball

Confession:

I'm not big on baseball.

You have to understand, though, I was born with Spina Bifida.

As a kid, I couldn't do things a lot of the other kids could do.

I still played park league ball, though. Yes, I wanted to be like the other kids. And I could run back then.

Mom talked to all the coaches and made sure they knew my situation.

Which also meant that I took my place in the right field. You can't get hurt or sue anyone from there. Trust me. Not in Little League, at least.

When I went up to bat, the coach always gave me the bunt signal. I'll admit, I could bunt the ball right down the third-base line. It would never go out of bounds either.

Fifty percent of the time, I'd be safe at first. The other fifty, I'd get thrown out.

But the guys on base always made it to their next base, too.

I didn't think I was any good at baseball, though.

If some kid managed to hit the ball to right field, it would catch me off guard.

I'd have to throw down the bug I was playing with and run toward the ball.

Usually, I'd run right into one of the other players.

One time, I caught a ball that was hit straight to me.

I just reached up and grabbed it out of the air.

Later, I found out it was a very important play.

The coach gave me the game ball. I was so happy.

I don't remember if the bases were loaded, but there were people on base.

The other team had two outs.

The ball got hit to right field, and I ran and caught it. That made three outs, and the game was over.

I can still see the coach's face when he gave his big speech.

He looked right at me and then tossed me the game ball.

He said, "Lynn, you saved us from losing. Here. You deserve this."

Wow.

Truth be told, I probably didn't even know if we were winning or losing.

I just caught the ball that got hit to me.

I never played any ball outside of park league.

So, I grew up not being a big baseball fan.

I do know this, though. In this house, we root for the Braves.

125: Lynn's Secret Chili Recipe

Let me start this entry by saying that I love chili.

Throw in some cool weather and leaves falling on the ground, and you're in business.

When I lived on my own, for that brief time in my life, I learned how to cook my own chili.

I take great pride in my chili. Most Southerners do.

I got the recipe from a very wise older gentleman I met in Huntsville, Alabama.

And now, I'll tell you what he told me:

"A little bit has to do with the type of bean you use, and a little bit has to do with how you season the ground beef as you cook it.

The rest has to do with the special blend of herbs and spices that you add."

I personally take great pride in my herbs and spices, and I'm going to break them down for you.

For this chili, I use spices derived from seeds. Here are some examples:

- Allspice
- Angelica
- Anise

- Annatto
- Black cumin
- Black pepper
- Brown mustard
- Caraway
- Cardamom
- Cayenne pepper
- Celery seed
- Coriander
- Cumin
- Dill
- Fennel
- Fenugreek
- Juniper berries
- Lovage
- Mace
- Mustard
- Myrtle
- Nutmeg
- Paprika
- Pepper
- Pimento
- Sichuan pepper
- Star anise
- Tabasco pepper
- Tamarind
- Vanilla
- White mustard
- White pepper

And here are a few examples of common herbs found in North America:

- Wild mint
- Horsemint
- Love root
- California bay
- Tarragon
- Sagebrush
- Juniper
- Wild onion

Now, what you'll need to do from here is go find your own wise man and get his secret chili recipe, because like most Southerners, I ain't giving mine out.

It *is* delicious, though.

Mmm-mmm, good.

126: Medical Update

I had an appointment with my Urologist today.

You may or may not know, but I developed Hydronephrosis Kidney and Ureter years ago.

In short, Hydronephrosis Kidney is swelling of the kidneys due to a build-up of urine.

In other words, my urine does not get out of my body quickly enough.

Over the years, it hasn't gotten worse, which is a good thing. It's been status quo.

Status quo, in this case, is good.

You may remember that last year I received a stent in my right kidney.

It's time to change that stent out, and my Urologist would also like to put a stent into my left kidney.

So, this coming Wednesday, I'll check into my hospital to have the stent in my right kidney swapped out for a new one and have my first stent placed into my left kidney.

My Urologist does not foresee any issues during the procedure.

I'm not sure if it will be outpatient. I think it's typically outpatient, but last year I stayed overnight.

I'll keep you updated if I learn anything new.

That's all for now.

127: Daily Drive

I haven't been quite myself lately.

I've been in a bit of a mental fog.

During my daily morning drives, I've noticed the number of deer has gone way up.

So have the ducks.

This morning, I saw six deer and two adult ducks with six baby ducks following behind.

I have to drive slowly because of the deer.

They'll jump right out in front of you.

Today, the deer were on the side of the road, and as I approached, one of them decided to run across the street.

Had I been going over twenty, I'd have hit it.

Rabbits are out in numbers as well.

Then, just when I thought I'd seen everything, *it* ran across the road.

A mink.

I'm pretty sure it was a mink.

Imagine you're watching a movie from the 1940s to the 1960s. Now, imagine a little old lady in the movie wearing a mink around her neck.

That's what ran out in front of me.

I didn't know that minks lived in the U.S.

I had to look it up.

Turns out, minks can be found in every state.

It could have been a weasel.

They both look a lot alike.

Either way, it was a pretty good drive this morning with lots of wildlife. Happy Halloween.

128: Pre-Hospital Checklist

The hospital called and asked me to come in to take a COVID test tomorrow before my Wednesday appointment.

Today, I've been straightening up my room and getting my hospital bag ready to go.

I've posted about my hospital bag before.

It contains everything I might need, such as wafers, bags, and other medical equipment.

It should last me about five to seven days.

I also cleaned up my room because I like to return home from the hospital to a clean space.

When my doctor's office calls tomorrow, I'm hoping they can tell me if I'll be staying overnight or if it'll be outpatient.

Personally, I hope I stay overnight.

I know, I know. Why would anyone wish to stay overnight in a hospital?

But over the many years of having procedures done, I've been sent home only to end up going back.

So, it's just easier to stay overnight and make sure all is well.

The nurses treat me like a king.

The food is good, and I binge-watch *The Andy Griffith Show* on my laptop.

I can usually get through the first five seasons.

Usually, as soon as a nurse walks in and sees me watching *The Andy Griffith Show*, they say, "Oh, I remember you."

If I do stay overnight, I'm pretty sure I'll have to be by myself due to the pandemic.

And… if I'm staying for something minor, like this, I kind of like to be alone.

Now, if it's something major… I get scared.

And like most big babies, I want my momma there with me.

This procedure shouldn't be anything major, though.

That's all for now.

129: 11/2/2021 Update

The doctor's office called to confirm my procedure scheduled for tomorrow.

I'm to arrive at the hospital at 10 AM for a Noon procedure.

I asked if it would be outpatient or if I'd be staying.

The nurse said they were planning on it being an outpatient procedure.

She added, "Of course, that can always change."

Nothing to eat or drink after midnight either.

That's pretty typical.

In the morning, I can take all my meds except for my diabetes medicine.

I can drink water to swallow the pills.

Tonight and in the morning, I'm supposed to shower with antibacterial soap, which I keep on hand.

Mom took me out for lunch today.

Before any procedure or surgery, Mom or Papa, or both, have always taken me out to eat.

Today, Mom took me to "Pappadeaux."

It was fantastic food.

I took pictures, and hopefully, I can write about it after the procedure.

My mind is too preoccupied to type anything up right now.

That's all for now.

130: Stent Procedure 11/3/2021

At 10:00 AM, Mom and I arrived at the hospital to check in.

I was scheduled for my procedure at Noon.

At 10:30 AM, we were taken back to a private room with a bed, a TV, and equipment to take my vitals. I was told to get undressed and put on the robe. I did as I was told.

They also let us know that two others were ahead of me.

At 12:30 PM, Mom and I were very quiet. Then came 1:00 PM. We both had the same thought going through our minds.

See, I was once scheduled for a 45-minute surgery. That surgery took a turn for the worse and ended up taking my doctor over 9 hours to complete.

My doctor would later tell me, "You dang near died on me."

All the appointments after mine were canceled that day.

My oldest brother told me that the doctor came out of the OR after 9 hours with blood on him, visibly upset, and told the family I was alive and stable.

He then explained what had happened. I won't go into that here, but it wasn't good.

I ended up staying in the hospital for 36 days.

I was fed through a feeding tube the entire time.

So now, here we are today at 2:00 PM, and Mom and I start to worry that something might have happened in the OR again.

At 2:30 PM, I asked the nurse to turn off the overhead lights so I could close my eyes and nap.

I also said a prayer or two for the person in surgery.

At 3:00 PM, Mom and I talked about the time my 45-minute surgery turned into 9 hours.

She said, "They'll probably admit you and plan on doing the procedure tomorrow. Something has happened in that operating room."

"Or cancel my procedure altogether," I replied.

At 4:00 PM, the nurse, who had been checking on us all day, came in and let us know that the team had finished in the OR, and my doctor would be coming to see me next.

When he came in, we knew he couldn't tell us what had happened.

Mom reminded him about the time he performed that 9-hour surgery on me.

"So, we understand," I said to my favorite doctor.

"We prayed for y'all," Mom added.

"Thank you for that," he replied.

My doctor is a Christian. We've talked about it.

He then explained the plan of action.

"I'm going to go through your ileostomy and replace the stent in your right kidney. Then I plan to place a stent in your left kidney as well. Either way, I don't plan for you to stay the night. You'll spend some time in recovery, then about 45 minutes with the nurses. You'll need to eat, drink, and keep everything down before you can leave. All in all, you'll spend about 2 hours with them before you go home."

"Sound good to you?" he asked.

"Yep. Sounds like a plan. Let's get this thing done."

I was wheeled in my bed into one of the many operating rooms. This one looked and felt familiar. They probably all do.

I saw the operating table and knew my part. I'd scoot from the bed onto the table. I've done it a million times.

A mask was placed over my nose.

"This is just oxygen, Mr. Thomas. We'll put you to sleep through your IV."

"Okay, tell me when you push the juice into my IV, please."

"It's in you, sir."

I began my routine. I always try to say the Lord's Prayer until I fall asleep.

"Okay… Our Father, who art in Heaven… um, Z, Y, X… um, 99, 98, Hallowed be thy name…"

I woke up in recovery.

As always, I immediately looked around and checked my body to make sure nothing went wrong.

I saw that I was indeed in the recovery room with other patients. Not in the ICU.

My nurse was sitting at the end of the bed, charting everything.

"How are you feeling, Mr. Thomas?"

"Actually, I feel fine. I'm not even in pain. Did everything go well?" I asked.

"Everything went fine."

"Did he get the stent into both kidneys?"

"Yes, sir. The right kidney and left kidney both have stents. It went fine."

"I haven't had anything to eat or drink since 7:30 PM last night. Can I have some water or ice, please?"

"Yes, sir. Here's a cup of ice. You can suck on it."

I took the ice and sucked on it.

I broke the rules and quietly chewed it, too.

It tasted so good. It tasted like it came straight from Heaven.

Shortly after, I was wheeled into another section.

In this section, I was given some peanut butter crackers and Diet Coke.

My job was to keep everything down.

The Diet Cokes were tiny cans. I'm guessing 8 ounces.

By the time I finished, I'd eaten a blueberry muffin, a pack of peanut butter crackers, and some kind of health nut bar.

I'd also consumed four of those tiny cans of Diet Coke.

Around 6:00 PM, they told me I could get dressed and go home.

I got dressed, and they wheeled me out to the vehicle.

On the way home, I had Momma stop by Milo's to get me some burgers for dinner.

I hope and pray that the patient who went before me is doing well tonight.

All in all, it went well for me.

I'm to get my stents changed out every year from now on, and I don't see a problem with it.

That's all for now.

Thank you all for your thoughts and prayers.

Growing up with Spina Bifida was difficult.

Heck, the teen years are hard for everyone.

People do judge a book by its cover, even if they don't mean to.

For one, I could walk.

When people saw this young teenage boy walking, running, and playing, they didn't think he had Spina Bifida.

I did walk with a limp.

Although sometimes, the limp wasn't as bad as on other days. My brothers told their friends about me.

A few other people figured it out on their own.

I didn't tell anyone, though. I kept it my secret.

I never felt like I fit into the "Spina Bifida" world.

And no, I've never felt like I fit into any "normal" world either.

One summer, I met a friend named Tommy.

Tommy and I hit it off that summer.

I was a younger teenager, and I would only be home in Alabama for a short time.

At night, Tommy and I would play tennis on the local courts. Yep. I once played tennis.

My late brother Tony also played.

He was much better and faster than me.

But Tommy and I were an excellent match-up when it came to tennis.

One night, Tommy asked me to come over to his house. I accepted.

When we arrived, Tommy introduced me to his whole family.

He introduced me to his mother, his father, and his older brother, "John."

John was in a wheelchair.

Later, I asked Tommy what was wrong with his brother.

"He was born with Spina Bifida."

I immediately felt terrible.

I didn't think it was right that I could walk while John was in a wheelchair.

I hadn't told Tommy about my Spina Bifida, and I sure wasn't going to tell him now.

Tommy spoke so highly of his older brother.

You could tell that John was Tommy's hero.

In John's bedroom hung all types of Rock and Roll memorabilia. I believe he had a Gold or Platinum Record that the band Skid Row had given to him.

He also had drumsticks, guitar picks, and other gear that rock bands had gifted him.

In addition, he had met many of those bands in person.

I felt bad just being in John's presence.

As I said, I didn't think it was fair that I walked while he couldn't.

It got even worse.

I found that I couldn't look John in the eyes.

My friendship with Tommy began to slip.

It eventually tapered off completely.

Later on, when I was around 19 and in college, I ran into Tommy again and asked how his brother was doing.

"He passed away. His kidneys quit working."

"I'm so sorry, Tommy. I'm so…"

I began feeling sick.

I held my stomach because it started to hurt.

"How old was he?"

"Twenty-five."

"I'm sorry. I… I… am sorry…"

"It's okay. John had a great life.

We're all Christians, and we know we'll see him again. It's okay."

I left and got into my Camaro.

I put in my Skid Row CD.

I turned the volume up and cried as I drove home that night.

As I said earlier, I've never felt that I fit into the "Spina Bifida" world.

And I've never felt that I fit into the "normal" world either.

But that night, I wished I had told them. I wished I had told them I had Spina Bifida, too. I wished I had known John better.

I was just a stupid kid, though.

And the teen years are hard for everyone.

132: Health Update 11/9/2021

I haven't posted much since getting my stents placed in my kidneys.

I got my stents on Wednesday.

Everything was going fine, and yes, my kidneys were a bit sore, but nothing I couldn't handle.

Then, on Friday, I became ill.

My symptoms were:

- Temperature of 100.4
- Cold sweats
- Head felt "full" (if that makes sense)
- Nasal drainage
- The shakes
- All-around crummy feeling

I immediately called my doctor, but it was already after office hours.

I left a message.

It felt like the flu or just the "crud."

I took a home COVID test, which has always been accurate for my family, and it came back negative.

I went ahead and started taking my antibiotic, just in case there was an infection.

I also kept a very close eye on my body temperature.

I spoke to my doctor's office during this time, and they also felt like my symptoms sounded more flu-like than anything related to the kidney stents.

By Monday, I was feeling a lot better, and my temperature had returned to normal.

Today is Tuesday, and my kidneys are no longer sore. I feel fine.

I'm guessing it was just a 48-hour bug.

Throughout the whole thing, I watched my temperature closely to make sure it never hit 101.

That's the magic number for me.

If my temperature ever hits 101, I have to go to the hospital.

I used three, yes, three different thermometers to check it.

At no time did it go over 100.4.

If my kidneys had gotten an infection from the stents, I believe it would've hit 101.

So, like I said, I'm guessing it was just a 48-hour bug.

That's all from me.

133: A Busy Day 11/11/2021

It's been a pretty hectic day today.

I had two doctor appointments.

The first was just a check-up, where I found out everything was fine with my stent procedure.

In fact, I'm now putting out more urine through my urostomy than I used to before getting the stents.

That could mean my hydronephrosis is improving, but I'll have to wait until my next kidney scan to know for sure.

The second appointment was about my ulnar nerve and "tennis elbow."

Back in 2019, I had surgery on the ulnar nerve in my right arm.

Now, in 2021, my left arm is doing the same thing.

It's from typing my journals so much.

In fact, I've typed over two million words since January of 2016. That's true.

This time, instead of doing surgery, the doctor will give me a shot in my left arm to ease the pain.

Then, two weeks later, I'll get a shot in my right arm.

They can't do both arms at the same time.

Both arms have been hurting, which has kept me from typing as much as I'd like.

When I got home, Mom and a friend were putting up the Christmas trees.

Yep, plural.

This year we'll have three Christmas trees.

We always have a large gathering at Thanksgiving, and Mom wanted the trees up before everyone came.

We had Christmas music playing and "White Christmas" on the TV.

We still have one more tree to decorate tomorrow.

I'll post pictures when it's done.

All in all, it was a busy yet happy day.

I hope yours was too.

That's all for now.

134: Morning Drive 11/12/2021

I got up around 4:30 AM with my usual Spina Bifida-related pain.

I did my usual thing and went for an early morning drive.

Something about that drive makes me feel better.

Maybe it's the position my driver's seat is in.

Maybe it's the old-timey radio shows I listen to.

Maybe it's the wildlife.

Maybe it's all of it together.

All I know is that it helps.

We live on a mountain that used to be called "Rattlesnake Mountain."

That name doesn't sell houses, though, so the mountain now has a more proper name.

It still has plenty of rattlesnakes, though.

This morning the mountain was foggy, and the wildlife wasn't out like usual.

But it was still a peaceful drive.

There's an owl I see from time to time.

He sits on a fence post overlooking a field.

Every time I pass by, his body is facing the field, but his head is turned completely around, watching me.

It's a bit creepy.

Mr. Owl was there the first time I passed, so I planned to get a picture on my next trip around.

But when I came back, he was gone.

Next time, I'll get that picture.

Around 6 AM (yes, I drove around that long), I saw the duck family.

They were out in full force today. Twelve of them, I think.

I stopped the car to let them cross the road.

And since I was stopped, I went ahead and took a few pictures of them.

Now I'm back home and about to pour another cup of coffee.

Good morning, all.

That's all for now.

135: Mr. Owl

It was 2:30 in the morning when I pulled off to the side of the road, stepping out into the cold stillness of night.

Nobody drives down this back road at this hour, not unless they're up to something or, like me, just looking for peace. I left the headlights on, casting a soft glow over the fence post and the big tree I know so well. That tree is Mr. Owl's tree.

I call him "Mr. Owl." It's a simple name, but it fits. He often sits right on that post beneath the tree, watching over the open field like he owns the place. Not tonight, though.

I craned my neck and stared into the dark branches above, hoping to catch a glimpse of his silhouette. Nothing. No rustle, no sound. Just the soft breeze of a quiet mountain night.

"Whooo," I called up into the branches, half-hoping he'd answer. Nothing.

I got back into my vehicle and resumed my early morning drive, cruising through the foggy mountain roads, the heater blowing gently, my Old-Timey radio show playing Gunsmoke this time. Sheriff Matt Dillon was chasing down another outlaw.

By 3:45 AM, I was back in our driveway. Mr. Owl never showed.

I crawled into bed and drifted off to sleep, warmed by the memory of my drive, even if I didn't get the picture I was hoping for.

Tomorrow's another chance.

136: To the Cabin

The last family checked out of the cabin on Saturday, and the next ones had to cancel. That left a rare opening in our usually packed schedule. Funny how a cancellation can feel like a blessing.

Papa took the opportunity to call in the plumber to check on the new septic tank and field lines. He'll be arriving Tuesday, so I'm heading up to the cabin today to meet with him. The next guests check in on Thursday, which means I'll need to be out by Wednesday morning. Just a quick trip.

I only packed a small suitcase, but my medical supplies? Enough for three weeks. I know it seems like overkill, but years of experience have taught me to always be prepared. Life can flip you upside down when you least expect it. Ever seen "Planes, Trains, and Automobiles"? Yeah. That.

I also swung by the pharmacy to refill my insulin and pick up a bottle of antibiotics, my go-to safety net for trips. I used up the last of it after my kidney stent procedure.

Taking my time, planning to leave after 11 AM.

Gonna shower now and hit the road.

137: Trip to the Cabin

I pulled out of the driveway around 11:30 AM CST and punched in the cabin address. GPS said I'd arrive at 6:23 PM EST.

Challenge accepted.

Naturally, I cued up "East Bound and Down" from *Smokey and the Bandit*—tradition. Let's see if I can shave a few minutes off that ETA, safely, of course.

It takes about an hour to reach the interstate from home. When I merged onto it, my arrival time had already moved to 6:22 PM. A small win.

Now, I'm not a fast driver, I set cruise control right at the speed limit and let it carry me forward smooth and steady.

By the time I hit Chattanooga, it was still 6:20. That's a good sign. Chattanooga traffic can be a bear, but going mid-day usually helps, and it did this time too.

I decided to try the Sweetwater exit instead of my usual Lenoir City one. GPS said it'd be faster. I took its word for it.

As I cruised through Townsend, TN, I had it in the bag. GPS now read 6:16 PM.

And then… the flashing lights.

An ambulance passed me. I said a quiet prayer. A few miles later, I was bumper to bumper—there'd been a wreck. From the looks of it, no one was seriously hurt. Just enough to throw off the whole trip.

I finally pulled up to the cabin at 6:47 PM.

Didn't beat the GPS, but I'll take a safe arrival over bragging rights any day.

138: Cabin Update – 11/17/2021

It's 7:00 AM CST, 8:00 on the cabin clock, and I'm sitting in my usual chair, sipping coffee, just before heading home.

This trip was a short one. Drove in Monday night, heading out Wednesday morning. Never even unpacked the suitcase.

But I did check off every item on my list. Mission accomplished.

Last night, I gave in and went to Golden Corral for dinner. I was planning on another burrito, but buffet food called to me. Sometimes, comfort food just wins.

On the way up, I stopped at a Tennessee rest area, the first one past the border, and grabbed some gold one-dollar coins from a change machine. Slid in a ten, and out came ten shiny gold coins.

My waiter last night got a gold coin tip. I made sure he knew they weren't quarters.

"Oh, I love getting these," he said, grinning. "I get 'em now and then."

I smiled. Felt like a little piece of nostalgia traded hands.

Believe it or not, I ended dinner with cottage cheese, peaches, and pineapple for dessert. Never thought I'd be a cottage cheese kind of guy, but here we are. And it was good.

This morning, I ran down the mountain to grab some cash for the cleaning lady and treated myself to a large cup of coffee. Can't hit the road without it.

Headed out now, "East Bound and Down" queued up again.

Until next time.

139: Sweetwater, Tennessee

Driving through Sweetwater, Tennessee, I felt the urge to pull off and stay the night. I'd passed signs for "The Lost Sea," flea markets, antique shops. it's a charming little town with a heartbeat of its own.

So, I hopped off the highway and checked into the Days Inn. With my AAA card, I got a room for about $78. Can't beat that.

There are plenty of places to eat in Sweetwater, everything from fast food joints to cozy sit-down spots, but right now, food isn't the priority.

Truth is, I'm just tired. One of those tireds that seeps into your bones.

So, I've got the A/C turned low, the TV humming softly, and I'm going to crawl under the covers and rest.

Maybe tomorrow I'll explore.

Or maybe I'll get back on the interstate and head home.

We'll see.

For now… just rest.

140: Sweetwater – Day 1

I woke up at 5 AM local time in Sweetwater, Tennessee.

Some mornings, I swear it feels like I've been hit by a jolt of electricity in my sleep, like my whole body's been rebooted by lightning. Today was one of those mornings.

I got dressed and headed out to the front desk in search of coffee.

In the breezeway, I stopped to button up my shirt. That's when the real comedy began. I fumbled with the buttons like I'd had one too many, standing there like old Otis Campbell from *The Andy Griffith Show*. After several long minutes, I finally got three buttons done up and figured that was good enough. Thankfully, I had an undershirt on underneath.

When I got to the office, I found one of those fancy single-serve coffee machines, the kind without a pot. You just push a button, and it dispenses straight into your cup. The problem? No cups. No lids. No straws. The machine didn't even look like it was turned on. And the front desk? Empty.

So, I trudged back to my room, where there was a coffee setup of its own.

Now, when I say "small coffee pot," I mean *tiny* enough to make two humble cups of weak hotel brew. Still, two cups of something warm and caffeinated beat no cups at all.

It wasn't great, but it wasn't bad either. I drank both cups, then decided to call down and check if the lobby coffee was up and running.

"Front desk, can I help you?"

"Yes, do you have coffee made at the front desk?"

"Yes, Ma'am," came the reply.

Ma'am.

Again.

I rolled my eyes, mistaken for a woman over the phone, which happens more often than I care to admit.

I thanked her anyway and made my way back to the front. Sure enough, the machine was up and running now. Cups, lids, and straws all laid out neatly. I filled two cups to take back with me.

With real coffee in hand, I finally felt ready to face the day.

That's all for now.

141: Bert's Story

His name was Bert.

I met him at the motel in Sweetwater. We got to talking over breakfast, and before long, I knew I'd remember this man.

Bert was ex-Navy, served from '76 to '84. Tall and lean, about 6 feet and maybe 150 pounds. He looked like he'd weathered a lot of storms but still had a kind of strength in his eyes.

He told me he'd just gotten out of the hospital after a blood clot in his lung. They'd had to do surgery.

"I'm a Crackin' times two," he said, grinning.

I blinked. "What's that mean?"

"In the Navy, if you go around the world once, they call you a Crackin'. Go twice, and you're a Crackin' times two," he explained proudly.

Bert had planned to re-enlist in '84, but life had other plans. His grandparents needed him back on the dairy farm. So he came home.

"It worked out," he said. "That same year, I met my wife, Gail. Married her the next."

"How old were you?" I asked.

"Twenty-six when I got out. Twenty-seven when we married. I knew when I saw her. She was the one."

He paused, his eyes softening.

"She was my teammate. That's the secret: being a team. You do what's best for the team. And never go to bed mad."

We ordered coffee. Bert declined food at first, but once I mentioned cornbread, he was off.

"Gail could cook anything from scratch. Her yeast rolls were better than any store brand. Her cornbread, three inches thick, golden crust, soft inside." He chuckled. "She called one of our cows Lucy, short for Lucifer. Meanest cow you've ever seen. But Lucy adored Gail. Let her milk her without a fuss."

He stared out the window for a minute, as if Gail was standing just on the other side of the glass.

"She loved feeding people. She loved *people*, period."

We sat quietly for a bit.

"You want anything else to eat?" I asked.

"No, no. I'm good. I want to thank you, though."

"For what?"

"For not judging me. People see someone homeless, and they judge. But you didn't ask how I got here. You just sat and shared a meal with me."

I looked at him. "You're a good man. I can feel it. The world's full of good people like you. It's just the loud ones, the bad ones, that get all the attention. But the quiet ones, the ones who care? They're out there."

He nodded slowly.

"Three years ago, when Gail died, everything changed. I weighed 230 before she passed. I'm 150 now."

He looked down at his hands.

"But going to the hospital turned out to be a blessing. They got the VA involved. A husband and wife team, both military, helping veterans like me. They got me this motel room and are working on getting me permanent housing."

He smiled a little.

"They're even getting me dentures. Said it'd take ten to twelve days. I told 'em I hadn't had any in over a year, so what's twelve more days?"

I grinned. "I'll bet you're counting every one."

He laughed. "Oh, I am."

I stood up. "I'm leaving soon, but I'm going to keep praying for you. Is there anything else I can do before I go?"

He looked up at me, and a quiet smile crept across his face.

"You've done enough," he said. "Thank you."

142: Iron Bowl

Alabama or Auburn.

If you're born in the South, there are certain rules you're just expected to know:

For starters, tea is sweet. Always sweet.

Directions are given in landmarks, not street names. "Go past the old apple tree and take a left" is perfectly acceptable.

And when driving down a country road, you are expected to lift your fingers in a subtle wave to the driver passing by, even if you don't know them.

But if you're born in Alabama, there's one rule that stands taller than all the rest.

You must be a die-hard fan of either Alabama or Auburn football. No exceptions.

I remember in the third grade, we took turns being "door greeters" at school. Kids would stand by the entrance and hold open doors, shouting things like:

"Auburn fans come through this door!"

And the kid on the other side would counter, "Alabama fans over here!"

Then they'd count how many walked through their door. The kid with the most fans won. That was our version of voter outreach.

At that age, I didn't even fully understand football, but it didn't matter. You were either Crimson Tide or War Eagle. And whichever side you picked, you stuck with it.

All the sane folks in my family picked the right team. My oldest brother, well, he had his own ideas about sanity.

Every year, the entire state of Alabama sets aside its differences and gathers around the TV for one sacred event — the Iron Bowl.

It's Alabama versus Auburn. A game that doesn't just matter. It *is* the matter.

When the Iron Bowl is on, nothing else is happening. Not really. The President could be on every major channel declaring the end of the world, and someone would yell, "Turn it off, the game's on!"

If you're caught inside a Dollar General or Wal-Mart while the Iron Bowl is on, folks look at you like you're either lost or have been recently dropped on your head.

That's how serious football is down here. That's how serious the Iron Bowl is.

I'm watching the game. And if you're from Alabama, you already know which side I'm on.

143: Iron Bowl Post Game Post

"Woo-hoo! We're in overtime!" I yelled, rushing into the living room.

We were watching the Iron Bowl, and Alabama had just tied the game.

Mom came in right behind me and plopped down on the couch.

"I was on the phone with Rhonda," she said. "'Oh my gosh, Alabama just tied it up!' she yelled. And I said, 'I gotta go. Bye!'"

Then she looked at me and said, "I might need to go back to my room. I don't wanna jinx it."

"Momma," I told her, "The outcome of this game doesn't depend on you at all. It depends on the shoes I'm wearing."

We laughed.

Iron Bowl 2021:

Alabama: 24

Auburn: 22

Roll Tide.

144: Snow Globes

If you've known me long enough, you know that this time of year, I make snow globes.

It's something simple I can do with my hands, even when I don't feel strong. Doesn't take much muscle, but it does take a little creativity. More than folks might think.

This year, I bought a six-foot folding table, a real "crafts table." Today, I set it up and pulled out the supplies I bought back in October from the local hobby shop in Gardendale.

They'd been sitting in the corner since then, still wrapped up in the protective paper from the clerk.

I unwrapped the first item and

blinked. A ceramic Easter Bunny.

Then came a parade of baby chicks, spring flowers, and all things pastel.

"Where in the world did this come from?" I muttered.

I called Mom in to see if she had picked any of it up.

"I wouldn't buy that," she said. "Hand me your receipt."

I gave it to her. She scanned it.

"None of this is on here. You got the wrong bag."

Well, great.

The kicker is, I can't even remember what I originally bought. I just know it wasn't Easter décor. And most of what I now have is too big to fit inside a snow globe anyway.

I guess I'll have to go back to the store and explain. I'm not even sure how to begin that conversation.

145: Latest On Me

I know I haven't been posting much lately.

My arms have been hurting; Tennis Elbow in both of them. Typing isn't just uncomfortable. Some days, it flat-out hurts.

Still, I went through my calendar for December and counted seven doctor appointments. Two of those are for shots in each arm to help with the pain. I'm honestly looking forward to them.

Today, I built three snow globes using leftover pieces from last year. After I finish one, I let it sit for a day or more to let the glitter, my version of "snow," settle at the bottom. I call that the "Sitting Phase."

It looks like December is going to be full of doctor visits and healing time.

That's all for now.

146: 2021 Snow Globes

Just wanted to share a few pictures of what I've been working on.

I've noticed that the glitter makes a big difference in how the snow globes look. I'm out of the good stuff; the heavy silver glitter. All I've got left is the extra fine kind, and it's more like dust than snow. Doesn't float right. Doesn't sparkle either.

I picked up a can of clear Rust-Oleum spray meant for hobby projects. Says it works on glass, wood, and plastic. I'm going to try sealing a few wood figurines and see how they hold up inside the globes. Those are just for me. I want to see how they look in a year.

Most of what I'm using this year comes from pieces I already had from the past two Christmases. I'm trying to get creative with what I've got.

That's all for now.

147: Latest 12/3/2021

I went to the doctor today and got a steroid injection in my left arm for my Tennis Elbow. The doctor numbed the area up pretty well, and

I've got to say, my arm feels a lot better already. I'll be getting the same shot in my right arm in about ten days.

Snow Globes

This morning, when I woke up, I noticed that everything inside my snow globes had come unglued.

That's when it hit me. Last year, I had the exact same problem.

I remembered I'd gone out and bought a better glue, one that actually worked. I dug around in my hobby drawer and found it. Sure enough, there was a sticky note on the bottle, written in my handwriting: "Lynn, use this glue! The other stuff doesn't work! Repeat, use this glue!"

So I sat down and re-glued all the objects inside the globes. It looks like I'll be able to make 14 snow globes this year; that's how many empty ones I could find at the hobby store. I bought every last one they had on the shelf.

Lately, I've been going through a lot of gas on my morning drives, and the wildlife hasn't been out in the same numbers. So tomorrow, I'm going to skip the drive and try sitting in my recliner instead. Might just watch the Bob Ross painting channel on Pluto TV.

Right now, I'm watching *Gunsmoke: Return to Dodge* and hoping to get inspired to write. Marshal Dillon looks like he's in his sixties.

I've got an appointment with my endocrinologist on Monday. I'm actually looking forward to that.

That's all for now.

148: Moments Past

May 28, 2005

We stood in a circle, hand in hand, forming a prayer chain around Nana's bed.

Pawpaw had just finished saying one of the most beautiful prayers I'd ever heard. I never knew he had those words inside him.

"Lord, I commit Nana's spirit into Your hands," he said.

And that was it.

Nana exhaled her last breath. The room went completely still.

The hospice nurse took her pulse, as did my cousins, who are both registered nurses. No pulse.

Then, the hospice nurse, who had witnessed this hundreds and thousands of times, spoke softly.

"Do you feel that? It's her spirit leaving her body. I can feel it."

Just then, the little lap dog, who had been sitting quietly at the foot of the bed the entire time, let out a loud howl.

It wasn't a sad howl. Not a painful one either.

He stared up at the ceiling above Nana and started yapping with excitement.

Papa and I glanced at each other, both a little stunned. Then we looked back at the dog.

Whatever he was seeing, he was happy about it.

Yes, that's the best way to describe it.

He was happy.

149: Santa on a Fire Truck

12/4/2021

I saw Santa Claus today riding through the neighborhood on a fire truck.

He had one of his elves with him too.

They were being chauffeured around to wave at all the neighborhood kids. By the time I made it outside, they'd already passed my house.

But this little kid is old enough to drive. So I hopped in my truck and caught up with them.

Sure enough, there they were, riding on top, waving at everybody.

Santa and his elf waved at me like they'd known me all my life. And I waved right back just as big.

It made my day.

150: Diabetes Update

I saw my endocrinologist today. He handles my diabetes, among other things.

My A1C was 7.4%—down slightly from my last reading of 7.5%. The lower, the better, of course. My goal is to get back to 5.8%, which is where I was just a year ago.

I'm still fairly new to managing diabetes, and I'm learning as I go.

When I first started, I would eat my meal and then wait to see how high my blood sugar spiked before giving myself insulin. Now, after enough trial and error, I can usually give a pretty good estimate ahead of time. So these days, I take my insulin about twenty minutes before eating. It's made a noticeable difference.

The appointment went well, and I'll follow up again in four months.

That's all for now.

151: Eye Care and Diabetes

As I mentioned before, I've got quite a few doctor appointments this month. I'll try to share updates after each one.

Today, I saw my ophthalmologist.

If you're living with diabetes, then you probably know how it can mess with your eyes—blurred vision, pressure, eye strain, and more. Some people have even gone blind because of it. Mary Tyler Moore is one example that always comes to mind.

That's why it's important for me to get regular checkups.

The doctor did every exam available today. I even paid an extra $35 for a specialized test. I'm happy to report that everything looked good; no burst blood vessels, no signs of glaucoma, no diabetic retinopathy. That was a big relief.

She told me I only need glasses when I'm working on the computer and writing. That's a win in my book.

Unless something changes, I'll see her again next year.

That's all for now.

152: The Long Night

When I was about ten years old, it wasn't unusual for a kid to stay home by himself. Today, you'd probably have Child Services knocking at your door. But back then, things were different.

One night, my dad got called in to work. He worked for the power company, and when the power went out in someone's area, he was on call. That evening around 8 PM, he got the call.

Mom had gone somewhere with both of my brothers, so I was home alone.

Now, let me paint the picture. Our house looked like something right out of a scary movie. We lived right by the woods and the train tracks. I had watched enough *Unsolved Mysteries* to convince myself there was a killer who walked those tracks. I was sure he'd eventually make his way to our door.

The wind was howling. The trees were bending and creaking. And this ten-year-old boy was in full panic mode.

Every sound outside convinced me someone was in the basement. So I picked up the phone and dialed "0" for the operator—that's how you got the police back then.

"Operator, how can I help you?"

"Yes, ma'am. Can you connect me to the police, please?"

"Certainly. One moment."

"Police Department, how can I help you?"

"Is Blackey workin' tonight?"

Blackey was a local police officer everyone knew. He was kind, easy to talk to, and I figured if I needed rescuing, I'd rather it be him.

"He's not in tonight."

"Oh. Well, can you send someone out to check on me?"

The officer on the line said, "Sure. Can you tell me what's going on?"

"I think someone's in our basement."

I gave them our address and waited.

I had my pellet gun with me. It was pumped six or seven times and ready. I figured it would at least leave a welt.

The officer showed up, and I met him outside in the driveway, pellet gun in hand.

"You alone, son?" he asked.

"Yes, sir. My dad works for the power company. He got called out."

"Ah, yeah, lots of lights are out tonight. We had a storm not far from here."

I was done with the small talk.

"I think someone's in our basement."

"Is the door out back?"

"Yes, sir. Can't miss it."

"Wait here, and I'll go check it out."

"Mind if I follow you?"

"I'd rather you stay right here. You'll be fine."

"Okay, sir." And I waited.

While he was gone, I fired a shot into the woods, just in case. Then I pumped my pellet gun back up. If something moved, I was ready.

The officer eventually came back.

"You're safe and sound. There's nobody in the basement. I walked around the whole house. You're good."

"Okay. Thank you, sir. I feel better."

I didn't really feel better. But I didn't want to be a bother, so I let him go.

About ten minutes later, the wind picked up again. The trees creaked. And I reached for the phone.

"Operator, how can I help you?"

"Yes, ma'am. Can you connect me to the police again?"

It was a long night.

153: Live Nativity – Crossroads Baptist

Last night, I visited the Live Nativity at Crossroads Baptist Church in Hayden, Alabama.

They host it every year, and I always enjoy walking through. The Nativity tells the full story of Christ's life, from the angel appearing to Mary, all the way through Jesus's crucifixion and ascension into Heaven.

It's held from 6 to 8 PM, and it's dark outside, which I think makes the whole experience even better. There are real campfires, actors dressed in time-appropriate clothing, and each scene is lit just enough to bring it to life.

By the end of the walk, I felt spiritually refreshed. It reminded me why Jesus was born and why He died on the cross.

I only wish they'd keep it open longer each year. It runs for just a few nights. Tonight's the last one, starting at 6 PM.

They offer free hot chocolate and cookies, and they have portable toilets in case you need them. And if you have trouble walking, they'll let you ride in a cart.

I really enjoyed it.

That's the latest on me.

154: Thomas Christmas Party 2021

Today was the first Christmas party of the season. And it was a good one.

The "Thomas Christmas Party" is something I look forward to every year.

I took my late brother's two daughters with me. They live with Momma and Papa, and with me. So they're more like little sisters than nieces at this point. We do life together.

Now, I spent way too long overthinking what to wear to this party. I know it probably doesn't matter to most folks, but I kept thinking about how I used to notice what Papa wore when he took us places growing up. Sometimes he wore a suit and tie. Sometimes a dress shirt with a sweater. And even as a kid, I noticed.

So I figured… maybe these girls notice what I wear too.

At first, I thought, "Go all in. Suit and tie. Let them see I take this stuff seriously."

Then I thought, "Nah, maybe just slacks and a sports coat. Something calm and put-together."

I went back and forth like that all afternoon. "What do I want them to see me in?"

Because you just never know what sticks with kids.

Eventually, I settled on something I felt good in. Hope it landed right.

Before we left, I packed up a bunch of handmade snow globes to give to my aunts, uncles, and cousins. I also grabbed some sweet onions and green onions for the food table. I sliced the sweet onions and threw them in a Tupperware. The green ones went in a mason jar. That's a bachelor's contribution right there.

On the drive over, my fourteen-year-old niece asked me something serious—something that had clearly been on her mind. I'm not going to share it because it was between us, but after I answered, she made a comment that just… stopped me in my tracks. So honest. So sweet. And so wise for her age. I haven't stopped thinking about it since.

She's still got so much innocence in her. So much love. I hate that this world is the way it is sometimes. It's hard. It's cruel. And if I could freeze her in this moment forever, I would. Because hearts like hers are too soft for what's out there.

She and her sister have already lost both their parents. That's why Momma and Papa are raising them now. And maybe that's why I care so much about what shirt I wear to a Christmas party. Because I want to be a steady, strong presence in their world—even if that just means wearing something they remember.

The party was great.
The food was good.
And the company? Even better.
That's all for now.

155: 12/16/2021

Woke up this morning at 4 AM, as usual, with my spinal cord doing its best impression of a lightning bolt. Felt like I got zapped straight out of a dream.

Got dressed, shuffled out the door, and went for my usual morning drive. Classic Radio on XM, Channel 148. Around 7 AM, I started to feel a little better, so I came back home and sank into my recliner for an hour.

At 8 AM, I got back out and headed to the Piggly Wiggly to grab some things for the big family get-together on Saturday.

By 9:12 AM, I was in the checkout line. Yes, I looked at my phone and suddenly remembered something important.

"Holy cow, I've got a doctor's appointment at 10!"

I told the cashier, "Throw it all in the buggy. I've got to roll!"

Loaded everything into the truck and got on the road. That's when traffic decided to turn into a parking lot. I-65 was a mess, so I tried to take the Red Mountain Expressway instead, thinking I was being slick. Nope. 280 was backed up for miles because of a wreck.

I finally pulled into Grandview Medical Center at 10:15 AM. Fifteen minutes late and sweating it.

Walked into the office and said, "I had a 10 AM appointment to get a shot in my arm—so sorry I'm late, traffic was—"

She stopped me, "Wreck on 65 and 280? You're not the only one. Everyone's late today. It'll be about an hour. Want to wait or reschedule?"

"Oh, I'll wait. Not the wreck part. But glad I'm not the only one running behind, you know?"

Finally got my injection around 11:30. Arm felt better already.

Got back home, unloaded the groceries, and realized I hadn't even showered yet. So I did that. Sat back down in my recliner around 2:08

PM, flipped on the TV, and guess what was on? *Wings.* Remember *Wings*? That was a good show.

That's where I'm at now. Recliner, quiet house, familiar reruns.

That's all for now.

156: Merry Christmas – 2021

Merry Christmas!

Momma said this is going to be the best Christmas since 2009. Let that sink in. That's 12 years.

She's lost a son. A grandson. A daughter-in-law. Her mom and dad. And still, she says this might be the best one yet. That's not nothing.

She also said Thanksgiving this year was the best one we've had in a long time.

When I was growing up, we always spent Christmas Day at Nana and Pawpaw's house. Same with Thanksgiving. That was our spot.

Every year, Nana would buy each grandkid a new Christmas ornament. We'd all dig around the tree looking for our new one. She had so many grandkids, she had to make a shopping list just to keep track.

One year, she accidentally reused the same list as the year before, and every single grandkid got the same gift twice in a row. We all laughed about it. I wasn't mad. The year before, she'd given me a chemistry set, and I'd already used up all my Plutonium.

(That, right there, is the only acceptable reason to use an exclamation point: *Plutonium!*)

Back then, Christmas meant food, games, and laughter. Just a house full of noise and joy.

Then in 2005, Nana passed. And things shifted. Slowly but surely, families started celebrating separately. The big gatherings faded.

Didn't mean for this entry to go all nostalgic and sad, but hang tight, because here's the point.

Just before I sat down to write this, I passed three Christmas trees in the house. Two regular ones. And one covered in ornaments from all the grandkids over the past 20 years.

Momma was in her room with her Excel spreadsheet pulled up, checking off the gifts she's already gotten this year.

This Saturday, when we all get together, the grandkids will look for their new ornaments on the tree, just like we did.

There will be games.

There will be food.

And there will be laughter filling the house.

Because Momma said this will be the best Christmas since 2009.

And I believe her.

Merry Christmas, everyone.

157: Deer

It's 10:45 PM, and I just got back home from a really great get-together with some dear friends. I'll write about that tomorrow after I've had some sleep.

The drive home was long. I went through Fayette, Jasper, Cordova, Dora... I'm not even sure I've got that order right, but I eventually made it to the Warrior-Jasper Road. I was taking my time, driving about 45 mph in a 55 mph zone when it happened.

Out of nowhere, a deer came charging at my truck.

Not just any deer either. A 6-point buck. I noticed the antlers right away. Funny how your brain catches that kind of detail in a split second.

He looked mad like I had wandered onto *his* road, not the other way around. It honestly looked like he was trying to pick a fight with my front bumper.

I swerved, and thank the Lord, I missed him. Right as I did, I noticed I was passing "Autumn Lane." Strange how you remember little things when you're in a moment like that. Autumn Lane. Big ol' buck. 45 miles per hour.

That's the closest I've ever come to hitting a deer, at least that I can remember.

Before I left the get-together tonight, someone had warned me: "Watch out. The deer are really out tonight." Turns out they weren't just making conversation; they were right.

But I made it home. Safe. Heart still full from the night.

Time for bed.

158: Publishers Clearing House

So, good news. I won 2.5 million dollars and a brand new car today.

That's right. Publishers Clearing House called.

A man named "Alan" rang me up. My caller ID just said "Tennessee." No last name. No business. Just Tennessee.

"Hello?" I said.

"Yes, this is Alan with Publishers Clearing House. I'm calling to let you know you've won 2.5 million dollars and one free car today."

Now, I need you to understand something. Alan sounded like he hated life. Hated his job, his phone, his house, and probably his momma too.

So I said back, as dry as I could manage, "Yay…"

Then he asked, "Has anyone else called to tell you this?"

"No, Alan. You're the lucky first."

Alan started in on his pitch, but I had had enough.

"I gotta go, Alan. Bye-bye." Click.

But Alan didn't give up. He called again. Then again. In total, six calls.

And then I got to wondering… what if it *was* real?

I walked into the living room and told Momma, "So this guy named Alan says I won Publishers Clearing House."

"Give me the number," she said. "I'll call him back."

So, she does. Alan answers.

"This is Alan; you've won 2.5 million dollars today."

I looked at Momma and said, "Guess you didn't win the car."

Momma wasn't impressed. She told Alan, "This sounds like a scam."

Click.

Alan hung up on her.

So, I guess we're not millionaires. Or car owners.

But it made for a good laugh.

159: Christmas 2021

Christmas is different when you're single, don't have kids, and you've got a disability.

You find new ways to celebrate.

When I was little, I used to get things like corrective shoes and diapers for Christmas. Sounds rough when I say it like that, but I got the fun stuff too.

One year I got a full US Army get-up: uniform, backpack, BB gun, canteen, and even a little cook kit. Nana and Pawpaw got me a toy monkey that year too. Then there was the year I got a BMX bike. I had a good childhood, even if some of my gifts were more medical than magical.

These days, I make snow globes.

Handmade. Personalized. I gave them out as gifts this year to people I love.

I also played a little Secret Santa while out to eat. Looked for hats that said stuff like "Vietnam Veteran," then quietly picked up their tab.

"You need more coffee?" the waitress asked.

"Yeah. You see that guy with the vet hat? Bring me his ticket. Just tell him someone in the restaurant has family who served too."

That's it. That's the moment.

I'm not telling you this to brag about a 12-dollar meal. I just don't have a wife or kids, so my Christmas looks different. If you're in the same boat, maybe it gives you an idea or two.

I handed out 18 snow globes, maybe more. I thought I had made 15 total, but then I found five more blanks while cleaning up, so I kept going. Might make even more if I find extras buried in this room of mine.

I went to several Christmas parties.

One was with a group of women I absolutely adore. We went to a Chinese restaurant. Got the big table so everyone could spread out and I wouldn't feel too cramped. The whole night was hugs and laughter. Felt really good to be around people who love you just as you are.

Then we had the Foster/Thomas party. I was worn out from the night before, but still had a good time. Momma and Papa loved it. That's always the best part; seeing them smile.

The Thomas Christmas party was a highlight. Got to see folks I only see once a year. Gave out snow globes, ate some incredible food, and caught up on everyone's lives. One of my aunts told me I should bring my "famous" cheese tray next year. Might just do that.

And we'll have our family Christmas here at the house; just me, Papa, Momma, and my two nieces. I probably won't write much about that one. Some moments you just want to keep for yourself.

Later that same day, I'll ride over to my dad's house with the girls. More food, more laughter, more love.

Momma said this would be the best Christmas since 2009, and I think she was right.

Merry Christmas.

—*Pictured: My late brother and I, both dressed in our army outfits, BB guns and all. Also, me holding the monkey Nana and Pawpaw gave me.*

Merry Christmas again, y'all.

160: Dentist – That's Gotta Come Out

I can still hear my old dentist clear as day…

"Gold'll last till you're around fifty years old. The other stuff won't make it that long."

I was in my twenties. Young, full of confidence, and officially grown up—because I was getting my first crown. I chose gold, of course.

"Mom, guess what? I got a gold tooth. No, for real. A *gold tooth*. No, I'm not turning around and taking it back. It's in the *back* of my mouth. Dentist says it'll last 'til I'm about fifty. That's a long time from now…"

Fast-forward to December 2021.

There I was, laid back in the dentist chair. Felt like the man had both hands, a flashlight, and maybe a wrench stuffed in my mouth.

"That's gotta come out," he says.

"Hmm? Wadda ya sayin'?"

"I said, that gold crown? Tooth under it's gotta come out."

"Mm-mm, I'm closs to fiddy… Dentiss said I'd be 'bout fiddy… I'm fordy-sis…"

"We'll schedule you for January. That okay?"

"Mm-hmm. Glad I got the gold. Almost made it to fiddy…"

161: Early Morning Drive

Christmas wore me slap out this year.

I spent less money than usual—handmade snow globes instead of handing out gift cards—and somehow, it still took all the energy I had. So, Monday and Tuesday, I just crashed. Slept like a log.

Then, around 1 AM this morning, I shot straight up in bed, kicking and yelling. Dreamed about snakes again.

And when you sleep wearing a CPAP with a 6-foot hose, and you're also hooked up to a night-time urine bag with another 6-foot hose, it's real easy to dream that you're tangled up in snakes.

I hate snakes.

My dog, Tommy, was just sitting across the room, staring at me like I'd lost my mind. Probably scared him to death.

Between the dreams and my tethered spinal cord zapping me like a cattle prod, I knew I wasn't going back to sleep. So I got in the truck and went for one of my drives around the mountain.

One day I'll take Tommy with me, but not tonight. He's not a fan of riding in vehicles anyway.

I tuned the radio to "Radio Classics" on SiriusXM and caught a string of good ones—Jack Benny, The Great Gildersleeve, Philip Marlowe, and Dragnet. All of 'em had New Year's Eve specials going.

So yeah, I rang in 1940 through 1948 tonight.

Now I'm back in my room, Tommy's curled up nearby, and I'm hoping to catch a little more sleep before morning hits.

As long as I don't dream about snakes again. I hate snakes.

That's all for now.

162: 3 Dear Reader

My Aunt and Uncle introduced me to her—a preacher's wife, sweet as a glass of Momma's homemade sweet tea.

They told me she didn't get out of the house much, but she loved to read. We ended up connecting on Facebook, and before long, she was commenting on nearly every story I posted.

And every time, it was something kind and thoughtful. Always uplifting. She would thank me for sharing, and truth is, I really needed that encouragement. Writing like this, putting myself out there, it's not always easy.

She followed along when I went to Gatlinburg, reading every nightly update like she was right there with me.

Then, after I posted that I was finally back home safe, she commented:

"Thank you for taking me with you on your trip."

That one got me. Still gets me.

I realized I wasn't just writing for myself—I was taking someone somewhere, even if just through a screen.

Tonight, I found out she passed away.

I didn't know her long. But I'm grateful I knew her at all.

You'll be missed, sweet friend.

163: Betty White

Dear Ms. Betty White,

Thank you.

All of America loves you. I mean *all* of us.

Big, burly men with beards and muddy boots are gonna cry when they hear the news of your passing. I'm not even kidding.

We've got all kinds of people in this country—rich folks, poor folks, cranky folks, sweet folks, people of every color and every walk of life—and somehow, all of us love you.

I grew up watching you. *Mary Tyler Moore. The Golden Girls.* All the reruns in between.

Funny enough, I was watching you *on* The Golden Girls when I heard about your passing. Earlier that same day, I had even heard you on the radio.

You've always been so classy. Smart. Beautiful. Talented. Kind.

Thank you for showing us that in a world full of Blanche Devereauxs, it's perfectly okay to be Rose Nylund.

We love you, Betty.

Rest well.

164: Happy New Year 2022

5... 4... 3... 2... 1... Happy New Year!

My Aunt and I were standing on the porch of the cabin, watching the fireworks light up over the Gatlinburg Space Needle.

All around us, people were singing "Auld Lang Syne." It was like stepping back in time.

Earlier that day, we'd gone and had 1920s gangster-style photos taken. Yep, the whole outfit—hats, suspenders, the works. We were ready to head into the Roaring Twenties… 2020s-style.

But then… well, life hit pause.

COVID.

And just like that, the last two years have felt like one long blur. One long, crummy year.

Sometimes, I don't even feel like I *had* a 2020. Like it just… vanished.

But 2021 gave me some good moments.

—Went to Mt. Airy, NC for the Mayberry Meet-Up

—Made it to Gatlinburg a few times

—Laughed a lot more than I cried

So things are looking up.

Today, Momma made plates and took them to folks in the family who were sick or couldn't join us.

We had the classics: black-eyed peas, turnip greens, pork roast, cornbread, apple pie, and pound cake.

We said our prayers. We asked for health and happiness. And we're heading into 2022 like it's 2020 – Part II. The do-over.

Here's hoping this one sticks. *Happy New Year, y'all.*

165: The Smoke Detector

—Smoke Detector—

"Beep, Beep, Beep. Beep, Beep, Beep."

"Papa, the smoke alarm's going off…"

Papa can't hear high-pitched sounds worth a flip, so he's just sitting there calm as ever while the house is trying to tell us something.

"Papa! The smoke alarm is going off!"

"Which one?"

"Good question. Sounds like it's the one in the garage. …Wait, since when do we have one in the garage?"

"Go up to the attic and make sure nothing's on fire."

So I crawl up to the attic, flashlight in hand, expecting to find at least a puff of smoke or a flaming squirrel or something.

But nope. Everything up there is fine and dandy.

"It's not the attic," I say, heading back into the garage.

I look up and sure enough, there it is. One lonely smoke alarm stuck to the garage ceiling. Hadn't even known it existed until it decided to sing the song of its people.

Papa had popped some popcorn earlier, so maybe that set it off? The garage is right off the kitchen.

"Beep, Beep, Beep. Beep, Beep, Beep."

We fan it with a towel. It quiets down. Victory.

Five minutes later...

"Beep, Beep, Beep. Beep, Beep, Beep."

Back we go.

Now, we've got about fifteen other smoke alarms in the house, all hardwired together. You'd think if there was *really* a fire, at least one other one would join the chorus.

"I think it's broke," I say.

"Let's get the ladder, and I'll climb up," Papa says.

So we drag the ladder out, and Papa climbs up.

"Beep, Beep, Beep. Beep, Beep, Beep."

"It's not this one," he hollers down.

"What?!"

"It's not coming from this!"

"Well, it *has* to be!"

"Nope. Not beeping at all."

Now I'm walking around the garage with my ears perked like a hunting dog.

"You're right. It's coming from… right here!"

The garage was mid-clean-out, so we had a bunch of stuff in a big pile. I start digging like a raccoon going through garbage.

"FOUND IT!"

It was a smoke detector, loose, not even mounted to anything. Still fully alive and beeping its little plastic heart out.

Date on the back? December 28th, 2003.

No idea why it was still functioning, but I'll say this much: ACE Hardware batteries last a long time.

Battery came out. Detector went in the trash.

And that's how we spent thirty minutes chasing a ghost beep through the garage.

166: First Snow of 2022

We got snow!

Now, that might not mean much to folks up North, but down here, it's a big event. Churches cancel stuff. Schools shut down for days. People panic-buy milk and bread like they're stocking up for a blizzard.

It's 6:00 AM CST as I write this. Still dark, but I'd guess we got about an inch and a half. I'll know more once the sun comes up.

What's crazy is that just a few days ago, it was in the 60s, and we were under tornado warnings. Southern weather doesn't play fair. One minute it's shorts and sweet tea, the next it's mittens and cocoa.

Now, if you've ever had Snow Ice Cream, you know what's up. But we don't get to make it much down here.

So as soon as it's light, I'm taking a bucket outside to gather some good, clean snow. The fluffy stuff. None of that yellow mess.

Snow Ice Cream is a simple joy; sugar, milk, vanilla, and fresh snow. That's it. Tastes like childhood.

I've already cranked my truck. Heater and defroster are going strong just in case I need to make a run. Got a timer set to remind me to check on it. It's cold but peaceful.

The snow reminded me of the time I lived in Virginia. That was a good season of life.

Here's hoping this snow sticks around a little while longer.

That's all for now.

167: 1/5/2022

Today was one of the good ones.

First off, my blood sugar has been way better since I started using the Freestyle Libre System.

Instead of stabbing my finger six times a day, I can now check my levels with just a scan. Ten times a day if I feel like it. Twenty if I'm feeling wild.

It even sends daily reports to my Endocrinologist, which makes keeping up with my diabetes feel a little less like guesswork and a little more like teamwork.

Lately, I've been hanging steady between 85 and 90. Not bad at all.

We went to Chili's for supper. I had the steak with broccoli and a side salad, but let me tell you, Momma got the Cajun Shrimp Pasta, and *whew,* that stuff was something else.

I stole a bite, and now I know what I'm getting next time. If it's still on the menu, I'm grabbing it. Might even ask for a double portion.

After dinner, we swung by the pharmacy to pick up a few meds.

They had Christmas ornaments 50% off. And not just any ornaments; the *perfect size* for snow globes.

You better believe I bought up every last one. (I'll post a picture later. They're real nice.)

Now I'm home, dog's asleep, and I'm about to wind down watching "Wings" on TV. That show never gets old.

That's all for now.

168: Memories

At this point, I think just about everyone knows someone who's battled cancer—some who made it through, and some who didn't.

This story is from over fifteen years ago, but it's stayed with me.

There was a lady I worked with for more than a decade. She and I—well, we clicked. We could laugh for hours, cutting up in the breakroom, or we could sit in complete silence during lunch and not feel the least bit awkward. She once told me, "It's because we're comfortable with each other." And she was right.

She reminded me of good ol' American apple pie, born in the 1950s, one of the best eras in my book.

She once told me, with a little mischievous grin, that she'd been in an all-girl gang back in Chicago growing up. "Leather jackets and everything," she said proudly. It cracked me up. I couldn't even picture her that way. A Yankee with a rebel streak.

She married a military man, and they ended up down South, in Huntsville, where I eventually met her.

She was quiet with most folks, but not with me. We were lunch buddies, work buddies. We just got each other.

Then one day, she went home and found her husband on the floor. Gone. Just like that. I went to his funeral, my first time attending one where the person had been cremated. I remember wondering if that was a Northern thing.

Afterward, she and I used to joke about how grocery stores didn't sell food for people who lived alone. Everything was family-sized. She got it. I got it. We were both in the same boat.

Then came the day she showed up at my office, looking real serious.

"I wanted to tell you myself, before you heard it from someone else," she said.

But I already knew.

She had cancer. It was advanced. So advanced that there'd be no chemo, no radiation—just time. Not much of it.

She told me she'd prayed "that prayer", you know, the one where you ask the Lord to save you. It was important to her that I knew that. And I could see it in her eyes; she was at peace. She really was on cloud nineteen.

She was never a big talker, especially not about faith. So when she brought that up, I knew it meant a lot.

I went to visit her at home one day, probably the last day she had the energy for company.

"If you could have anything right now, anything at all," I asked, "what would it be?"

She didn't hesitate. "A real Chicago hot dog or pizza from UNO's." She said she'd tried making a hot dog at home but couldn't keep it down. The cancer had gotten to her stomach by then.

Before I left, I hugged her tight and told her I loved her. She said she loved me too. I knew that was our goodbye.

She slipped into a coma not long after and passed away. She weighed less than 80 pounds when she died.

Her funeral was packed. Folks came in from all over: East Coast, West Coast, South. She'd touched a lot of lives.

Her little brother gave a eulogy that lasted two full hours. You could hear the pride in every word. When he asked if anyone else wanted to speak, I found myself standing up without thinking.

I could've said a lot. I could've told them how she got saved, how we shared jokes, or how we just "got" each other.

But instead, I kept it simple.

"She was a good person to take a break with at work."

And that said it all.

169: Snow Days

When I was a kid, the forecast of snow meant one glorious thing: NO SCHOOL.

In the South, it doesn't take much. Just a whisper of snow, and everything shuts down. A half-inch? That's all we need for icy bridges and panic at the Piggly Wiggly.

Sometimes, schools would cancel classes before the first flake even fell. Just the threat of snow was enough.

I remember sitting at the kitchen table, "working" on my homework, and if the weatherman even *mentioned* the word "snow," I'd casually close my books and slide them away.

Didn't know much about Algebra, but I sure knew this equation: Weekday + Snow = No School.

We'd stay up waiting for the snow like it was Santa. If they said it would start at 1 AM, then by golly, I was outside in my pajamas at 1:01 AM.

Some of my best memories happened on Snow Days. Learned a few hard lessons too:

— Riding a bike on ice? Not smart.

— Igloos really are warm inside.

— Walking the icy rails of the train track? Another bad idea.

— If you're going to walk on a frozen creek, test it first with a big ol' stick. Or better yet, let your brother go first.

Snow Days taught me things. And they reminded me to pay attention to my body, too. With my Spina Bifida, I don't feel the cold in my legs and feet the same way. I had to watch for frostbite before I even knew what it was.

But now… now the kids don't get Snow Days.

Since the pandemic and the rise of virtual school, the minute snow hits, they just switch over to computers. Doesn't matter if there's a foot of snow or just a dusting; school's still on.

Tonight, the weatherman's calling for more wintry weather in parts of North Alabama. And wouldn't you know it? The schools have already announced: *Virtual Learning Day.*

That just doesn't sit right with me.

What are kids supposed to do on a Snow Day now?

No sledding. No snowmen. Just screen time and typing.

If I had kids, if I were able, I don't think I'd change my mind.

Because for me, some of life's best joys came wrapped in snowflakes.

And I'd hate to see a generation miss out on that kind of magic.

170: 1/8/2022

The morning kicked off around 6 AM.

I got dressed, stepped outside, and headed for my truck to begin my usual drive. On the way out, I made a quick stop by the fridge and grabbed a Diet Coke for the road—it was perfectly chilled.

I climbed into the truck, fired it up, and cranked the heat.

At the first stop sign, I cracked open the Diet Coke.

Now, there's a scientific explanation for what happened next— I've even looked it up before, but I can't recall the exact details. What I do know is this: the moment I opened the can, the Coke instantly turned to slush. I absolutely love it when that happens.

And let me be clear—it wasn't slushy beforehand.

Something about pressure, temperature, and carbonation all align just right, and... boom! Slush. It's like a little morning miracle.

I smiled and said to myself, "It's gonna be a great day."

I pulled into the local fast-food joint and ordered my usual breakfast.

When I got to the window, the lady leaned out and said, "The car in front of you paid for your order."

Now, around here—and maybe in other places too, that kind of gesture comes with a bit of etiquette. We call it "Paying it forward" or sometimes, "Keep it going."

So I said, "Keep it going. I'll pay for the car behind me."

From there, I swung by Dollar General and picked up some cleaning supplies. Today's the day I finally tackle cleaning my room.

With everything going so well, I made plans to meet up with a friend and hand-deliver his Christmas gift—I hadn't had a chance to give it to him yet.

And yes, sir. It's shaping up to be a mighty fine day.

That's all for now.

171: Evening 1/8/2022

What a wonderful day it's been.

I finally caught up with a good friend and handed him his Christmas gifts.

We decided to grab a bite at our go-to "sit-down" spot—The White House Restaurant. It's one of those local places where the food's always hot and the waitresses already know your drink order. We spent over an hour just talking and catching up on life. It felt good to reconnect.

On the way home, I stopped by the store and picked up some over-the-counter antacid medicine for Mom. Her heartburn's been acting up again, and I figured she could use the relief.

Now, I'm curled up at home watching *Downton Abbey*. I love that show. I've probably seen the whole series at least six times, but nights like this, I like to pick a couple of favorite episodes and just settle in with them. Okay, more like two or three.

And that's where I'll leave it for tonight.

That's all for now.

172: National Championship 1/10/2022

I felt like I needed to mark today with a post. After all, it's 1/10/2022.

What makes it special? Tonight is the National Championship Game—7 PM CST. Alabama versus Georgia. Both teams from the SEC. That's a big deal.

So naturally, I'm pulling for Alabama.

I'm camped out in my recliner, watching the game unfold. Now, if you've followed me or read any of my posts, you already know—I'm not a huge football fan. I don't follow stats, I don't know who's been traded, and I don't yell at the TV. But football meant a lot to people in my life. Especially my late brother.

He was the biggest Alabama Crimson Tide fan I've ever known.

If Alabama was playing, everything else could wait. He'd be glued to the game—on TV, radio, or however he could find it.

Back in the '90s, when we were living in Virginia, we didn't always get the Alabama games on TV. Didn't matter. He'd dig around, find the game on some distant AM station, and tune in with a Walkman radio and headphones.

I remember once, he showed up to a formal sit-down event with his earphones in—listening to the Tide while everything else went on around him. I think it was Paw Paw's idea. Truth be told, my brother, Paw Paw, my uncle, and my cousin were all wearing earpieces that day. All of them, diehard fans through and through.

Then in 2010, my brother passed away suddenly, from a brain hemorrhage.

And almost right after that, the Alabama Crimson Tide caught fire, winning games, championships, and making history.

These days, it seems everyone in the country knows Alabama football. Everyone knows the name "Nick Saban." And every time I watch a game, I feel a tug in my chest. He's missing all of this, and he would've loved it more than anything.

He would've been in Heaven—well, he is.

Love you, brother.

Miss you every day.

Roll Tide.

173: 1/12/2022

It was a full day today.

I started the morning around 6 AM.

Went out for my usual early drive and was greeted by the usual company—plenty of rabbits and deer. The "Duck Family" made their appearance too, waddling right across the road again. I had to stop and let them pass, and it still tickles me every time. They move like they own the place.

After that, I pulled into my local fast-food joint and grabbed my regular breakfast.

Then, I took my truck over to the car wash. It was way too cold to get it washed, but I did go ahead and vacuum it out. Sometimes, that's all you can manage in this weather.

For Christmas, my Aunt gave me a $50 gift certificate to Hobby Lobby. I drove out that way and used it to buy a small table to replace the piece of furniture next to my Lazy Boy Recliner. I'm happy with it—fits the space perfectly and looks nice too.

At 2 PM, I had an appointment with my Psychologist. Yes, I openly and proudly admit that I see a Psychologist. Mental health matters—especially when you're living with a disability. It's easy to fall into depression if you're not careful.

The appointment went well.

Afterward, I took a slow drive through the countryside. It was a beautiful day for it—sun shining, sky clear, just the kind of quiet that makes you breathe deeper.

I hope your day was a good one, too.

That's all for now.

174: Spina Bifida – The Birds And The Bees

No two people born with Spina Bifida are alike.

The condition affects everyone differently.

When I was born, doctors told my parents I likely wouldn't be able to walk.

After my Spina Bifida was surgically repaired and it was finally safe to lay me on my back, my mother began a daily routine. She would lay me down, gently take my feet in her hands, and rotate my legs like they were pedaling a bicycle. She did this every single day—sometimes for more than an hour at a time.

Eventually, I began to move my legs on my own. One day, I pulled myself up and stood—and Momma cried.

Now, I'm going to skip over a lot and get to the story I want to share.

Over the years, I've met several parents of children born with Spina Bifida. And almost every time, the same question comes up— *Will my child be able to make love and have children?*

And my answer is always honest: *I don't know.*

What I can offer is my own story. I share this not for pity, but so people can understand what this part of life can look like for someone like me. I'll try to use proper medical terms, and I ask you to read it with maturity and respect.

By the time I was sixteen, I knew something wasn't right.

This was back before the internet could give you answers. All I had was the public library, the Encyclopedia Britannica, and two brothers who were, let's just say, *not especially helpful* in that area.

The library wasn't much help either.

So, I made an appointment with my Urologist—Dr. Morgan. He was brilliant. I felt sure he could help me figure this out.

Now, I don't remember every detail. I think my brain has blocked a good bit of it out, but here's what I do remember:

After some testing, I was referred to a specialist in Erectile Dysfunction. She was a woman, and I was embarrassed. I still remember that part clearly.

In the end, the conclusion was this: my penis had not developed properly and would not grow. My body also didn't produce sperm, which meant I wouldn't be able to have biological children. I also couldn't achieve an erection, which meant I wouldn't be able to make love to a wife.

For a teenage boy, that was devastating news.

And I had to come to terms with it—quietly, alone, and in a world that expects young men to act like everything's fine.

I also had to figure out how to appear "normal" when everything in that part of life felt broken. But that's a story for another day.

And no, there weren't any surgical options for me. I looked into it. Maybe there are now, but to be honest, I don't care anymore.

The Bible says not every man is called to marriage. I believe that with all my heart.

I truly believe I'm one of those men. I'm called to be single, and I'm grateful for the life I have.

I have nieces and nephews, a wonderful family, and close friends. My life feels full.

So, when parents ask if I think their child will one day be able to make love or have kids, I always answer with care: *I just don't know.*

But I'll say this—when I visit the Adult Spina Bifida Clinic, I see married couples all the time. One partner, sometimes both, are in wheelchairs, and they'll have one or two children with them. Clearly, their experience with Spina Bifida is different from mine.

Like I said, no two cases are ever the same.

That's all on that topic.

175: Feeling 'Blah'

I've been in a bit of a "Blah" mood lately.

Can't quite shake it. But I know it'll pass—it always does.

So, I decide to go for a drive.

As I head down one of the quieter roads, I pass a small farm. A husband-and-wife team are already hard at work—just like they always are.

Most days, I see them out there: mending fences, hauling hay with the tractor, or working with the cattle.

I give them a wave as I go by.

The sight reminds me of the farmland back in Virginia—fields stretched as far as the eye could see.

I learned to drive on those winding country roads, probably around the ripe old age of fourteen or fifteen.

It was in a beat-up blue van from the '70s. I'd swear it was the same kind of van that always shows up in those old cop shows, tearing down alleyways with the fuzz in hot pursuit.

But that's a story for another day.

I pass another field, this one full of horses.

It brings back memories of horse-drawn buggies driven by Mennonites.

Good memories.

Again, a story for another day.

Eventually, I make it to the highway.

It's just after 6 AM, and the roads are already packed with folks heading into work.

I find myself thinking about my last job. Actually, I don't think of it as just a "job"—it was my career. And I miss it.

One time, I showed up to work in full uniform—except for the fuzzy house slippers I forgot I was still wearing.

That, too, is a story for another day.

I flip on the radio—XM Channel 148, "Radio Classics"—and head toward breakfast.

At the local fast-food joint, I pull into the drive-thru and order my usual.

"That'll be six dollars and thirty cents. Pull up to the window, please."

I pull up.

"The car ahead of you paid for your meal," the woman at the window says.

It's happened before—I've written about it.

So, I say, "I'll pay it forward. Cover the car behind me."

She looks at the screen and says, "Are you sure? That'll be fifteen dollars and thirty-six cents."

"Ouch," I say, but I pay it anyway and move on.

When I get home, I sit down and start typing out a story from a memory that came to me during the drive.

It's not ready to share yet.

So, for now, it's a story for another day.

That's all for now.

176: Mayberry Meet-Up 2022

I went ahead and made my reservations for Mt. Airy, North Carolina this July—for the annual "Mayberry Meet-Up."

You might remember that last year, my Aunt and Step-Grandmother went with me for the event.

This time around, it looks like Momma and my Aunt will be tagging along.

There's something special about this trip.

Something truly unique about people from all over the country gathering together just to sit and watch *The Andy Griffith Show.*

People who still believe in the simple things in life.

Love Thy Neighbor comes to mind.

To put it plainly: these are my people.

The hugs are long. Sometimes fifteen minutes long.

The smiles linger.

The laughter is soft but sincere.

It's a place full of folks who just want to feel connected.

I feel at home there.

And I can't wait to get back.

That's all for now.

177: Upcoming Trips – 2022

I know it's been a while since I've gone on any real trips, but the truth is—I just haven't had the chance… or the money.

Well, the money part still hasn't changed, but the travel part is about to.

Lately, I've been putting together a list of short upcoming trips—Southern road trips, quick getaways, call 'em what you like.

One of the trips is with my Aunt. We're planning to visit Elvis Presley's birth home.

She and I also have another trip scheduled to Mt. Airy, NC.

And there's a possible third trip back to Mississippi in the works, too.

Between March and May, I've planned another Mississippi trip—this one with my Dad.

We'll drive about four hours to a "Place" I'm keeping secret for now—I want it to be a surprise.

We'll stay overnight, then drive home the next day.

So, yes, multiple trips to the great state of Mississippi.

I'm also thinking of reaching out to a dear friend of mine who lives in Mississippi. We'd pass right through his area on our way to the "Place."

(You know I'm talking about you, "M.")

All of these are budget-friendly trips… or at least I *hope* they are.

Before any of that, though, I've got a trip planned back up to the Cabin to take the Christmas decorations down. Yep. We didn't schedule a proper time to go back and do that.

But I do hope the guests who've stayed since the holidays enjoyed the festive setup.

In the next few days, I'll make that drive and take care of it.

I've gotten the go-ahead from my doctor, and I'll be taking some prescribed antibiotics along with me—just in case.

And that's the latest update on me.

That's all for now.

178: Half Shell Oyster House

Today, I had a craving for oysters on the half shell.

Unfortunately, the only restaurant I knew of that served them closed down during the pandemic.

So, I called my uncle—Uncle "Unc!"

He told me to check out a place called the "Half Shell Oyster House."

Next, I called my Dad and asked if he wanted to tag along.

Turns out, he was in the mood for oysters too.

I picked him up around 12:30 PM, and we hit the road to Birmingham, Alabama.

The restaurant's located in a really nice, modern part of town.

Let me just say—it's upscale.

Very classy on the inside. So much so that I felt a little embarrassed being *that guy* taking pictures of the décor or snapping photos of my food.

So, you won't find many pictures from this outing.

For starters, we ordered stuffed crab cakes and fried green tomatoes.

Then came the oysters.

I got a half dozen on the half shell and a half dozen Oysters Bienville.

Dad went for the classic oysters on the half shell.

The restaurant had a calm, peaceful atmosphere—perfect for a quiet conversation.

Dad and I talked about our upcoming trip to Mississippi, and even tossed around ideas for a few more.

And, yes—I ordered another half dozen oysters on the half shell once I'd cleaned my plate.

They were that good.

Uncle Unc! was right. He usually is.

After lunch, I drove Dad back home. Gave him a hug and told him, "I love you."

It was a good day.

That's all for now.

179: Tooth Extraction – 'Gowd' Crown

Today, I went to the dentist to have a tooth "extracted."

Now, I'll be honest with you—I would've much rather heard my dentist just say he was going to *pull* my tooth.

Instead, he says, "Mr. Thomas, we're going to extract that tooth today."

I glanced over at the tools on the tray and saw *The Tool.*

No matter how clean and clinical they try to make it look, we all know—it's a pair of pliers. And he's going to use it to yank a tooth right out of my head.

After numbing the left side of my face, my dentist got to work on the far-back molar on the bottom.

He picked up *The Tool*, and I closed my eyes.

Now, it's easier to tell you I simply closed my eyes… than to admit I might have passed out.

"You're going to feel some pressure," he said. "That's normal. What I really need to prepare you for is the cracking sound—you're going to hear a cracking sound. That's normal too."

So there I was—feeling pressure, hearing my dentist grunt like he was tightening lug nuts under a car. I half expected him to mutter something about a busted furnace.

Then, I heard the crack.

"Ahh, there we go. Got it," he said.

"Don't lose the crown!" I shouted.

Well, what actually came out was: "Don't oos my gowd! I want my gowd!"

That's how I sounded with gauze packed in my mouth.

When I got home, I showed my niece the "treasure."

"This is older than you," I told her.

She looked at me and said, "Sounds like you got a little lisp now, too."

I grinned and showed her my treasure again.

My "Gowd.

180: Rock Star

Lately, I've been living life as a Rock Star.

Yep—headlining the biggest stadiums across the world.

My last concert? I played in front of one hundred and fifty thousand fans.

All of them screaming my name.

I handled the rhythm guitar, lead guitar, *and* lead vocals.

I ran through everything from my album *Dark Side of the Moon* to *The Wall*.

Then I shifted gears into my Southern Rock catalog.

Of course, I closed out the night with my most iconic song—"Free Bird."

There I was, singing "Free Bird" at full volume, getting ready to drop one of the greatest guitar solos of all time when it hit me…

Have I even heard Ronnie Van Zant sing "Free Bird" in the past twenty years?

Seems like I'm always the one doing the singing when that song plays.

Some country drives are quiet and peaceful.

Others? Full-blown arena tours.

I love playing the Rock Star.

181: 1/29/2022

Mom and I were home alone tonight, so I thought I'd pick up some food and fix us a nice meal.

Something simple but tasty. So, off I went to the good ol' Piggly Wiggly.

I picked up a pack of pre-stuffed mushrooms, as well as a container of sliced mushrooms.

I got both because the stuffed ones only come six to a pack, and I wasn't sure if Mom would even like them.

For the sliced mushrooms, I grabbed a bottle of Worcestershire sauce to sauté them in. I also picked up some pre-cut sweet peppers and onions to go along with them.

Next, I chose two good-sized baking potatoes; not too big, just right.

Then I grabbed a can of asparagus. I know fresh is an option, but I actually prefer it straight from the can.

I also picked up a couple of ears of corn.

And from the seafood section, I grabbed a small, ready-to-serve shrimp platter.

As soon as I got home, I tidied up the kitchen and got to cooking.

Within two hours, Mom and I were sitting down to a nice little dinner for two.

Everything turned out delicious.

182: Pizza Hoagies

Mom and I were home alone again today.

So for lunch, I figured a Pizza Hoagie would hit the spot—and it's easy to make, too.

My late brother taught me how to make them back when I was younger.

Off to the "Pig" I went.

At our local Piggly Wiggly, I picked up everything we needed: sub sandwich rolls, pizza sauce, shredded mozzarella cheese, pepperoni, hard salami, ham, bell pepper, and onion.

Back home, Mom and I each built our own hoagie just how we liked it.

You pop them in the oven at 400 degrees for about 13 minutes.

(Temperature and cook times may vary… blah, blah, blah.)

Golden Flake "Hot" Chips go perfectly with it.

Mmm-mmm, good.

183: Gatlinburg February 2022

Today I packed up my clothes, toiletries, and medical supplies for my return trip to the Cabin in Gatlinburg.

I'm planning to wake up around 3 AM and hit the road.

The main goal this time around is to take down the Christmas decorations.

I figure as long as they're down before Valentine's Day, we're still in the clear.

I'm honestly excited to be getting back on the road again.

Planning to stay for about twenty days or so.

So, join me for the journey to Gatlinburg. We roll out at 3 AM.

184: Gatlinburg February 2022 part 2
I have arrived!

I've arrived!

This morning, my alarm went off right at 3 AM.

My dog, who was curled up in his bed, gave me *the* look.

If you're a dog owner, you know the look I mean. The "Wherever you're going, I'm not coming" look.

Thankfully, I had showered before bed and laid my clothes out for the morning.

I got dressed, kissed my pup goodbye, and by 3:30 AM, I was on the road.

The drive up was smooth and quiet. I had old-time radio shows playing as I eased my way north into Tennessee.

I got off the exit at Sweetwater to grab breakfast at *The Dinner Bell*.

It's a family-owned restaurant run by a brother and sister and has been in business for 46 years.

There's a gift shop inside, much like what you'd see at a Cracker Barrel—filled with unique little items you won't find just anywhere.

The food is good, the prices are reasonable, and I enjoy walking through the shop area after a meal.

This was only my second time eating there, but Mom told me that my great-grandfather also liked dining at that very restaurant.

Since I wasn't sure about the current road conditions in the mountains, I decided to avoid the backroads this time and stuck to the interstate.

I came through Pigeon Forge instead of my usual route through Townsend.

At about 10:45 AM Eastern Time, I pulled into the Cabin.

My plans for today are simple: make out the couch and go back to sleep.

I've got my travel camera set up so Papa and Momma can check in on me.

And I've got *Downton Abbey* playing on the TV.

It feels good to be back in the mountains.

That's all for now.

185: Cabin – Day 1

Good morning!

The day started around 7 AM EST.

I got up, made myself a cup of coffee, and checked to see what I had brought along for breakfast.

I've been trying to be better about bringing groceries with me instead of waiting until I arrive to do all my shopping.

But as it turns out, I forgot to pack the bologna and cheese.

So, off to Food City I went.

Once I got back to the cabin, I fried up some bologna and made cheese toast in the toaster oven.

Oh, and had another cup of coffee, of course.

That's all for this morning.

186: Cabin – Day 1 – Evening

A long nap was had today by yours truly.

Around 3 PM, I had a telehealth visit with my psychologist.

I was impressed—he immediately recognized that I was at the cabin just by the chair I was sitting in and the background behind me. Very observant.

The appointment went well.

Afterward, I went out and picked up ten large tote boxes to pack away all the Christmas decorations.

You may or may not remember, but I had purchased brand-new Christmas decorations specifically for the cabin when I decorated it back in December.

…And now I need storage for all of it.

I'm excited to share that Momma is planning to come up this weekend to help me out. If she can, my Aunt will come with her.

That'll also give me a chance to go see the *Hatfield and McCoy Dinner Show* in Pigeon Forge. I didn't want to do that one solo.

The town is practically empty right now.

I counted a total of four cars as I drove through Gatlinburg on my way to the Dollar Store. On the way back, I counted twelve.

Tonight, I stopped by McDonald's for dinner.

Tomorrow, I'll start packing up the Christmas decorations— somewhere in between naps.

That's all for now.

187: Cabin – Day 2 – Morning

Rough night's sleep last night.

I woke up with my spinal cord shocking me, painful and relentless.

I sat up, swung my legs off the couch, and noticed something strange: one of my socks was missing. Still no idea where it went.

I got up and shuffled to the coffee maker, dragging my pee bag across the floor behind me. Started the coffee.

Took my morning meds and gave myself my insulin.

I glanced out the window—it rained through the night, and now the fog is thick over the mountains. The whole view outside is misty and grey.

I'm not even hungry this morning, so I'll probably skip breakfast and have an early lunch instead.

The big task for today is packing up the Christmas decorations.

But first, I've got to find that missing sock.

That's all for now.

188: Pottery House Cafe and Grille

I had skipped breakfast this morning and was craving an early lunch—something light.

My friend, Lee Ann, had recommended the *Pottery House Café and Grille*, located at *The Old Mill*. It sounded like just the thing for a day like today.

I got dressed and put on my favorite sweater.

At 11:30 AM EST, I arrived and parked around back.

It's a charming little restaurant that reminded me of *The Creamery* when it was still open in Cullman, Alabama.

They have entrances at both the front and the back, plus plenty of patio space for outdoor dining.

The history of *The Old Mill* is fascinating.

Everything—from the bread you eat to the plates you eat off of—is made right there. I'd definitely recommend checking out their website for more.

I was seated next to the fireplace, which I enjoyed.

The menu has a variety of soups, salads, and sandwiches—just what I was in the mood for.

They also offer heartier options like Black Angus Burgers and Ribeye Sandwiches.

I ordered a bowl of *Baked Potato Soup* and a side salad.

(For just a buck and a quarter more, you can have your soup served in a bread bowl.)

It also comes with two slices of in-house baked bread.

I had tea with my meal.

My waitress was friendly and attentive, and the atmosphere was warm and inviting.

The total came to about thirteen dollars.

I left her a tip in gold $1 coins.

If you're ever in the area, give *The Pottery House Café and Grille* a try. It's located at *The Old Mill*.

That's all for now.

189: Cabin – Day 3 – Morning

Truth be told, I came up to the ol' cabin hoping to get snowed in.

Almost every guest who stayed here this past month got to see snow.

But today, I woke up late—*really* late.

10 AM EST.

I had a hard time getting up, as usual, because of the spinal cord "zaps."

I looked outside, and it was still raining. Fog had rolled in thick.

You can't even see the mountains in the distance—heck, you can't even see the neighbor's cabin.

A lot of fog.

"Nope… I'm not gonna see any snow," I thought to myself.

Right now, I'm sitting in my chair with my feet propped up.

I need to get up and make a pot of coffee, but I wanted to journal first.

The good news is that Momma, my Aunt, and I think my Uncle are all coming up for the weekend—maybe even staying a little longer. I'm not sure of the exact plans.

They should be arriving tonight.

Today's agenda is to tidy up a little so they arrive to a clean cabin.

Not that the place is messy—I haven't even been downstairs. That part of the house is spotless.

I just need to straighten up the upstairs area where I stay when I'm here.

Also, I've got to stop by CVS and pick up a few things.

I'll grab lunch while I'm out.

That's all for now.

190: Cabin – Day 3 – Evening

I spent today straightening up the cabin and taking a shower to get ready—Mom and my Aunt are on their way.

Unfortunately, my Uncle didn't come with them.

According to the "Life360" driving app we use, they're about an hour out.

The forecast is calling for snow tonight—not much, just a light dusting.

But for those of us staying above the snow line, that can sometimes mean quite a bit more. So, I've gone ahead and built a fire.

Two women staying in the cabin next door asked if they could park in our driveway. Their car couldn't make it up its own.

I told them that was perfectly fine.

I also called Mom to let her know there'd be a strange vehicle parked in the driveway when she arrived. She understood.

Their driveway must be soaked from all the rain we've had, on and off, all day.

I'm holding off on taking the decorations down until Mom gets here.

She didn't get to see them this year and wanted the chance to enjoy them for a bit first.

I have to be out of the cabin by the 17th and the renters arrive on the 18th.

So, I've still got plenty of vacation time left.

Earlier today, I went down to the gas station at the bottom of the mountain and was greeted with a big ol' "Hey, Lynn! Welcome back!"

It felt like I was "Norm" from *Cheers*.

I'll probably stop in each day just to say hey to the fellas.

That's all for now.

191: Cabin – Day 4

Not much to report from the cabin today.

I woke up around 5 AM, while Momma and my Aunt didn't get up until about 9.

I built a fire, and the three of us lounged around on the couches watching TV—mostly documentaries about old Hollywood stars.

We also watched a few episodes of *Autopsy: The Last Hours of...*

It dives into the final moments of actors' and actresses' lives—people like Marilyn Monroe and others.

Momma made her famous Butterbean Pie, and we all ate on that.

It was delicious, as always.

Goes real well with a splash of hot sauce. Mmm-mmm.

We don't have any set plans for tomorrow yet. Just playing it by ear.

The sun stayed out all day, but I don't think the temperature ever made it above freezing. It stayed cold.

Everyone's gone to bed now, and I thought I'd journal before turning in myself.

That's all for now.

192: Cabin – Day 5

I woke up this morning at 5:00 AM EST and decided to journal about yesterday's events.

Yesterday, we packed up all the Christmas decorations.

Mom loaded some boxes into her vehicle, and I'll be taking the rest in mine when I head out.

For dinner, we ordered a large pizza, breadsticks, and two salads from *Ski Mountain Pizza*.

Before we ate, we sang "Happy Birthday" to my Aunt—it was her 21st birthday… again.

While we ate, we had *The Hallmark Channel* playing in the background.

Now, I'm not usually one for that channel, but this particular show was actually pretty interesting. It was about a "Butler School." Yep—a school that teaches you how to become a proper butler. I found that part fascinating.

And yes, of course, it also featured a young couple falling in love.

She had always dreamed of becoming a butler, and he had always wanted to be a chef.

But he comes from a long line of butlers—200 years, if I recall—and is expected to follow the family tradition. Still, his heart belongs in the kitchen.

That's a rough summary, because truthfully, I was paying more attention to the training side of things.

"I'd like to have a butler," I thought to myself.

This morning, we're taking my Aunt to *The Pancake House* for breakfast as part of her birthday celebration.

After that, Mom and my Aunt will head home.

I've really enjoyed having them up here with me, and I'll admit—it'll be a little sad to see them go.

That's all for now.

193: The Dishwasher

My eyes were blurry this morning—classic sign that my blood sugar was high.

I checked it. Sure enough, it was.

I gave myself a dose of insulin.

Next, I headed into the kitchen to load the dishwasher.

I filled it up, but I couldn't find any of those little detergent pods. Sitting on the counter, though, was a small bottle labeled "Dishwasher Liquid."

That sounded close enough… so I used it.

I closed the door, turned the dial to "Normal Wash," and walked away.

About twenty minutes later, I went to the fridge to grab a Diet Coke.

That's when I saw it: soap suds pouring out from under the dishwasher door. A lot of suds.

I rushed over, flung the door open—and the entire inside was a foam party.

I darted to the bathroom and grabbed several towels, then got to work mopping up the mess.

That's when I picked up the bottle again and realized my mistake. It read: "Dishwashing Liquid."

Yep—I had put dish soap in the dishwasher.

I cleaned up what I could, wiped up the floor, and started the washer again.

And again.

And again.

Until it finally stopped bubbling over.

On the bright side?

The dishwasher has never been cleaner.

194: Crafts Antiques & Collectibles

Today I drove over to Pigeon Forge, TN.

My original mission was to visit a candy shop and pick up some sugar-free candy.

Unfortunately, the store I usually go to was closed.

But right next door, I spotted a shop called *Crafts, Antiques & Collectibles*—and it piqued my interest. So in I went.

The manager was very friendly and let me know they were just about to close for the day. I told her I understood and promised I'd only take a quick look around.

The place reminded me of a flea market.

I'm guessing people rent little booth spaces, set up their items to sell, and then one manager oversees everything day-to-day.

There was a wide variety of treasures: collectible electric train sets, model planes, vintage cars and trucks, crystal, lead crystal, dolls, vinyl records, and even old gas pumps.

They even had a Dale Earnhardt trading card that I *think* was autographed. I took a picture of it.

I snapped photos of everything that caught my eye, just moving quickly from one booth to the next since I had limited time.

Honestly, I think I'll go back again when I have more time. Especially to look at those electric trains—I didn't even get pictures of them because I was too caught up in studying the details.

It was a fun and unexpected stop.

Afterward, I realized I was more in the mood for dinner than candy, so I swung by Taco Bell and headed back to the cabin.

That's all for now.

195: Cabin – Day 7

Today was a slow and easy one—I slept through most of it.

A good friend called, and we had a nice long chat on the phone.

Later, I drove down to the bottom of the mountain to catch up with the fellas at the gas station. I hung around and talked with them for about half an hour. Always good for the spirit.

Afterward, I headed over to McDonald's for a simple, budget-friendly meal.

Now, let me tell you about the McDonald's in Pigeon Forge—they've added a third window in the drive-thru. That's right. A *third* window.

And here's the best part: I was the only person in line.

I placed my order and pulled up to the first window to pay.

Then I drove to the second window, where they told me to pull forward to the third window to receive my food.

So I did.

At the third window, the same employee from the second window walked over, opened it, and handed me my food.

Same person. Different window. Same order.

And somehow… it made my night.

That's all for now.

196: Cabin – Day 8

The day kicked off around 8:00 AM EST.

I got up, folded the bedding on the couch, and settled into my chair for about an hour of morning TV—just enough to wake up properly.

Then I drove down the mountain to the gas station and picked up a Coke and a Honey Bun. A classic combo.

Back at the cabin, I took a shower, got dressed, and tossed a load of laundry into the washer.

I did a quick walkthrough of the cabin, tidied up a bit, and threw out anything that needed tossing.

This afternoon, I'm thinking about grabbing dinner at *Cherokee Grill*.

Although, I might change my mind and make a reservation at *The Peddler* instead.

My doctor recommends I eat a steak and baked potato once a week, and who am I to argue with medical advice?

I may also take a scenic drive through the country and stop at one of the many lookout points around here. The views go on for miles, and there's nothing like soaking up some natural beauty.

First things first, though—I need to clean out the inside of my truck.

A country drive just feels better in a clean ride.

That's all for now.

197: Cabin 2/9/2022

I'll be honest, I've lost track of what day I'm on at the cabin. It's either Day 8 or Day 9.

Today I took a long drive through the country.

I stopped at one of the scenic lookout points and stayed for about an hour.

I backed the truck into a space, dropped the tailgate, and perched there with a cold Diet Soda—just enjoying the peaceful view and thinking about life.

Several families stopped by while I was there, most of them taking selfies or trying to wrangle everyone together for a group photo.

The kids were running around and laughing, and the moms were doing their best to keep everyone still long enough to snap a picture. It was nice to watch—pure vacation joy.

Afterwards, I drove over to *Cherokee Grill* for dinner.

I ordered the 14 oz. ribeye with a loaded baked potato and had sweet tea to drink.

No complaints there—it was a good meal.

Back at the cabin now. The temperature hit the 60s today, and the sky was a brilliant blue with just a few clouds.

Right now, it's about 50 degrees outside.

Too warm for a fire tonight.

I'm heading to bed shortly, but wanted to journal before I do.

That's all for now.

198: Cabin 2/10/2022

I woke up at a decent hour today—8:00 AM EST.

I took out the trash and drove down to the station to grab a case of Diet Cokes. A cabin essential.

Yesterday, I straightened up the place and caught up on my laundry.

I also cleaned the ashes out of the fireplace and brought up twelve sticks of firewood from downstairs.

Then, I prepped the fireplace for its next fire by stacking the wood just right—ready to light.

Today, I'm in the mood for some solid BBQ.

There are several BBQ joints in the area, but I think I'll give *Calhoun's* a try today.

I've never eaten there before, but I've heard good things.

I'll be sure to take some pictures and share my thoughts when I get back.

That's all for now.

199: Calhoun's

Today, I finally made my way over to *Calhoun's* for some BBQ.

They've been listed as the #1 BBQ restaurant on several review lists, and I wanted to see if they lived up to the hype.

The restaurant is located right next to *Cherokee Grill*, and the interior has a similar feel; warm, upscale, and comfortable.

I was seated quickly, and since I had already studied the menu online, I knew exactly what I wanted.

I ordered the Half Slab of Ribs, Creamy Coleslaw, and Smoky Mountain Baked Beans. Tea to drink.

A bread basket came out first, and it had a little bit of everything: cornbread, a biscuit, a dinner roll, and even a sweet roll, which I saved for dessert.

The ribs and slaw were both really good. The ribs were tender and flavorful, and the slaw had that creamy Southern texture I like.

The baked beans, however, threw me off a bit. They tasted more like chili, specifically, the kind you'd put on a hot dog. Now, I love hot dog chili, but paired with ribs and slaw? It felt a little out of place. Still, not bad—just unexpected.

While I was eating, I noticed the local Fire Chief being seated.

We've spoken

before, years ago, when I first started coming to Gatlinburg alone, I gave my medical information to 911/EMS just to be safe.

The Fire Chief actually called me personally to say he'd received my file and that I'd be in good hands if anything ever happened. That call stuck with me. I've never forgotten it.

I didn't want to interrupt his lunch, especially since he was dining with someone else—it might have been a business meeting for all I knew.

Instead, I handed my waitress my card and asked her to cover his lunch.

I told her to let him know, *"Thank you for all you do."*

Then I headed out.

So far, I've had BBQ from:

Three Jimmy's

Calhoun's

Bennett's

Once I've tried a few more, I'll do a little ranking.

That's all for now.

200: Lynn Takes The Tram

Today, I did something I've wanted to do for years—I took the Tram.

I've always been too nervous to ride it before, mainly because it doesn't have a restroom onboard. Disabled folks think about things like that. We don't just think about it—we worry.

This morning, I didn't eat anything. I also limited how much I drank because I knew: today was the day. The day I'd ride the Tram.

It's about a ten-minute ride from Gatlinburg to Ober Gatlinburg.

The highest point? 2,800 feet above sea level—1,500 feet above Gatlinburg.

And, according to the operator, just one second to the bottom… if it falls.

I was ready to chicken out. But when I found out it was only a ten-minute ride—and the Tram was already there with the doors wide open—I felt like I could handle it. So, I climbed on board.

Inside, there were leather straps hanging from the ceiling to hold onto during the ride. I grabbed one and never let go.

The Tram swings—forward, backward, side to side—like a cruise ship caught in a storm.

The younger passengers let out excited "Woo-Hoos!" with every sway.

I, however, counted every second. I know for sure—it's exactly ten minutes. I counted.

I had planned to take a picture of our cabin from the Tram and get it enlarged and framed.

That didn't happen.

I *did* see our cabin.

But with my balance issues, I wasn't about to let go of that strap—not even for a second. My legs and feet don't have much feeling, so letting go would've meant falling flat.

I now know this: you get a *great* view of the cabin from the Tram.

In fact, if you wave from the cabin, the passengers can see you.

When we reached the top, I hopped off and walked around for a bit. My plan was to stay ten minutes and catch the next Tram back.

They have an ice rink up there. I skated on it when I was younger—good memories.

Outside, artificial snow blanketed the mountain, and people were skiing.

The place hadn't changed much over the years.

There are food stands, a restaurant, and several little shops up top.

I snapped a few pictures and then rode the Tram back down to Gatlinburg.

I have to admit—I felt proud of myself.

I finally did something that *worry* had kept me from doing since childhood.

It was a good day.

201: A Bad Morning

I woke up at 3:00 AM EST.

My spinal cord was acting up again—this particular pain only hits once every six months or so, but when it hits, it *hits* hard.

The moment I got up, my spine bent me over—literally. I couldn't even stand up straight.

It's always a reminder: my brain and spinal cord are in charge of this body. Not me.

I took a hot shower.

On top of the spinal pain, I was also dealing with acid reflux and stomach cramps.

Normally, I'd take some Alka-Seltzer or Pepto, but I hadn't brought any with me.

I knew I had to get to a pharmacy. So, I got dressed and slowly made my way to the truck.

Stepping outside, I saw it had snowed. Not much, and nothing stuck to the pavement, but the truck had a soft dusting on it.

I climbed in, cranked the engine, and turned on the heat.

"Suspense" was playing on the old-time radio channel as I made my way down the mountain.

It was nearly 4:30 AM. The streets were completely empty—Gatlinburg was a ghost town.

I figured Walgreens or CVS wouldn't be open yet, so I planned to stop at a gas station instead.

But the ones in Gatlinburg were closed, so I drove to Pigeon Forge and found one that was open.

I picked up:

Pepto

Alka-Seltzer

Water

I chugged some Pepto right there in the parking lot.

Then, I poured out half the water and dropped in two Alka-Seltzer tablets to dissolve.

Once ready, I downed that, too.

Within a few minutes, I felt better. So much better, in fact, that I started thinking about breakfast.

But I decided to head back to the cabin and eat later.

Right now, I'm back in my chair, watching TV and journaling this rough morning.

Still sipping Pepto, but thankfully, I'm finally walking upright again.

That's all for now.

202: Your Secret Admirer

Happy Valentine's Day from the Great Smoky Mountains.

Many years ago, back in elementary school, every Valentine's Day, each student would bring cards to hand out to every other classmate.

So, if there were twenty students total (including you), you'd end up with nineteen cards—one from each of the others.

The night before Valentine's Day, Mom took me to K-Mart, where we bought a box of cards.

Each card said the same thing: *"Happy Valentine's Day!"* and came with a red sucker attached.

We were instructed to sign every card with our names.

There was a girl in my class named Bridget (some names may have been changed for this post), and I liked her.

So, I decided I'd sign *her* card as "Your Secret Admirer."

My brothers warned me she'd likely go around the room asking all the boys if they were her "Secret Admirer."

They said I could either man up and say "Yes" or chicken out and say "No."

I figured I'd worry about that if—and when—it happened.

First, I needed to make sure the card made it to Bridget's desk.

At school, when it was time to pass out our cards, the teacher had everyone stand and walk around the room delivering them.

Perfect.

Bridget was up and moving, which gave me a chance to slip the "Secret Admirer" card directly onto her desk without her seeing.

Mission accomplished.

Then I handed out the rest of my cards like normal.

I sat and waited, quietly watching her return to her desk and start opening her cards.

When she got to mine, I saw her pause.

"Happy Valentine's Day! From: Your Secret Admirer."

She looked up and scanned the room. I quickly looked down at the floor.

If she caught me staring, she'd know it was me.

And I wanted it to stay a secret—at least for now.

Just like my brothers predicted, she got up and started walking around, asking boys if they were her Secret Admirer.

That's when I started to panic: *What am I gonna say when she gets to me?*

But then I noticed something.

She wasn't asking *all* the boys. She was only asking the ones she liked.

She never even came to my desk.

In fact, she walked *right past* me… and went straight to Johnny's desk to ask if he was her Secret Admirer.

And that's when I learned:

Even as a "Secret Admirer," you can still get rejected.

I never tried that stunt again.

That was also about the time I started questioning the wisdom of my older brothers.

Happy Valentine's Day.

203: Cabin 2/14/2022

Today, I spent the afternoon walking the streets of Gatlinburg, popping in and out of shops.

The smell of food being cooked up and down the strip was absolutely heavenly.

Every time a candy shop or restaurant door opened, a wave of sweet, warm air would drift out—and I soaked it all in.

I stopped into the hot sauce store called *All Sauced Up*.

They had samples set out for customers to try.

Some sauces were so strong they made your eyes water just from the smell.

Others had a nice flavor without being too spicy.

Next, I wandered into *The Chocolate Monkey*, where I bought a candied apple for nine bucks.

But this wasn't your average candied apple.

This one was smothered in caramel, rolled in nuts, and drizzled with both white and dark chocolate.

After that, I made my way toward *Fannie Farkles*, stopping here and there along the sidewalk.

Once at Fannie's, I ordered a sausage dog with peppers and onions, plus a foot-long corn dog.

Eventually, I made my way back to the truck.

For the record, I paid fifteen dollars for my parking spot today.

Now, I'm back at the cabin and about to eat—*in moderation*, of course.

Afterward, I'll take a nap.

That's all for now.

204: Cabin -Evening Update- 2/15/2022

My FreeStyle Libre blood sugar sensor needed to be changed out today. Unfortunately, they only last for 14 days.

So, I had the local CVS call my pharmacy back home to get the prescription so I could pick up a new one.

Since I've started using the sensor, I've been able to lower my insulin dosage. It's truly been a game-changer for me.

My blood sugar stays in range 93% of the time. I know because the software tells me.

It also sends my readings directly to my endocrinologist, which helps him keep track of my diabetes.

I know I post a lot of pictures of food, but you should know I eat it all in moderation.

(Enough about that.)

While I was out, I stopped by Outback Steakhouse for a steak, baked potato, and Bloomin' Onion.

Okay, maybe just a *little* more about that.

With Bob Seger loaded up on the radio, I took as many backroads as I could on my way back to the cabin.

The sky was clear, the sun was out, and the temperature was in the 60s.

I rolled the windows down and sang *"Against the Wind"* as I cruised along the winding roads of the Great Smoky Mountains.

At times, the Tram passed overhead.

At one scenic overlook, I pulled over, hopped out, and soaked in the view.

Mr. Seger kept playing in the background.

I had the place to myself, and it was perfect.

Then I made my way back to the cabin.

And yes, the steak was great.

That's all for now.

205: Bye-Bye Gatlinburg

I've decided to go ahead and head home today.

Originally, I had planned to leave tomorrow, the 17th.

But I woke up this morning with a rare burst of energy—and I've learned to take advantage of days like this.

Tomorrow, I might not have it.

I'm going to take my time packing and getting things together.

It may be noon before I actually pull out.

I already stopped by the station and grabbed some cash from the ATM for the drive home. I also filled up the truck with gas.

This morning, I found the milk frozen. Turns out, someone had set the fridge to level 9.

(9 is the coldest setting. 5 is normal.)

I dialed it down to 6.5.

Turns out, slushy milk is actually pretty good in cereal. I know that now.

I hadn't eaten cereal or used the milk yesterday, so I guess it had time to freeze up.

I think I'll drive home through Pigeon Forge instead of going over the mountain through Townsend.

It's been a great trip.

I didn't do too much, but I still had a wonderful time.

Time to get this day started.

That's all for now.

206: The Bacon Burger

I stopped by one of the local fast food joints today.

When I pulled in, the drive-thru line was out to the road.

So, I decided to go inside and eat.

Inside was chaos. About twelve people were standing around the registers.

Some were waiting on their food, some were returning orders that had been messed up, and then there was a Walmart worker on her lunch break, waiting to place her order.

And then… There was I.

I stood behind the Walmart worker. She was wearing the company vest with a name tag clipped to the front. Her name was *Brenda*.

"I'd like a chicken sandwich with a large fry and a Coke, please," she said.

The cashier asked for her name to attach to the order.

"Brenda," she replied.

She stepped aside, and I walked up to place my order.

"I'd like a bacon burger, large fry, and a Diet Coke, please."

"Can I have a name for the order?"

"Lynn."

And I stepped aside next to Brenda.

While we waited, more people walked up to the counter, most of them with incorrect orders.

I thought to myself, *They're off today. This crew isn't working together.*

Then they called, "Brenda!"

She grabbed her food and sat down.

"Lynn!"

I got my order and sat a table or two away from her.

I bowed my head and said grace before unwrapping my bacon burger.

"They gave me a dang bacon burger," I heard Brenda mutter.

I looked up.

"I ain't got time to wait in that line," she said, and began eating the bacon burger anyway.

I smiled, unwrapped my food, and took a bite.

And that's when I realized…

I was eating a chicken sandwich.

And I smiled even bigger—thinking about all my blessings in life.

207: The Cabin – Update

The cabin could have caught fire.

We were blessed that someone was staying there.

Even more blessed that it was a friend.

They arrived Thursday night. Everything seemed fine at first. But then, a windstorm hit overnight—along with some snow.

When they woke up and started using the electricity, something was clearly off.

First, turning on the hair dryer made the *upstairs lights* come on.

Then, the microwave wouldn't work. Neither would the Keurig.

The internet was out as well.

They got in touch with me, and together we contacted the power company.

To their credit, the power company arrived quickly.

They found the issue: the "neutral" line from the power pole to the cabin had broken during the storm.

They shut off the power and repaired the line.

But the damage was already done.

Several appliances had been fried, along with the hot tub.

The internet equipment was also burned out.

So now, I've got to head back up there Tuesday to get things sorted out.

New guests are arriving Saturday (I believe), and I'm hoping to have everything back up and running by then.

Thankfully, the current guests have been incredibly kind and understanding.

That makes all the difference.

That's all for now.

208: The Cabin – Arrival

It's 2:00 AM EST, and I've made it safely back to the cabin.

It rained the whole drive, which made the trip a bit longer than usual.

I also avoided going through the mountains via Lenoir City—I figured it would be too wet and unsafe.

So instead, I got off at the Pigeon Forge exit (407).

The internet line outside is definitely down.

I'm using my mobile hotspot to post this and to run the upstairs TV.

So far, I know the upstairs TV works (because I'm watching it), but I haven't tested the ones in the bedrooms yet.

From what I can tell, more than 50% of the light bulbs in the cabin are out.

That's as far as I'm getting tonight—I need sleep. Tomorrow's going to be a full day of inventory and repairs.

I'm here to document everything that's been burnt out and to try and get the internet running again.

(I can't physically move the hot tub… and yes, the hot tub got burned out too.)

If you didn't catch the earlier update, a high windstorm came through a few nights ago and snapped the neutral cable on the power pole.

Without a working neutral line, a lot of the electrical devices in the cabin were damaged or destroyed.

The power company came quickly and ran a new line.

I walked back there with my flashlight tonight and saw the fresh cable in place.

I'm hoping this will be a short trip. We've got guests arriving Friday or Saturday.

That's all for now.

209: Cabin Inventory

I woke up at 7:00 AM EST and brought in my medical supplies and luggage.

Being a single guy has its perks—like not having unpacked from my last trip. Most of my stuff was still in the vehicle, ready to go. I did have to restock my medical supplies, though—mainly colostomy bags and urostomy bags. Other than that, I was set.

The internet cable is down.

Thankfully, the equipment itself appears to be fine.

I had bought an APC UPS and plugged all the gear into it. It protects against surges, and this time, it paid for itself.

Spectrum told me they'd be out between 4 and 5 PM tomorrow.

I was surprised. I expected the usual "Noon to 5" window.

Nope. 4 to 5 PM. That's progress.

I took inventory of everything that got damaged. It's a decent list:

The hot tub, several kitchen appliances, and around seventeen light bulbs are out so far.

In the meantime, I'm using my mobile hotspot to watch TV and work on my laptop.

The fellas at the station warned me that another windstorm is expected tonight—possibly with 60 MPH straight-line winds.

We'll see what happens.

That's all for now.

210: Headed Home

It's currently 3:00 AM EST.

The wind is howling against the cabin.

It's not raining, but the ground is soaked.

I left a box of "Hillbilly Taffy" on the table for our next guest.

It's locally made, a little Smoky Mountain treat.

Time for a hot shower and clean clothes.

If all goes well, I'll be on the road by 4:30 AM EST.

This time, I'm heading back through Pigeon Forge rather than taking the mountain road to Townsend. Probably safer with this weather.

That's all for now.

211: 2/26/2022

I slept like a rock after getting home yesterday.

Didn't wake up until 5:00 AM. 6:00 AM "Cabin Time."

That's about 17 hours of sleep. I must've needed it.

The first thing I did was let our dog, *Tommy*, outside.

Then I got started unloading the vehicle.

I had taken Mom's car to the cabin this time since my truck is still waiting on repairs. I didn't want to drive it with ongoing issues.

The truck needs new brakes, and maybe a few other things.

When I crank it in the morning, it makes a strange noise, kind of like a hydraulic or power steering issue. Once it warms up, the sound disappears.

The brake wear is from all those mountain drives.

I usually put it in second gear going downhill to ease up on the brakes, but still, some wear is inevitable.

After unpacking Mom's vehicle, I noticed it needed a good vacuuming.

So I took it to the car wash.

The car wash is close to CVS, and I've been wanting to try the "NeilMed Sinus Rinse" they sell there.

Mom uses it and swears by it. They had several kits, so I bought two.

I'll find out tonight if it works for me.

Before leaving earlier, I turned on my germ-killing light in the bedroom and locked the door.

The instructions warn that it can be harmful to people, pets, and plants.

Locking the door ensures everyone's safe while it does its thing.

When you live in a small town, it's almost guaranteed you'll run into someone you know.

Sure enough, I bumped into a friend at CVS. We chatted quickly, he was clearly in a hurry, and then made plans to catch up later in the week.

I've got a doctor's appointment on Monday with my urologist.

Any appointment with him is important. Actually, with Spina Bifida, *every* medical appointment is important.

He'll likely check my kidneys to see how the hydronephrosis is progressing.

Hopefully, there's been no change, or even some improvement.

With the new stents, I'm optimistic.

We'll find out on Monday.

That's all for now.

212: Health Update

I saw my urologist today for a regular checkup.

You may remember that I had stents placed in both of my kidneys about four months ago. The goal was to help improve my hydronephrosis.

Hydronephrosis is typically easy to manage in most people, but with me having a urostomy, it's a bit more complicated.

I told my doctor that my urine output had increased since the stents were placed. He was glad to hear that.

I also mentioned that I had to switch from using a 2000cc nighttime urine bag to a 4000cc one while I sleep. That's how much the output has improved.

He scheduled a scan to check if the dilation in my kidneys has gotten any better.

I also gave a urine sample.

All in all, I felt good about today's appointment.

I'll post an update after the scan results come in.

That's all for now.

213: 3/1/22

I dropped my truck off at my cousin's shop to get the brakes changed and have him give it a full look-over. I told him there's no rush—he can take his time.

After that, Papa and I went shopping.

We hit up Sam's and the Pig.

Papa bought everything at Sam's, and I took care of the list at the Pig.

When we got home, I realized I had picked up the wrong items on more than a few things.

So, back out I went to correct my shopping mistakes.

The truth is, I've been in a bit of a funk lately. And I really need to pull myself out of it.

I think I'll text some friends from school—see if anyone's up for meeting for lunch sometime soon.

That's all for now.

214: A Call From A Friend

A good friend called me today. We go way back.

As soon as I picked up, he said,

"Well dang. I just remembered I already told you the story I was gonna tell you…"

So, I told *him* a story instead, one I hadn't shared before. Not one I can post here, mind you, but definitely one he hadn't heard yet.

Life for the two of us hasn't gone the way we once thought it would.

He's moved from Alabama to Arkansas.

I've rented out my house and moved back home to live with my parents.

No one's life goes exactly as planned. No one's.

We didn't talk long, but the call was exactly what I needed to lift my spirits and pull me out of this funk I've been in.

I felt a whole lot better after we hung up

215: Alabama Day Trip

I'm going on a day trip with my Mom and Aunt tomorrow.

I'm excited, but at the same time, I don't want to jinx it by talk about it too much here. If everything goes well, I might have an amazing story to share tomorrow night.

Fingers crossed everything goes right!

216: Road Trip

I woke up this morning to my dog, Tommy, licking my hands.

The usual pain I feel in the mornings was surprisingly absent.

"It's gonna be a good day," I thought to myself.

I asked my Alexa what time it was, and she said 5 AM.

I got out of bed with a little extra pep, let Tommy out, took my morning meds, and made the bed.

Then I grabbed my laptop, plopped down in my recliner, and checked emails and my calendar while *Murder, She Wrote* played on the TV.

I'm excited about today. We're going on a road trip.

Mom, my aunt, and I are hitting the road, and I'm hopeful for something special to happen. Even if it doesn't go the way I hope, it'll still be a great day. Road trips always are. There's always a story to tell by the end.

I'm about to hop in the shower and get this day started.

It's gonna be a great day.

That's all for now.

217: Dixieland Delight

In 1969, Randy Owen and his cousin formed the country music group Alabama, and country music has never been the same since.

There are a lot of things Alabamians disagree on. Things like:

* Football – Alabama or Auburn
* Tea – Sweet or Sweeter
* Mayonnaise – Bama or Duke's
* Pizza – Pineapple or No Pineapple
* Trucks – Chevrolet or Ford

I could go on and on.

But when it comes to the supergroup Alabama, *everyone* agrees that we love them, and we're proud of their success.

You've heard of the "Six Degrees of Kevin Bacon"?

Well, in Alabama, we've got "The Six Degrees of Alabama."

Every Alabamian knows someone who knows someone who knows a member of the band. Every single one of us.

In 1981, Randy Owen and his wife opened up a small meat market, selling beef from the cows they raised on their ranch, the Tennessee River Music Cattle Ranch.

Today, *The Market at TRM* sells everything from oxtail to New York strips.

We found out about it through a friend, whose friend knows Randy Owen himself.

And that's where this story begins.

Papa and I had been looking for steaks at The Pig and Sam's Club, but the prices were outrageous.

A 6-pound brisket? $164.

Two sirloins? $30.

So we were ready to try something different.

Mom, my aunt, and I loaded up for a road trip to Fort Payne, Alabama, to visit *The Market at TRM* and check out the steaks ourselves.

Now, I'll let you in on something: I had this strange feeling that I was going to run into Randy Owen. I just had a hunch.

We plugged the address into the GPS and headed out. It's about a 1-hour and 50-minute drive from home.

But once we got about a mile away, the GPS started acting up and sending us in circles.

Eventually, we saw a private drive labeled Randy Owen Drive and figured, "Hey, this must be it!"

We followed the drive to a big barn and house, parked, and got out.

And there we were… walking around in Randy Owen's front yard.

I guess that's why the road has his name on it.

There was a large house behind a privacy fence, so we weren't *right* up in the yard, but still pretty close.

Mom pointed at the open barn door.

"This might be it," she said.

We walked in. The walls were covered with old newspaper and magazine clippings about the band, stapled up like wallpaper.

"This ain't it, y'all," I said. "That's his actual house right there. He's not gonna have a meat market in his yard."

Mom kept calling out,

"Hello? Hello?"

I added,

"Mr. Owen, if you can hear me, please don't have your handlers beat me up. We're just trying to find your meat market, sir."

Three cats came out and rubbed up against me.

"I'm petting Randy Owen's cats, Mama," I said.

Eventually, we gave up and drove back down the road.

"There it is!" someone shouted.

Sure enough, we had found the real market.

It was a small building, shaped like a gazebo with walls, windows, and a front door.

We walked inside and were greeted by Mr. Owen's granddaughter, Randa, who runs the place.

While chatting, I asked,

"Does Mr. Owen ever come over here?"

"Oh yes," she said. "He pops in from time to time. You never know when. That house across the road is his."

"I thought so," I said. "We may have… accidentally visited."

I added,

"Now, if you *know* for a fact he won't be stopping by today—like if he's out doing a concert or something—don't tell me. I want to believe he could walk through that door at any moment."

She smiled.

"He really could."

They had specials posted, so I took photos. The place was stocked with everything I asked for—sirloins, jams, pickles, salsa, chow-chow, even homemade vegetable soup.

I ended up getting six sirloins, a jar of salsa, chow-chow, and blueberry jam. Total? $74.

My aunt bought the $90 special. Pictured, of course.

Mom stocked up, too. Steaks, jellies, the works. I don't know her total, but it was a haul.

Randy Owen didn't show up, and I'll admit that bummed me out.

I had such a strong feeling I'd run into him.

Still, there's always next time, and there *will* be a next time.

I still want to visit the Alabama Museum nearby. Maybe even stay overnight and make a weekend of it.

All in all, it was a fantastic day.

That's all for now.

218: Sleeping The Day Away

Wow—I slept the entire day away.

I guess I was still worn out from yesterday.

We didn't get home until late in the evening, and I'd been up since before 7 AM.

I got up this morning and went out for breakfast.

After I got back, I crawled back into bed, planning to nap until about noon.

Instead, I woke up at 9 PM.

Our dog Tommy is curled up on his pillow, fast asleep as I type this.

Murder, She Wrote is playing in the background. I've been keeping it on lately—not so much "watching" it as letting it play while I check emails or type.

Angela Lansbury's voice is soft and soothing. Honestly, I sleep like a baby when she's narrating a mystery.

Still, I hate when I sleep the entire day away. I should've set an alarm for noon.

Now I'll probably stay up until about midnight, then try to get back to sleep.

That's all for now.

219: Oh Well

I got up early this morning with the urge to go for a drive.

I checked the clock. 5 AM.

"Perfect!" I thought.

I brushed my teeth and figured I'd shower after the drive.

I wanted to ride around and see the deer as the sun came up.

If I was lucky, maybe I'd spot that owl I sometimes see.

It likes to perch on the limb of an old tree—one that looks dead in winter, but come spring, proves it's very much alive.

I also thought I'd swing by the gas station at the bottom of the hill.

It's a family-owned place with a small deli that serves breakfast and lunch.

Their tenderloin biscuit is one of my favorites.

I figured I'd grab a coffee and say hello to a few familiar faces.

I let Tommy outside and climbed into Mom's vehicle—still borrowing it while my truck's in the shop.

I hit the garage door opener, and the door slowly lifted.

I cranked up the car, looked in the mirror, and—there it was…

Papa's truck, parked right behind me, was blocking the way.

Nope. I'm not waking Papa up, and I'm definitely not going through anyone's pockets for keys.

It's just not right.

Oh well.

Honestly, I should probably shower first anyway…

And truth be told, our coffee at home isn't half bad.

Good morning, everyone!

220: 3/7/2022

It rained today up here on top of the mountain where we live.

We've got a great view of the storms as they roll in.

I stood by the window and watched the rain inch closer and closer—until finally, it reached us in a downpour.

I've been watching a lot of *Murder, She Wrote* lately.

Angela Lansbury's voice is kind and gentle—like a grandmother's.

She's such a sweet lady on the show. I half expect her to offer the murderer a bowl of homemade vegetable soup after catching them.

And it's just about the only mystery show I can solve on my own.

Well... almost. Sometimes I'm wrong.

Speaking of homemade soup, we bought a jar of vegetable soup at *The Market.*

I think Randy Owen's aunt makes it.

We also picked up some jams and jellies she canned.

Today, Mom made a pan of cornbread and heated up that soup. It smells delicious.

I'll grab a bowl a little later.

This week, I see my Pulmonary Doctor, also known as my Sleep Doc.

I'm actually looking forward to that check-up.

That's all for now.

221: Sleep Doctor

I saw my Sleep Doctor today.

The good news? I'm doing well on my CPAP.

The not-so-good news?

My Philips CPAP device has been recalled.

He gave me the website where I can register to receive a replacement unit.

I'm told it may take up to six months for the new one to arrive.

Still, I'm glad to have this appointment behind me.

He's one of the few doctors I only have to see once a year.

That's all for now.

222: The Bullies

I was about twelve, and it was summertime.

I was lying in bed watching TV when suddenly, my brother Tony ran into the room.

He lifted the mattress, tossed something underneath it, let the mattress drop, and then jumped into bed beside me.

"I've been here all night, okay?" he said quickly.

"Uh… okay," I said. "Mind telling me what's going on, and what you just threw under the mattress?"

"You know those guys that have been picking on you?"

My eyes widened. "Yeah…"

"They won't bother you anymore. We all just fought it out."

"Wait, what?!"

"Yep. A bunch of us and all of them. They're done messing with you."

"Ummm… Tony. What's under the mattress?"

"Brass knuckles."

"What?! Oh crap. Is everyone okay?"

"Oh yeah. Everyone's fine. But like I said, they won't be bothering you anymore."

That group of guys had become my worst nightmare.

They were at least three years older than me—bigger, faster, and stronger. I was afraid of them.

They mocked the way I walked.

I have atrophied legs and feet, with some bone deformities, which causes me to walk with a limp.

Sometimes it's more noticeable than others, especially when I wear shorts.

I hated walking past those guys.

They'd mimic my gait.

They'd call me names.

Sometimes they'd block my path and wouldn't let me through.

There were always several of them, and just one of me.

Tony had found me crying in my room earlier that month.

I told him everything they were doing to me.

"I hate them! All they do is make fun of me and knock things out of my hands. They make fun of the way I walk and how my legs look."

Tony was always protective of me.

I didn't know he had plans to do something about it.

The next time I had to walk past that group of guys, I was nervous, really nervous.

They jokingly called me "Sir."

"I hope you're having a good day, Sir," one of them said as I passed.

I didn't say anything.

Eventually, they just stopped saying anything at all when I walked by.

Years later, after Tony died from a brain hemorrhage, my psychologist asked me:

"Lynn, you try very hard to right the wrongs done to your late brother. Why?"

Looking down at my legs and feet, I said quietly,

"Because he would've done the same for me."

223: Epitaphs

The sun was out today, and the temperature climbed into the 60s.

We've got the weirdest weather here in the South—but I'm sure that's true elsewhere too.

This weekend, things are supposed to get cold again, and the word "snow" is being tossed around.

But today was beautiful.

So I decided to take advantage of it and visit the family cemetery.

I walked around, reading the epitaphs carved into headstones.

You can tell a lot about a person just by what's written there.

Some of the more common ones I saw:

Gone But Not Forgotten

The Lord Is Close To The Brokenhearted

In Loving Memory Of

We Will Meet Again

Rest In Peace

I once visited Frances Bavier's grave—she played "Aunt Bee" on *The Andy Griffith Show.*

Her epitaph reads: *To Live In The Hearts Of Those Left Behind Is Not To Die.*

I've also visited George Lindsey's grave—he played "Goober" on the same show.

His epitaph says: *I'm Glad I Made You Laugh!*

My brother's headstone reads:

A True Fisherman Is One Who Will Persist At His Task For Hours.

His footstone adds:

He Who Is Generous Shall Be Blessed, For He Gives Some Of His Food To Those In Need.

My Nana wrote her own poem for her epitaph.

But my favorite of all is my Pawpaw's.

It simply says: *I'm OK.*

Like I said, you can tell a lot about someone just from reading their epitaph.

224: 3/11/2022

I got up at 4 AM this morning.

Asked Alexa for the forecast.

Today's high: 70.

Tonight's low: 27.

And yes, the "S" word—*snow*—is being thrown around again.

Weather in the South is... unpredictable.

I've got a busy morning ahead.

First up: breakfast with Papa and his friends.

Then I'm picking up my truck from the shop.

My cousin's garage took care of it. It had a few issues, but now she's ready to get back on the road.

After that, I'm meeting a childhood friend for lunch—Mexican food. I'm thinking steak fajitas... though that could change when I see the menu.

After lunch, the plan is to head home, sink into my La-Z-Boy recliner, and watch some TV.

At least… that's the plan for now.

Good morning!

Hope you have a great day.

225: Surprise Birthday Party

Lately, I've been as busy as a social butterfly.

Two birthday parties in one week. *Two!* Count 'em.

The first was a surprise party for my first cousin on Papa's side. She turned the big 6-0, but she doesn't look a day over 44.

The party was held at the Woodall Building in Springville, Alabama.

Papa, Mom, and I got ready and headed that way.

I even wore my sports coat for the occasion.

The Woodall Building dates back to the 1880s.

It started as a wagon and buggy assembly plant.

Today, it's used for weddings and birthday parties like this one.

When we walked in, the place looked beautiful.

And if you know me, you know, I'm a hugger.

I hug, and I say "I love you" often. Life has taught me that much.

I'd been there maybe ten minutes and had already hugged over twenty people.

Then someone shouted, "She's almost here! One minute out! Everyone, get ready to yell 'Surprise!'"

The excitement was real.

I couldn't help but wonder: did she suspect anything?

Her husband opened the door for her.

And the moment she walked in, the whole room erupted: "Surprise!"

Her face said it all; she had no clue.

She was genuinely shocked and totally delighted.

People clapped. People cheered.

And I got to give another hug, and tell one more person I love them.

Happy birthday, cousin. I love you.

P.S. — I'll share the story about the second party in another post.

226: A Day In The Life

I had a pretty typical day today.

It started with neurological pain, bone pain, hip pain, and leg and foot pain.

In a word, *miserable*.

I sat in my recliner for a bit, trying to gather myself, then finally got up, took a shower, and got dressed.

First stop: CVS.

But before that, I dropped off two bags of aluminum cans with a man in the community who recycles them.

Many of us around here save our cans for him. It's a small way we help out.

At CVS, I grabbed a few essentials. I don't get my prescriptions filled there—I use our local, family-owned pharmacy for that.

Speaking of which, that was my next stop.

Our local pharmacy is a "mom-and-pop" shop. Everyone knows me by name.

On my way in, a familiar face stopped me.

"Hi, Lynn. I'm Jim. I read your posts on Facebook and just wanted to say hey."

"Oh yeah, I know who you are! I see your posts too. It's nice to finally put a face to the name."

We talked for a few minutes—got to know each other a bit. It was a nice conversation.

Now, when we run into each other again, we'll have more than just Facebook in common.

I walked inside and up to the counter.

"Hey, Lynn. Been to Gatlinburg lately?"

"Nah, the cabin's booked most of March and April. I might be able to get back up there in May."

"Wow, and y'all don't even advertise, right?"

"Nope. Just good ol' word of mouth."

After a few more minutes of chatting, I paid my bill and headed to Dollar General, one of my most frequented spots.

Honestly, I go there two or three times a day sometimes. I'm sure I'm not the only one in this town who does.

The employees recognize me, even if we haven't exchanged names yet. That'll happen eventually.

"How was your last trip to Gatlinburg?" one asked.

"It was great. Stayed for—oh, twelve days? Maybe fifteen."

"If you lost count, it must've been a good one!"

"Yep."

As I waited in line, a man behind me held just a single pack of baby diapers—Huggies, I think.

"You can go ahead of me, sir. You've only got the one item."

"No, thank you. I'm in no rush whatsoever."

"You sure?"

"Positive."

I smiled to myself.

He's probably just trying to stay away from the chaos at home a little longer, I thought.

Another employee walked by.

"I see you got your Diet Cokes."

"Yep—three six-packs for twelve dollars."

I asked the man behind me again, "You sure you don't want to go ahead?"

"I'm sure, sir. I'm sure."

"Okay. I just feel bad."

I put my items on the counter.

"Cram it all into one bag if you can. The fewer bags, the better."

"Yes, sir. I can do that."

I paid, then headed home.

When I walked in, Mom called out,

"We got pizza and breadsticks today. Help yourself."

"Alright. That sounds great—it'll hit the spot."

I let Tommy inside, grabbed a slice of pizza, and went back to my room.

Now I'm sitting in my recliner. The TV is playing in the background.

Tommy is staring me down, hoping for a bite of pizza.

I smile, give him a dog treat, and take a bite of my slice.

It's been a good day.

That's all for now.

227: Medical Entry 3/16/2022

At 2 AM on 3/16/2022, I woke up with tremendous pain in my lower back, on both the left and right sides.

Classic *kidney pain.*

I got out of bed and immediately emptied my nighttime urine bag so I could start tracking output.

(To monitor properly, I needed to begin at zero cc's.)

Still in a great deal of pain, I pulled out my emergency hospital bag and did a quick check to make sure everything was inside.

It holds enough colostomy and urostomy supplies to last seven days, along with toiletries, undershirts, shorts, and other essentials.

I had every intention of heading to the hospital.

I took a 1000mg Vitamin C tablet.

The pain was intensifying. I was soon down on my knees in agony.

Fifteen minutes had passed since I emptied my urine bag… and there was barely any output.

For context:

I don't have a bladder. My urostomy bag *is* my bladder.

I also have a Foley catheter connected to the urostomy to help with urine flow.

But mucus—something my body produces a lot of—can sometimes clog the catheter.

And now, I was beginning to suspect exactly that.

Barely able to stand, I made it to the bathroom and opened my medical supply drawer.

I grabbed an irrigation syringe, hooked it to the end of my Foley catheter, and gently suctioned out a fair amount of mucus.

I reconnected everything.

Within a minute, over 300ccs of urine had drained into the bag—

And my pain started easing.

Within ten minutes, I had over 800ccs of urine in the bag—

And the pain was virtually gone.

I wanted to share this entry to give you a glimpse into what it's like living with a urostomy.

This is real life for many of us.

It's now 3:30 AM.

I'll go ahead and post this to my patient portal as well.

That's all for now.

228: Dolly Parton Rock N Roll Hall Of Fame

Dolly Parton has been nominated for the Rock & Roll Hall of Fame.

On her social media accounts, she responded with something along the lines of,

"Thanks, but no thanks."

Okay, I'm paraphrasing a little.

Then the Rock & Roll Hall of Fame replied with something like, "We'll let the voters decide whether you're in or not."

Again, loosely paraphrased.

I get it.

I've often wondered how some of the inductees even made it into the Hall of Fame.

It includes rappers, country singers, lovey-dovey singers, and even disco artists.

If you go to their website and look through the full list of members, some names will make you scratch your head.

The only way I can make sense of it is like this:

That person, group, or genre probably inspired someone who eventually wrote a great rock and roll song.

(Have you ever heard anyone say "beautiful rock and roll songs?")

I'm sure Dolly has inspired plenty of people who went on to create great rock and roll music.

In short, if the Bee Gees can be in it, then Dolly Parton can too.

229: The Kissing Conest

I was around twelve years old.

Four other guys and I were playing together at some apartments when two girls about our age came walking up.

One of them, for the sake of this story, was named Amy.

If I like a girl, I call her "Amy" in my stories. I can't give out real names—my childhood friends read these.

I didn't know the other girl; I had never seen her before.

Amy and I were in the same class at school, and I'd always thought she was pretty.

"Hey boys, who wants to have a kissing contest?"

she asked.

All five of us immediately raised our hands.

(Alert: what comes next is not the most sanitary thing in the world... but hey, it's no worse than a kissing booth.)

Amy explained the rules:

She would kiss each of us and then choose the top two kissers.

After that, she'd kiss those two again and choose the *best* kisser.

We lined up.

I think I was third.

When it was finally my turn, I closed my eyes and leaned in.

Wow.

That was my very first kiss. And afterward—my world wasn't the same.

Amy announced that Jason and I were the top two kissers.

So, round two.

She kissed us again to decide who the best kisser was.

Guess what? I won.

I went home that night floating on cloud nine.

Later that night, I decided I would ask Amy to go steady with me.

That was going to take some real guts, but I was *in love.*

The next day, I got up early, took a shower (which is a big deal when you're twelve), and put on my brother's cologne.

I might've even added a little of Dad's aftershave—who knows.

I headed to the apartments and walked over to the tennis courts where all the kids usually hung out.

And there she was…

…holding hands with Jason.

I turned around and walked away.

Even the guys who used to pick on me didn't say anything as I passed by.

I think they could see the heartbreak written all over my face.

And that's the story of my first kiss.

But wow—what a kiss.

230: The Biker

I felt better today. So good that I went shopping for a few things.

I pulled up to Dollar General.

There was a nice motorcycle parked in the lot.

I don't usually notice "Normal" looking Motor Cycles. That's why I noticed this one. It was extra nice—lots of Chrome.

I go inside, grab a buggy and start my shopping.

My shopping is usually pretty fast. I go and get my stuff and get out.

I came upon an older lady wearing a motorcycle helmet down the first aisle. I moved over to give her room. She grabbed something off the shelf and moved on.

"These aisles are way too close together," I thought

Down the second aisle, I came upon her again. And again, I moved over. She grabbed something off the shelf and moved on.

"I'm really getting in her way…"I think.

On the drink aisle…you guessed it. I ran into her again.

"I'm really sorry, ma'am, I just keep getting in your way," I said to her.

She replied, "No, not at all. Every time I've had to stop for you, I've found what I was looking for on the shelf. You've been a big help today," and she grabbed something off the shelf and moved on.

231: Morrison The Cat

We have this cat here at our house. It's one of four.

This cat, "Morrison," and I have had a bizarre relationship.

He sneaks up on me while I'm sitting down and jumps up on my stomach. My stomach that has two bags hanging off it.

I protect my stomach just as much as men protect their, um, delicates. Maybe even more.

Not just because of my bags, although that's reason enough, but I also have a hernia in my stomach area, and after over thirty surgeries in my abdomen, I just like that area to be left alone.

So, I immediately freak out and jump out of the chair, making him fall off me. He then runs away and stays away from me for the next two weeks…

This has been going on for two years, I guess. Maybe more.

Tonight, though, he changed his method.

Tonight, he came up to my chair, stood up on his back legs, and meowed at me.

I then tapped on the chair's armrest, and he jumped up on the armrest.

And then I began petting him until he fell asleep on the armrest.

232: The Family

I was at the hospital at 3 AM, because, well… that's apparently where I hang out at 3 AM. Where do you hang out at 3 AM?

In Triage, I was sitting in a chair, arms wrapped around my stomach, telling my nurse, "They're seven minutes apart, I tell ya. I've been timing 'em."

"I've never heard of that. That's really weird."

"Yeah, it is. Every seven minutes, like clockwork," I said. "I called my doctor, and the after-hours nurse told me to come to the hospital. Every seven minutes, my colon knots up. I'm worried it might be another intussusception or something…"

My nurse replied, "We'll have to get a scan. For now, have a seat in the lobby and let me get you all set."

"Okay," I said, walking back out to the lobby.

The lobby was empty, which was a relief. Every seven minutes I could let out a yell of pain without feeling self-conscious.

Then a young man came running through the doors.

"I need a wheelchair! Where do I get a wheelchair? Never mind, I see it!" He grabbed one and rushed back outside.

Seconds later, he came back through the doors, pushing his pregnant wife at top speed. I guessed they were no older than twenty.

The husband shouted, "She's thirty-nine weeks, her water's broken, and they're one minute apart! Oh yeah, and I called!"

The man behind the desk immediately picked up the phone, called the Labor and Delivery Department, and relayed everything word for word.

"They're on their way down to get you two!" he said.

The husband leaned down, kissed his wife's sweaty forehead, and told her, "It's going to be alright, baby. I promise. I love you so much."

Looking into her husband's eyes, she replied, "I love you too, baby," and took his hand in hers.

Two nurses arrived and whisked Mommy and Daddy off to Delivery.

I was alone again in the lobby… and speechless. I couldn't help but get misty-eyed at what I had just witnessed.

"Mr. Thomas, we're ready for you now. Follow me, please," my nurse called.

I walked over. She turned to me and said, "Every seven minutes, huh?"

"Yeah," I answered. "Like clockwork."

233: ER Visit

I had been sick for over five days.

And for those five days, I also had a torn-up stomach.

I ate a lot of tomato soup during that time, along with Campbell's Cream of Potato Soup.

I was pleasantly surprised by Campbell's potato soup and Progresso's tomato soup with basil… but I digress.

At 8 PM, my colon began to hurt. It felt like it was twisting and cramping up.

The pain was sharp, lasting about a minute each time.

I lay down, hoping to get some sleep.

A little after 1 AM, the pain still hadn't let up.

I called my primary care physician's office and got the after-hours nurse.

I told her exactly what was going on, even mentioning that the pains were coming every seven minutes apart. I had timed them.

She pulled up my chart and reviewed my doctor's notes. Then she said, "It could be many things with you... all of which require a doctor. I advise you to go to the ER."

I keep a hospital bag packed at all times for situations like this. I grabbed it, told Papa what was going on, and headed for the hospital. It was about 2:30 AM.

Around 3:00 AM, I arrived.

The lobby was empty. Completely still.

I walked up to the counter, gave my name, and explained why I was there. Then I began filling out paperwork.

I was triaged quickly, and by 3:45 AM, I was in a room in the back.

The doctor began pressing on my abdomen, focusing on my colon. Each time he pressed, I nearly came out of the bed.

I explained that I had been sick for more than five days.

He asked if my colostomy had been functioning normally during that time. I told him my stomach had been upset the entire time.

He ordered a scan of my abdomen.

The results came back clear. Everything looked fine and appeared to be working as it should. No twists or obstructions were visible.

The doctor said he believed my colon was simply irritated, likely because my stomach had been upset for so many days.

To which I replied, "You tellin' me I've pooped too much?"

He prescribed me medication for gastrointestinal spasms and sent me home.

The medicine has helped, and I've been taking it easy. My stomach is no longer torn up.

That's all for now.

234: Momma's Pecan Pie

No true Southerner can call themselves a true Southerner without knowing how to make at least one type of pie.

It doesn't matter if it's fruit or nut, as long as they know how to bake one.

So, I learned how to make a pie — pecan pie, to be exact. And it's delicious, if I do say so myself.

This is my momma's recipe, and she's the one who taught me how to make it.

I'm proud to say I've baked her pecan pie three times now, and the last time, I didn't even need to look at the directions.

Do you want the secret recipe?

First, plant a pecan tree, because fresh pecans are the key.

Second, get your own secret recipe — because Momma's is going to stay with me.

It truly is delicious.

That's all for now.

235: 3/26/2022

Our power went out around 3:30 PM.

It's happening more and more often in this area.

All I can say is thank goodness for cell phone hotspots and laptops. I had just finished charging my phone.

I have two pecan pies ready to go into the oven, but instead, they're sitting in the fridge.

We have a gas stove, but the oven still needs electricity to light. I can light the top burners with a lighter, but I'm not about to try lighting the oven that way — although I'm sure it could be done.

Before I sat down to write in my journal today, I lit two candles. The flickering is nice to watch.

Someone posted on our HOA Facebook page that the ETA for the power is 6:30 PM. I'm hoping they're wrong.

Today, I spent a little over ninety dollars on ingredients to make ten pecan pies. Not only are they delicious, but they're also inexpensive per pie. Some of the ingredients will be enough for twenty or more pies.

I'm going to stop here. Papa just came back from shopping and said he believes the power will be back on soon. He mentioned it's already on in other parts of the neighborhood.

That's all for now.

236: Visiting Huntsville

I had to drive to Huntsville today for a doctor's appointment.

After it was over, I decided to visit the place where I used to work.

Standing there on the grass, I felt nostalgic.

Much of my life had taken place right on that spot.

Back then, there was a building here. I was standing where my office once stood.

The building was torn down several years ago, and I was amazed at how quickly the earth reclaimed the space. Grass now grows where I once worked. You couldn't even tell a building had been there.

I waved at people as they drove by.

They looked at me like they were wondering if I belonged there — maybe even debating whether to call security.

All the other buildings were still standing and were now being used by a new company.

I had driven through the back gate as if I still belonged. After all, I'd passed through that gate so often in my life that it felt natural. I half-expected security to pull up any moment and ask me to leave.

Until then, I wanted to take in the moment.

There was a time when I would have sworn to you that I'd work in that building for the rest of my life.

Now there's not even any proof it ever stood here.

"Can I help you, sir?" a man asked as he got out of his vehicle.

"Do you remember the building that once stood here?" I asked him.

"Oh yeah. It was torn down several years back."

"Well, I worked most of my life right here where I'm standing. And… I guess it's time for me to go now. Sorry to have bothered you."

I got in my vehicle, drove out the back gate, and headed home.

237: Almost a Road Trip

I had a road trip planned for today, but due to the weather, we pushed it back.

You see, it's officially tornado season.

I'm not going to reveal the destination just yet, because I still plan on going once the weather improves.

Here in the South, tornado season is something we take seriously.

I guess every state has something they have to deal with. Ours is tornadoes.

Some states get earthquakes, others get hurricanes. The colder states get snow. We get tornadoes, or, as some folks call them, "naders." Our tornado season runs from March until the end of May.

Trips around here have to be planned with bad weather in mind.

Last Wednesday, we had terrible weather, and it seems we're going to have more tonight.

If everything had gone according to plan, we would have left this morning and returned Friday.

We don't take tornado warnings lightly here in this part of America.

My hometown of Fultondale, Alabama, has been devastated by tornadoes many times over the years. It seems that just when the town recovers from one outbreak, another comes along.

When I was in school, we had tornado drills. If I remember correctly, the school bell rang three times to signal the drill. After the bell, each student would calmly get up, form a single-file line, walk out to the hallway, and sit with their back against the wall.

It was important to bring a hardback book with you. You used it to cover your head.

Many people here also keep helmets on hand for tornado outbreaks, and they have saved lives. Schools may have helmets for students nowadays. If not, they should.

So, I was supposed to go on a road trip today, but, as I said earlier, it's been postponed.

I might try to get away for something this weekend, if the weather is good.

That's all for now.

238: 3/31/2022

I stayed up until 11:30 last night, watching the weather.

Alabama did get some severe weather.

Several possible tornadoes were spotted while Alabama's favorite weatherman, James Spann, gave live updates.

The whole state tunes in to watch Mr. Spann during severe weather.

We didn't lose power, but many Alabamians did.

While watching, I started thinking — why is it that people only rush to buy bread and milk when bad winter weather is forecast?

During severe weather season, you're actually more likely to lose power and be stuck at home than you are during a half-inch snowfall.

I'm beginning to think that when severe weather is predicted, we should stock up on bread, milk, and bologna.

Once we got the "all clear," I fell asleep.

That's all for now.

239: The Train Museum

I've always loved trains.

When I was younger, we lived right next to a set of train tracks — maybe thirty yards away, if that.

Whenever the evening train passed, I would go to my special spot to wave at the engineer. From there, he could see me clearly, and I could get an up-close look at the train.

Every now and then, the engineer would toss me a bottle of water with the "Seaboard System Railroad" or "CSX" logo on it. That was a big deal for me.

As a kid, I wanted to grow up to be one of two things: a train engineer or the rear brakeman. The rear brakeman was the person who sat in the caboose. Remember cabooses? Eventually, trains stopped having anyone stationed there.

More than once, I ran up to a caboose and climbed on to peek inside. Nowadays, most trains don't even have a caboose.

My late brother once got in trouble for hopping onto trains. He made the mistake of giving the engineer his real name and our home phone number. I'll just say I never made that mistake.

When I was young, my dad would take me to the CSX train yard outside Birmingham. We'd park and watch the trains, and sometimes walk over to a parked one to get a closer look. Rules were a lot looser back then.

I'm leaving some details out of this story — and for good reason.

Recently, I learned that Alabama has a train museum: the Heart of Dixie Train Museum. Dad and I have made plans to visit it next week.

This isn't the road trip I mentioned earlier, it's a new one.

I'm hoping to step inside the trains, see everything up close, and take plenty of pictures. I also plan to write about the trip, so you can come along with me.

Right now, the trip is scheduled for April 5, weather permitting.

That's all for now.

240: Morning Ritual

I got up today at about 6:30 AM.

I went to the fridge for my morning Diet Coke and discovered I was out.

Unless I'm traveling, the first thing I drink in the morning is a Diet Coke.

When I'm on trips, I drink coffee. I don't know when or why that started, but it did.

If I go out for breakfast, I drink coffee. In fact, I drink coffee if I go to Waffle House or Huddle House for dinner. Actually, if I go anywhere in the morning that serves coffee, I'll drink it. But at home, the first thing I drink in the morning is my Diet Coke. I still can't believe I let myself run out.

Dollar General sells three six-packs of Coke for ten dollars, but they don't open until 8:00 AM. So, I made myself a cup of coffee — black, no sugar — and waited until they opened.

At Dollar General, I was the first customer. The workers were outside talking with one another. I don't know their names, but they know me from my frequent visits.

"Good morning!" they said energetically.

I thought to myself, *They must've already had their Diet Cokes.*

"Mornin'!" I replied, trying to sound just as energetic. I was faking it.

"I'm sorry for my appearance," I said. "I haven't had a shower or anything. I realized I was out of Diet Cokes, and I haven't had one yet."

"Oh, we understand," one said. "I have to have my Mountain Dew first thing or I'm a wreck."

"Yep," I said. "And I'm a wreck right now."

I grabbed a buggy and headed to the drink section.

The sign read, "Three six-packs for $10."

I grabbed three, tossed them in the buggy, and went to the register.

From the fridge at the counter, I pulled out a cold Diet Coke and set it down.

I placed one of the six-packs next to it and said, "I've got three of these. You don't have to bag 'em."

I paid, went out to the truck, and opened my Diet Coke. It made that familiar fizzy sound.

"Ahhhhh," I said after the first drink.

I waved to the employees as I pulled away. Now I was ready to get the day started.

It was going to be a great day.

241: A Good Day

It's been a good day.

I ended up making a second trip to Dollar General. After that, I headed to my hometown of Fultondale, Alabama, to pick up my CPAP supplies from my healthcare provider there.

Later, Mom made chicken and dressing.

Here in the South, we never call it "stuffing." It's always "dressing."

One of my favorite things to eat is raw dressing. It's delicious.

Mom's dressing is made with cornbread, boiled eggs, celery, and a few other things. Everything is already cooked, so "raw" dressing isn't really raw. The eggs are boiled, the cornbread is baked, and celery is celery. Still, I like it raw more than I do baked.

I've mentioned before that I love *The Andy Griffith Show,* or "TAGS," as we fans call it. On Monday nights, many of us meet online to chat about TAGS. It starts at 7 PM CST.

So I need to wrap up this journal entry so I can get to the chat room.

That's all for now.

242: Bread, Bread, Bread

I was looking for something to eat for lunch today.

I walked into the kitchen and started poking around in the cabinets, or maybe cupboards. I know there's a difference, but I'm not sure what it is.

I checked the countertops, then the fridge, then back to the cabinets/cupboards, then back to the countertops.

That's when I realized something: we love bread.

We really do. Mom even taught me how to pick the best loaf at the store. You pat the top to check if it's soft. The softer, the better.

We even have brands we'll buy and brands we won't touch. Bread is treated with the same loyalty people here in the South give to mayonnaise. And for the record, the correct answer is "Bama."

Right now, in our house, we have hoagie bread from the Piggly Wiggly bakery, artisan bread, Hawaiian sweet rolls, and two brands of white sandwich bread — Wonder and Sunbeam. We also have hamburger buns and hot dog buns.

Looking at all of it, I thought about how often bread is mentioned in the Bible. A lot. It might just be the perfect food.

I took some artisan bread, toasted it, and made myself a chicken salad sandwich.

We do love bread, and my lunch today was good.

243: Train Museum Canceled

I woke to the cracking sound of thunder and lightning.

It was so loud that my eyes opened instantly, and I was wide awake. I wasn't even groggy. Thunder does that to me if it's loud enough, and this was loud, a sharp crack followed by a deep boom.

"Dang it, it would happen today," I thought.

Today was the day Dad and I had planned to visit the Train Museum.

In an earlier post, I had said the trip was "weather permitting," and, as is typical for April, it's supposed to rain all day.

I had been in touch with one of the nice ladies who works there, so I felt I should let her know as soon as possible. I got my laptop and sent her an email, letting her know we were canceling for today and would try again next Tuesday or Saturday. On Saturdays, you can actually ride one of the trains, but only on Saturdays.

So, it looks like it will be a typical April day in 'Bama: rainy.

I'll try to make it a good day anyway.

You try to have a good day as well.

Love you,

Lynn

PS: April showers bring May flowers.

244: Dana

When I was about eighteen years old, I worked at the local pizza place.

My female boss there was nineteen or twenty, and her name was Dana. She was a looker.

At the time, I was taking classes at the local college. Dana took classes there too, working on her prerequisites so she could transfer to The University of Alabama.

During this time, Dana and I became best friends.

I knew everything about her, and she knew everything about me — everything except that I had spina bifida. I kept that a secret.

We loved working together, and since she made the schedule, we were often paired up. We both loved '60s and '70s music. Dana was a big Doors fan, and I was a big Pink Floyd fan. We got along great.

I also played guitar back then and had dreams of becoming a rock star. I even told her my band's name — "White Diamond." It sounds cheesy now, but at the time, I thought it was awesome. I didn't tell anyone else that name.

I described what the front cover of our CD would look like, and one day, she brought her camera to work so we could take pictures for it. The truth was, I wasn't even in a band, and my playing was nowhere near good enough.

Eventually, Dana got accepted into the University of Alabama and moved to Tuscaloosa. By then, she was over twenty-one. I drove down to visit her.

We spent the whole day together, including over an hour in a music store, talking about music and acting like fools. She even bought us a "Best Friends" necklace, the kind with a heart split in two. One half was mine, and one half was hers.

Back at her place, a single-wide trailer decorated with tie-dyed sheets on the walls and ceilings, The Doors playing in the background, I decided to tell her about my spina bifida. It was tough. She was floored and silent for a moment.

Then she changed the subject, telling me she had tried some drugs. Now I was the one floored and silent.

She asked me personal questions about my condition, and I answered honestly, even telling her that I couldn't make love and that my body didn't produce sperm.

I remember her saying "Oh..." while The Doors' "Break on Through" played.

Then she told me about a guy she had met who took photos for adult magazines.

"Oh..." I replied.

She asked why I had never told her about my spina bifida. I told her it wasn't easy to explain, especially since I didn't use a wheelchair and "looked normal on the outside."

I half-joked, "You're not going to start taking nude pictures or something, are you?"

"Nah," she said. "Just nice to get offered."

We talked a little more, then I drove home. Before I left, we hugged. "I love you," I told her.

I called her the next day, and the next ten days after that. No answer.

I finally called her mom, who told me Dana had gone missing. She hadn't heard from her in over two weeks and had filed a police report. Her mom asked me to tell Dana to call her if I heard from her.

I told her mom about everything Dana and I had talked about during my last visit.

Still, I didn't believe she was actually missing. I figured she just didn't want to talk to me after learning about my spina bifida.

I began to hate my spina bifida. I saw it as something awful, something bad.

I tried calling her several more times, with no answer. Each time I spoke to her mom, she said Dana was still missing.

Life went on. I grew older.

To this day, I don't know what happened to Dana. I'm not sure if I was in love, but I've thought about her often over the past twenty-six years. At this point, I think I'd rather not know what happened.

Not all stories have a happy ending.

245: Health Update

I went to my endocrinologist today for my three-month diabetes check-up.

He was very happy with my numbers.

My A1c was 6.8, down from 7.4 three months ago.

With my FreeStyle Libre monitor, he could see a detailed report of my daily blood sugar levels.

Since starting the Libre, my daily insulin has dropped from 16 units to 10 units.

He was so pleased with my progress that he said I could start coming in every six months instead of every three.

That's all for now.

246: Floyd's Hat

To get to my doctor's office, actually, to get to any of my doctors, I have to drive through Birmingham.

Specifically, I pass through two well-known areas: one appropriately nicknamed "Malfunction Junction" and another simply called "280..."

And yes, that's exactly how you say it — "Two eighty...," with the ellipsis at the end.

I had just gotten home from a doctor's appointment yesterday when I got a call from the same office I had just left.

"Mr. Lynn, you left something here..."

Before she even finished her sentence, I had already decided in my head that whatever it was could just be thrown away.

"It's a hat that says 'Floyd's Barber Shop, Two Chairs No Waiting.'"

"Oh! I'll come back and get it. Thank you for letting me know."

That's my favorite hat.

247: Pecan Pie

Well, I guess I'm decent at making pecan pies.

The family members who have tried mine have all complimented me on them.

And when you do something well, people will ask you to do it again and again, which is its own kind of compliment.

So, Momma came to my room today and asked if I could make a pecan pie tonight. Naturally, I said yes.

And for those of you who will be happy to hear it, I do clean up behind myself as I go. Yep. By the time I'm done, the only proof I've been in the kitchen is a finished pie cooling on the counter.

248: Nickels

I've often wondered why counterfeiters can't make their fakes identical to real money. Don't get me wrong — it's a good thing they mess up. And I am completely against counterfeiting. Dead against it. It is not for me.

When my late brother and I were kids — I was about thirteen or fourteen — we got into trouble for using a copy machine to copy dollar bills.

Technology was new to us back then, and so were vending machines that accepted paper money.

At the time, you could copy a dollar, walk over to a vending machine, insert your fake bill, and still get your drink.

I cannot stress enough how wrong that is to do. Fortunately for my brother and me, we were caught before the month was up, which put an end to our short-lived "life of crime."

Francis Leroy Henning was a man who took counterfeiting a lot further. You may have heard of him.

In 1939, he got in trouble for counterfeiting bills. He clearly didn't stay in jail long, because by 1953 he was caught again, this time with a new scheme: counterfeit nickels.

Don't laugh. A nickel went a lot further in 1953. A loaf of bread was about fifteen cents back then.

It's estimated Henning made up to half a million counterfeit nickels. He even used different years on them — 1939, '44, '46, '47, and '53.

It was the 1944 nickels that ultimately got him caught. The Secret Service arrested him.

Here's the interesting part: some of his coins are thought to still be in circulation, and they're now considered collectibles. I'm guessing it's illegal to collect counterfeit coins, but I could be wrong.

Henning's story is a fascinating one. If you get the chance, look him up. One other odd fact, his profits weren't as big as he had hoped. It cost him about 3.5 cents to produce each nickel.

Oh, and if you ever come across one of his coins, don't tell me. I promised myself I'd never get mixed up with counterfeiting again.

249: Ridin'

The day started with me taking my niece to school early this morning.

I don't know if my niece actually likes listening to old-time radio, but that's what we listen to when she rides with me.

The truth is, that's what we listen to every single time, either one of my nieces rides with me.

When I was growing up, rides with my Nana, Pawpaw, or my Tot Tot always had their own soundtrack, or lack thereof.

If I rode with Tot Tot, we didn't listen to anything at all. I'm not even sure the radio in his truck worked.

We'd roll down the windows, and as we drove down the road, we'd share drinks from a gallon milk jug he'd filled with water. I felt like a big boy, sharing a milk jug with my Tot Tot.

With Nana or Pawpaw, it was always gospel music, unless Pawpaw had brought along his Ray Stevens tape. If he had, we listened to "The Mississippi Squirrel Revival" as we rode along.

Nana would fuss at Pawpaw for bringing that tape, but when the part came where the squirrel got loose, I'd always catch a smile sneaking onto her face.

Those are good memories for me.

I can't tell you how many times memories like that have pulled me out of a depression. Sometimes, they're all we have left of the people we love.

And I hope that someday, when my nieces are grown, they'll remember listening to "Bob Hope" or "Johnny Dollar" with me as we cruised down the road.

Maybe tomorrow I'll even bring a gallon milk jug and see if I can get her to drink water from it.

Though I have a feeling she won't go for that.

250: Love

I had a breakdown today.

It started over the littlest thing — they usually do. But if you follow the trail of emotions far enough, you eventually get to the real reason.

Today, the truth hit me hard, and I started wailing out loud. It was intense.

I remembered one particular surgery, my thirty-somethingth, when my late brother had to care for me every single day for weeks.

He was the one who took care of me after most of my surgeries. Not because the rest of the family didn't want to, but because it just worked out better that way.

That surgery was on both my abdomen and my perineum. ("Taint," as some call it — though that's not the medical term.) They went inside me in two different places.

At that point in my life, I wore extra-large Depends. Embarrassing.

After the operation, my abdomen was stitched up, but the perineum incision was left open, packed with gauze. It would take weeks for it to close.

Every day, someone had to take out the old gauze, clean the wound, and put new gauze inside. I couldn't do it — my abdomen had been cut open and sewn shut. I couldn't bend, couldn't move much at all. I was helpless.

My late brother did it for me, day after day.

The first time he did it, I remember thinking he'd laugh when he saw me like that. But instead, his eyes filled with tears. That made me even more embarrassed.

"Okay," he said, "I've washed my hands, got my gloves on... I guess I use this thing here to take the gauze out."

"They're called forceps," I told him. "After you take the gauze out, you've got to use the antibiotic, or antibacterial medicine, to clean the inside. Just... don't hurt me, brother."

"Okay, I'm starting now. Don't move."

I could see the nervousness in his eyes, so I looked straight up at the ceiling instead.

He counted as he worked. "One gauze, two, three, four, five... ten! You had ten pieces of gauze in there."

"Then you have to put ten back in," I said. "And remember to clean the wound with the medicine."

"Okay, I put the medicine in the hole. Can you feel it?"

"No," I said. "I'm numb from my spina bifida. But remind me to tell you something after you're done."

"Alright, I'm going to start putting the gauze in now. One, two, three, four, five, six... ten. That's all that will fit."

Then my brother changed my diaper. His thirty-year-old brother's diaper.

Every day, for weeks, he came to my room, changed the gauze in my perineum, and changed my diaper. He wiped me.

That's love.

And that thing I wanted to tell him after he finished?

I said, "Every time you put the forceps in the hole, I feel and taste metal in my mouth..."

He laughed.

Eleven years after his passing, I still have breakdowns.

251: The Disabled Garden

Over the years, I've enjoyed gardening — small gardening.

I'd get down on my hands and knees to plant the vegetables I wanted to grow. Each day, I'd pull weeds from the garden and water the plants.

Now, don't think I'm talking about a *big* garden — that's what my Tot Tot, Dad, and uncles had. Big gardens, the kind you tilled with a tractor. My late brother had one of those too.

Me? I had a tiller attachment for my weed eater, perfect for tilling my *little* garden.

But nowadays, I've stopped gardening altogether. I can't get down on my hands and knees anymore, so I haven't grown anything for several years.

Then God stepped in.

We had a storage building put up on the property.

It's a nice building, but it sits up on cement blocks. There's about a three-foot gap between the bottom of the building and the ground. You've seen cars up on blocks? Well, it's the same idea, except instead of a hot rod, it's a storage shed.

Mom took one look at it and said something like, *"I'm not having a building up on blocks. Cover that up!"*

(Thank goodness she's not on social media anymore.)

So Papa had a raised flower bed built to cover the gap and hide the blocks.

He told Momma she could plant some lovely flowers in her new flower bed.

But later, I noticed something. "Hey," I said, "this is waist-high. I could plant a garden here without bending over at all."

Yes, without even realizing it, Papa had built a raised garden… for me.

I've been calling it "The Disabled Garden."

And no, I didn't take over Mom's flower bed without asking. I saw she hadn't planted anything yet, so I asked her first.

Long story short — I know, too late — I've planted a garden. I don't have to bend over. I just walk up to it, dig a hole, and plant. Easy.

I planted vegetables I've always had good luck with, plus a few things I've never grown before:

- Tomatoes – You can't plant a garden in the South without tomatoes. Your family will disown you. Your friends will throw them at you as you get out of your truck at the local general store.
- Bell Pepper
- Eggplant
- Squash
- Broccoli
- Basil
- Strawberry

Maybe I planted too much. I was excited. It might get crowded fast.

It's mostly things Mom likes, the broccoli is for my niece and me.

It'll take some work, but it'll also give me something fun to do.

And just so you remember, this is a *small* garden. Not a big one.

Eighteen plants in total.

That's all for now.

252: Good Friday Night

It's Good Friday, 2022. Nighttime.

I can't sleep, so I decide to go for a ride. It's after 10:00 PM.

The moon is full, the sky is cloudy, and I can see flashes of lightning in the distance. Thunder rumbles somewhere far away.

The moment feels familiar, like I've lived it before. The air is fresh, and even the smell brings something back to me. Something from a long time ago.

Standing in the driveway, it clicks: *Moundville, Alabama.*

Growing up, every year, my family would pack up and head to Moundville to camp out for Easter.

Back then, Moundville was privately owned. Each year, the owner would put on a big sunrise service atop one of the mounds.

We kids — strike that — we cousins would go out at night to play. Our parents told us not to leave the park and to be back for breakfast. Life was good.

We played chase, pulled pranks, even fished — all night long.

Sometimes, we'd sit on top of a mound and talk about life. Six or seven cousins, ages ten to sixteen, smoking cigarettes we'd gotten *somehow* (that's another story), staring at the sky and getting serious about our futures.

I think those nights brought us closer than anything else. Talking about life will do that.

The moon was full, and the sky looked just like it does tonight — clouds rolling in, lightning off in the distance.

It wouldn't rain on Saturday. Almost never did. But Easter Sunday? Almost always. Rain or shine, though, the sunrise service went on.

Afterward, Mom would put on an Easter Bunny costume and hand out our baskets, each one made special for that kid. One year, Uncle Dale wore the costume instead. Hilarious.

And the food — I could eat breakfast five times. Lunch five times. Just going from campsite to campsite, visiting with family, sitting around the fire with my *third* breakfast in hand.

Life was good.

Strike that — life was *great.*

I love this moment.

253: 4/21/2022 – Early Morning

I got up early. I was in pain. I had even slept in my La-Z-Boy chair the night before.

First thing, I reached for my phone to scan my FreeStyle Libre and check my blood sugar.

As soon as I scanned the sensor, the phone beeped… and went dead.

"Great. Gonna be a great day," I muttered, dripping sarcasm.

With gas prices the way they are, I haven't been driving much lately. But today, I didn't care. I got up from my La-Z-Boy, dragged myself out to the truck, and took off.

While driving around, I had to stop for a line of ducks crossing the road.

I didn't even roll down my window to yell, *"Hey! Why y'all crossing the road?!"*, and normally, I get a kick out of doing that.

I drove around for about fifteen miles before heading home.

As I pulled into the driveway, my truck *dinged* and the gas light came on.

"Oh, great…" I thought. I decided to give myself an hour or two before heading back out to get gas.

254: 4/21/2022 – Getting Gas

Eventually, I dragged myself out of my chair and drove to the gas station to fill up.

When I arrived, I realized my outfit of choice wasn't ideal: shorts, a white T-shirt, suspenders, and shoes — no socks.

Unfortunately, my two ostomy bags hang just low enough to show beneath a white T-shirt… and the gas station was *busy*.

"I forgot to put on an overshirt," I thought.

I decided my best option was speed: get out, start the pump, and retreat to the truck until it finished. Maybe no one would notice.

So I got out quickly, unscrewed the gas cap, swiped my card, and started pumping. Then I hopped back into the truck to wait.

When the pump clicked off, I returned it to the holder and got back in my seat.

"Pfew," I thought. "I don't think anyone saw my ostomy bags flopping around." I had been tugging my shirt down the whole time, just in case.

I cranked up the truck and headed home.

On my way out, everyone outside the station seemed unusually friendly, smiling and waving at me.

"This day is looking up," I thought, smiling and waving back.

But when I got home, I turned off the truck, glanced in the driver's side mirror… and it hit me.

Maybe this day wasn't looking up after all. At least, not yet.

Time for a shower. Everything's better after a shower.

255: 4/21/2022 – Day's End

The end of this day turned out far better than the start.

Momma had to run an errand with her sister, so I picked up one of my nieces while Papa picked up the other. We agreed to meet in Gardendale for dinner at "Ming's Garden."

I've been eating at Ming's since I was a kid. We went there when I made the honor roll, and I remember eating there the day the Challenger exploded. So it's always been a special place.

I arrived first, so I went in and got us a table. While waiting, I ordered an appetizer called the "Pu-Pu Platter."

You've probably heard of it — with a name like that, how could you not?

I texted Papa: *"I got us the Pu Pu Platter for an appetizer."*

My phone's autocorrect changed it to: *"I got us the Puppy Platter for an appetizer."* I didn't proofread before hitting send. We laughed about it later.

The nieces ordered steamed dumplings. I've seen those things all my life but had never tried them. I finally did, and they're actually pretty good. I'd eat them again.

We spent the meal talking about our day, laughing, and sharing food.

My fortune cookie said, *"It's time to start a new hobby."*

"I just started my garden," I replied.

Papa's fortune told him to forget his diet and eat desserts for the next month. I'm not kidding.

All in all, it was a great evening, a much better ending to a day that had started out pretty darn bad.

And yes, I know it's only 5:30 PM, but I'm calling it. This day is done.

I hope yours ends just as well.

That's all for now.

256: 4/24/2022

A quick journal entry.

I had a busy day yesterday.

I visited several garden centers, picking out plants for our front porch. I wanted to get the porch ready before Mother's Day.

I ended up purchasing seven plants from three different garden centers.

Once I got home, I hurried to clean off the porch, hang the plants, and give everything a good watering.

I'd say 90% of my day was spent getting everything ready for Mother's Day… only for Momma to tell me that Mother's Day is *next* weekend.

Boy, was I embarrassed.

Well, I'm ready for Mother's Day now.

My vegetable garden is doing well. The plants are getting bigger and stronger every day.

I'll post some pictures of it later.

That's all for now.

257: Flag Team

While sitting in the school pickup line today, waiting for school to let out, I watched the "Flag Team" lower the American flag and fold it.

It reminded me of when I got to be on the Flag Team in elementary school.

It was an honor to be chosen. For one week, my team and I would walk to the principal's office, collect the American flag, and head out to the flagpole.

Once in place, each person would take a corner of the flag.

The flag always started folded into a triangle, a shape meant to resemble the hats worn during the Revolutionary War. Others might call it a "paper football" shape. We'd carefully unfold it, attach it to the rope, and raise it. I can't recall for sure if I saluted as it went up, but that certainly sounds like something I would have done.

Then, around 2:00 in the afternoon, the Flag Team would meet back at the pole to lower it. I remember never letting it touch the ground because "Johnny," one of the kids on our team, always warned, *"Don't let it touch the ground. They'll have to dispose of it if it touches the ground."*

Once lowered, we'd carefully fold it back into a triangle and return it to the principal's office.

We did that for five days, and then a new team would be chosen for the next week.

Watching today's Flag Team, you could tell they took great pride in their job. I could almost hear one of them, probably someone named Johnny, saying, *"Don't let it touch the ground. They'll have to dispose of it if it touches the ground..."*

Looking back, it was actually a pretty stressful week. But now, it's a good memory.

258: 4/26/2022

I got up around 4:30 AM this morning.

"Jack's," a local fast-food joint, opens at 5:00 AM, and I thought I'd head over for a biscuit. I considered calling my uncle to see if he wanted to meet me there, but I ended up going through the drive-thru instead.

It was pouring down rain outside.

Good for the garden, I thought. God's water is always better than what comes out of the hose. A professional gardener once told me that.

At Jack's, I ordered a chicken biscuit combo with a Diet Coke.

The drive there and back was slow, super slow, thanks to the downpour.

When I got home, I ate my breakfast, took my morning meds, and hopped in the shower.

I'm hoping the sun comes out today. Gloomy days are depressing to me; I can't stand them. If it keeps raining, I might just crawl back into bed.

That's all for now.

259: Garden Update

I've spent a good bit of time working in our little garden.

Even though I don't have to bend over, and the work is minor compared to a big garden, it's still enough to wear me out by evening.

Today I weeded, watered, and planted extra basil. I like basil so much that I bought five more plants and placed them all in one large flower pot. They're *supposed* to be eighteen inches apart, but I'm going to see if they'll grow in this pot.

The plants are coming along well.

Strawberries are already growing on all the strawberry plants, and peppers are beginning to appear too.

Here are a few photos of everything. It's small, but perfect for me.

That's all for now.

260: Journal – 4/29/2022

I went for a drive first thing this morning. That's something I've had to cut back on since gas prices went up, but today was an exception.

I woke up at 5:00 AM.

The last thing I remembered was coming inside a little after 1:00 PM *yesterday* to take a nap. A serious nap. I undressed, got under the sheets, both signs of a *real* nap.

And here I was, waking up at 5:00 AM the next day.

Fourteen hours in bed had done a number on my bones, spinal cord, and muscles. I was hurting, and my spinal cord was sending shocks through me. So I decided on an early drive.

I stopped by the local fast-food joint for a biscuit.

I ordered the Number 1, large-sized, with a Diet Coke.

The cashier said, "I'm sorry, but we're out of tater tots right now. Will French fries do?"

I wanted to say, "I love you," but I didn't.

"Fries will be fine. Thank you."

When I got home with my food, I confirmed what I'd always suspected, French fries go great with a chicken biscuit.

The rest of the day went well.

I weeded and watered my garden, and Mom and I planted some flowers her sister and brother-in-law had given her.

By the time I came inside for dinner, I was good and tired. And it's nice to be good and tired when you sit down to eat.

I wonder if I can order fries every morning.

261: Bottle Rockets and BB Guns

Do Not Try This Anywhere. Ever.

I had a great childhood. Actually, I've had a great life.

For the cards I was dealt, ages zero through twenty were fairly "normal", and fun.

That's because I had a great support system.

Growing up, I played everything from chase to bottle rocket wars and BB gun wars. I went squirrel hunting, fishing, coon hunting, and—my favorite—dove hunting.

My friend Donny once shot and killed two doves with a single shot.

We didn't just hunt and fish for fun. We ate everything we caught or shot.

By age twelve, I knew how to clean and cook dove, squirrel, bream, catfish, and bass.

After school, Donny and I would meet at the train tracks with our .22 rifles and head down to hunt.

We'd shoot enough doves for each of us to take home for dinner. My favorite way to cook doves? Wrap them in bacon, brush with BBQ sauce, and bake in the oven. Mmm-mmm.

Bottle rocket wars weren't just about bottle rockets. Nope.

Smoke bombs and Roman candles were fair game too.

We also allowed PVC pipes as launchers. You'd light the bottle rocket, drop it in the pipe, hoist it onto your shoulder, and aim. Easy, and very effective.

One time, my bag of fireworks was sitting on the ground next to me. I watched, in slow motion, as a bottle rocket landed right inside the bag. My eyes went wide. I bolted and dove to the ground.

Seconds later, the whole bag went off. Then I heard someone scream, "Fire!"

Long story short, the fire department had to be called twice.

And BB gun wars? That's a story for another day.

What's my point? I'm not entirely sure. I've had plenty of bad things happen in life. But I guess it's this: even with a disability, I've had a good life, a fun life.

And I'm pretty sure it all started with my support system. Good family and friends who included me.

262: Top O' The River

Today, I had the pleasure of visiting the "Top O' The River" restaurant in Guntersville, Alabama, with Mom and Papa's Sunday School class.

It was my first time eating there.

The building is huge—two floors, seating up to 600 people.

Once seated, the waitress brought a hot skillet of cornbread, pickled onions, and slaw to start our meal. I ordered the "Pot O' Mustard Greens" to go with my cornbread and slaw. Highly recommended—the greens were outstanding. Honestly, *everything* was.

Mom and Papa ordered the fried whole catfish.

I, on the other hand, went for a full pound of Creole boiled shrimp. Yep, a whole pound.

Technically, it's an appetizer, but it's exactly what I wanted, and it was delicious. The spices on the shrimp were perfect.

We sat with over twenty others, talking about life. Candle supply shopping came up. Those of us with diabetes compared A1C numbers. We laughed loudly, shared food, and enjoyed each other's company.

It was a great day.

If you ever get the chance to try "Top O' The River," I highly recommend it.

Get there early. They open at 4:00 PM, and the place fills up fast.

263: May 1st, 2022 – Decoration Day

I woke up this morning around 5:00 AM.

It was windy and raining outside, so there was no need to water the plants or the garden.

By noon, the sun came out, and the day turned out beautiful.

Later, I visited my aunt and uncle. My cousin, their son, came over, and we all sat on the porch, chatting about life.

It was a great visit for me.

At our family cemetery, it's Decoration Day, always the first Sunday in May for us, so after visiting with family, I stopped by to visit family graves, including my brother's.

My blood sugar was low, so I made sure to grab a bottled Coke on the way. Bottled Cokes are the best. I even bought a bag of salted cashews to pour into the Coke. Traditionally, it's salted peanuts, but the store only had cashews. You work with what you've got.

While at the cemetery, I ran into more family members.

We hugged, chatted, and caught up. I made sure to get extra hugs before leaving. (I'm a big hugger.)

Now I'm back home.

I walked over to the garden to make sure everything looked good, and I checked Momma's plants as well.

It's been a great day, and I believe I'll sleep well tonight.

That's all for now.

264: The Pee Bag

I was going to tell a story about a strange date I had as a teenager. I typed it up, edited it, and then decided to go for a drive to think about it before posting.

Going for a drive would also give me a chance to finish the audiobook I'd been listening to—two birds, one stone.

So, I attached my 2000 cc urine bag to my urostomy. The bag has a six-foot hose, which is so long that I have to hold it or it'll drag the ground.

I climbed into my truck, set the bag on the floorboard, connected my phone to the truck's radio via Bluetooth, and started my drive.

Earlier, it had rained. The roads were wet, the sky cloudy, and the back roads were eerily empty.

I noticed I needed gas, so I headed toward the station.

While driving, I thought about that "strange" date. Strange is really the only word for it.

I pulled into the station. Nobody was there. The inside was closed, but the pumps stayed on for people like me who needed gas after hours.

I parked at pump one, turned off the truck, hit the button to open the gas cap, and started to get out, when I was immediately introduced to the cement.

"Crap! I forgot to unhook the pee bag! Again!" I yelled.

(It happens more often than I'd like to admit.)

I stood up, yanked my bag out of the truck, and walked to the pump. I slid my debit card into the reader and punched in my code.

"Declined."

"What?" I muttered.

Then it hit me—I'd been messing around with my bank's "Lock It" feature and had locked my card.

"Well, now I know it works," I thought.

I grabbed my phone, opened the bank app, unlocked the card, and tried again. Success.

Seventy-something dollars later, I was back on the road.

"It'd be weird if she also had spina bifida and wore a diaper, like me," I thought to myself, still mulling over that date. (Not to confuse you, I don't wear a diaper anymore. I did once, but now I have a colostomy and a urostomy.)

When I got home, I decided to go inside and post the "strange date" story.

I hopped out of the truck and immediately met the cement again.

I'll post the other story another day.

Good night, everybody.

265: Strange Date

As a teenager, I didn't date much.

I knew my health problems and my limitations.

I also felt I wasn't meant to get married—and if you're not getting married, why date?

Still, I went on a few.

I took one girl, Kim, to see *The Silence of the Lambs*.

Another, Lisa, to see *Anaconda*.

Then there was Shirley— "Shirl" for short.

Shirl was possibly the weirdest date I ever had. If it *was* a date. It lasted about thirty-five minutes.

It was supposed to be a typical night: dinner and a movie. I can't remember the movie title.

We met in a parking lot, and she hopped into my vehicle. I started driving down Highway 31 toward the restaurant. We were almost there when she suddenly yelled, "I gotta go back to my car! Take me back now, please."

It was as if she'd just gotten a secret signal saying, *That guy's on America's Most Wanted.*

And this was back when people didn't have cell phones, let alone text messages.

The whole thing reminded me of myself in my diaper-wearing days. Back then, I'd make a quick exit without explaining, sometimes climbing out of bathroom windows and walking home.

Without asking questions, I turned around and took her back. She got out, got into her car, and drove off.

Later, she told me over the phone that it wasn't going to work out. I was fine with that—after all, we hadn't really gone on a date yet.

The next time I saw her was over a year later in Walmart. She was with her husband. We said hello, and she introduced me to him.

"Better him than me," I thought.

I didn't mention our "date," but I decided to count it anyway. I have to keep my numbers looking respectable.

To this day, I still wonder what that was all about.

266: Birmingham, Alabama VA – Part 1
4/6/22

I hate typing on my phone, but with three hours to kill while Dad's eye surgery is underway, here I am, pecking away at the screen.

The Birmingham, AL VA is a place many in my family have used over the years.

I was up at 5:00 AM to make sure I could be here by 8:00.

That's because I have to get up early and move around a bit before my day truly starts.

At 6:45, I picked Dad up from his house, and we headed for the VA.

We parked in the parking garage, then caught the VA shuttle bus to the hospital. The people you see and meet here will make you stop and think. They'll make you respect the flag, stand for the national anthem, and cover your heart while standing.

The VA is full of people whose job is to help— "Ambassadors," they're called. And they are everywhere. Everyone has been extremely friendly.

I went to the café and ordered a big breakfast:
- Omelet with ham, cheese, onion, bell pepper, and mushroom
- Bacon
- Two pieces of toast
- Fried potatoes
- Coffee

I handed the cashier a ten and a five. She gave the five back and said, "Have a great day, Sweetie."

"Thank you, ma'am. You too."

After breakfast, I made my way to the "Family Waiting Room," which is where I'm typing this from.

I have three hours to wait. And wait, I will.

That's all for now. Please excuse any typos.

The Family Waiting Room at the VA was a comfortable place.

It had three couches and four recliners—real recliners that went all the way back so you could sleep in them.

A restroom was right next door, as well as the chapel. I visited both.

The Ambassador on duty kept everyone comfortable and entertained.

"Anyone need a blanket?" he asked.

Several people were lying down, trying to sleep.

One man shouted from his recliner, "Yeah, I'll take one."

"Yes, sir. You want anything else while I'm up?"

"It'd be nice if you could read me a story to help me go to sleep."

The room erupted with laughter. The Ambassador brought the blanket, draped it over the man, and then, just to keep the joke going, sat down beside him and opened the book he was reading, pretending to read it aloud. More laughter followed.

Normally, I prefer reading physical books, but lately, I've been enjoying the Kindle and Audible apps. I've even re-purchased books I already own in paperback so I can read them on Kindle or listen on Audible. I've gotten hooked on Audible, truth be told.

In the waiting room, I opened my Kindle app and started reading. I like that you have to swipe your finger to "turn" the page. I also like the built-in dictionary feature, though I had to turn it down a notch.

"I'm not that stupid," I muttered to myself while adjusting the settings.

After a few chapters, the Ambassador called out, "Thomas!"

"Here!" I replied.

"Phone."

He held up the receiver in the universal "you have a call" signal.

"Hello? This is Lynn."

"Hey, Mr. Thomas, everything went well, and he's in recovery. You can come to room six on the third floor."

I went to see Dad.

He had a clear patch taped over his right eye.

"He'll need to wear this for 24 hours," the nurse explained. "Then he can take it off."

"Yes, ma'am."

She handed him a wallet card explaining the lens he now had in his eye, for emergency workers, nurses, and doctors to reference if needed.

Dad got dressed, and we headed to the shuttle stop to ride back to the parking garage.

It was a sobering visit, seeing so many other soldiers. I said several prayers in the chapel and met a lot of genuinely kind people.

On the way home, we stopped for a BBQ plate for Dad to take with him.

By 1:30 PM, I was back home.

That's all for now.

268: Clowns and Bathrooms

People like me have a tendency to overthink and overworry. We think about things that probably will never happen.

For instance, I've always worried about the power going out while I'm in the bathroom changing my colostomy bag. Once that bag is off... well... let's just say you're "wide open."

And clowns.

I'm scared of clowns.

Don't get me wrong—I've been to the circus plenty of times, and I laugh at the clowns just like everyone else. But if a clown ever walked up to me in a parking lot in broad daylight, I'd probably wet myself. Thank goodness I have a bag to catch it.

I also don't like sitting too far from an exit in a room, or being in a room without a clock. My cell phone has helped with the clock issue.

So what's my point?

As soon as I got home today, I went straight to the bathroom. And wouldn't you know it, the power went out mid-change.

It was every bit as bad as I'd imagined.

The only thing worse would have been if, when the lights came back on, there had been a clown standing there with me.

About a month ago, Papa brought "Sparky" to his new home.

Each day, Sparky roams through the house, learning his new surroundings. We even step out of his way to let him "explore." The cats? Completely unbothered.

Right away, we put Sparky to work cleaning the floors. He works twelve hours a day, no breaks.

You see, Sparky is our new robot maid.

He's an iRobot Roomba.

His official job? Vacuum the floors. Every. Single. Day.

Papa wouldn't normally buy such a thing, but he had racked up so many credit card reward points that he used them to get Sparky.

And I love "Sparky." (I named him, by the way.)

At the breakfast table, we've learned to lift our legs and let him pass.

All of the rooms in this house have wood floors, and it's easy for us to dirty them up. Mom used to spend hours every week sweeping, muttering things like, "Land sakes alive! Just look at these floors."

When Momma and Papa remodeled this house in '05, they had no idea what was coming. They thought they'd spend their retirement here alone. They didn't know they'd be raising my late brother's two girls. They didn't know their son with Spina Bifida would move back home. They certainly didn't know the place would be overrun with four cats and three dogs—dogs that love dirt and mud.

Thanks to Sparky, our floors are much cleaner than before. The whole house is cleaner, actually, because we're more mindful about what we leave on the floor. For example, we make sure Sparky doesn't suck up socks by putting them on the table instead of leaving them on the floor. Mom's a lot happier, too.

Sparky has even mapped the whole house, so we can send him to vacuum specific rooms instead of the entire place. Mostly, though, he vacuums daily from 8:00 AM to 8:00 PM.

Tonight, however, Sparky decided he'd had enough and went into hiding.

"Where's Sparky?" Papa asked.

"Hmm, I don't hear or see him. He was in the den earlier," Momma replied.

The app on our phones said, "Can't connect to Sparky."

"Are we gonna have to get in our vehicles and roam the neighborhood lookin' for him?" I asked.

Mom found him under the hutch.

We might need to start giving Sparky a fifteen-minute break every couple of hours.

270: Mother's Day 2022

"Happy Mother's Day!" I shouted to Momma.

It was April 24th, 2022.

I had gone to three different garden centers and bought seven plants for her. I cleaned off the porch and carefully arranged each one, making sure everything was perfect.

"Here's your card. I love you, Momma."

"Well, thank you, Son. But… Mother's Day isn't today. It's not for a while yet. But thank you. I love you, too!" She grinned, trying not to laugh.

Embarrassed, I said, "It's not today? Are you sure about that?"

"I'm sure, Son."

"No way. I worked my tail off. It has to be today. You're joking."

"Nope. Not today."

I felt stupid. Stew-pid. Stewpid. S-T-E-W-P-I-D.

"We'll meet back out here on May 8th, then. In the meantime, I'm flat broke. So this is your gift." And I burst into uncontrollable laughter.

Every day since then, I watered all of her plants so they'd still look good by the real Mother's Day.

And… today is the day!

I had taken the original card back in April, saying, "I'll give this back to you on May 8th!" Somewhere along the way, I lost it. So I bought another one.

I'd kept her from going out front since the April mix-up. So today, she finally stepped outside and enjoyed her "new" plants—for the second time.

I handed her the card and one more new plant I'd bought yesterday.

"Happy Mother's Day, Momma. I love you."

It was a good day.

Happy Mother's Day to all the mommas out there.

271: My First Home

My first home was in my hometown of Fultondale, Alabama.

I lived there from birth until I was fourteen.

1432 Leora Avenue—it even rhymes.

It wasn't a big place, maybe 800 square feet: three bedrooms, one bath, and seven-foot ceilings.

We didn't have much back then, but we were rich in every way that mattered.

We had an old three-hundred-pound TV in the living room. On top of it sat a twelve-inch TV, the one we actually watched, because the big one was broken and far too heavy to haul to the dump. And on top of *that* TV was a big metal soup pot to catch rainwater from our leaky roof.

One thing we *did* have that many people didn't was a VCR.

Dad was a pro at programming it to record all his favorite shows.

Dad worked for TVA and got called out a lot. It seemed like he was always on call or "stand-by." He also ran a side business doing electrical work, and once a week, he attended Dale Carnegie classes to better himself. That meant he missed a lot of his shows.

Every day, he'd pop a blank VHS tape into the VCR and set it to record *Cheers* or one of his other favorites. We knew better than to mess with the VCR. Each tape was neatly labeled: *Cheers 01, Cheers 02,* and so on.

We had a small stream running through the yard, and Dad built a wooden bridge to cross it. On the other side, he constructed a full clubhouse. He went all out—electricity, bunk beds, a front porch. Later, we even put a TV in there, and Dad ran a cable line from the house.

The clubhouse was always "Base" during games of tag. It was our fort during capture the flag and BB gun wars. (Yes, we played BB gun war, bottle rocket war, and other games I'm pretty sure our parents didn't know about.)

I wish I had a picture of that clubhouse, but cameras weren't as common back then as they are now.

Also across the stream was a tire swing Dad hung for us. He always made sure we had plenty to do.

Black Creek ran nearby, and we'd catch bream, bass, and catfish there, then bring them to our little stream. We'd dam it up so the fish would have more room to swim. Crawdads and turtles were regular catches, too.

A tunnel ran under the road next to our house. We'd hide in it during hide-and-seek or any other game. Friends came over all the time.

When I spent the night at someone else's house, I couldn't sleep; the silence kept me awake. At home, the train tracks were right behind our yard. Every couple of hours, a train rumbled past, its horn blowing. I needed that sound to drift off.

We'd walk the tracks to our favorite fishing spot, "the Deep Hole," the deepest part of Black Creek. We could catch seventy or eighty bream a day there—though, in truth, we were probably catching the same fish over and over.

Coming home after a day of playing, Mom would have supper ready—one meat and several vegetables from our garden. Dad kept a huge garden, at least it seemed huge to us.

Every season, my granddad "Tot Tot" would bring his horse over to plow it. Then we'd plant seeds together as a family. Dad tended the garden all summer, and we all pitched in to pick vegetables when they were ready.

We had grapevines, apple trees, and peach trees.

In the living room stood a wood-burning stove, its small pipe running through the ceiling. On Christmas Eve, I always begged Mom and Dad not to light a fire—it would be hard enough for Santa to get down that little pipe without one burning on top of it.

The old home wasn't much, but it was full of love. Mom and Dad made it a home. We always had food, friends, and fun. In our eyes, we had everything.

I even found a photo of the house online—it looks different now. We didn't have a metal roof back then. In the back, you can see just how close those train tracks were.

Every time I see a kid outside playing, I'm reminded of my own childhood there. It might not look like much from the outside, but in his world, that kid is a king, and the world is his oyster.

272: May 12, 2022

I had an excellent day today—busy, but excellent.

The day started around 6:30 AM.

I got up, let "Tommy" the dog out, and took my niece to school. Papa took the other niece to hers.

When I got back, I turned on the hose and watered my garden, then all of Mom's plants.

By 10:30, I was hungry. I remembered we had lettuce and everything for a good salad, so I started chopping vegetables. I like to layer my salad, a trick my late brother taught me. It turned out great.

I'd also bought two mini watermelons from Dollar General. I cut one open and shared it with Mom and Papa.

After eating, I took a shower and a nap.

I woke at 1:00 PM and headed to get in the school pickup line for my niece. She gets out at 2:45 PM, and I pride myself on being near the front. Today I was second in line—I arrived at 1:20.

After picking her up, we all met at O'Charley's in Fultondale. I ordered the Louisiana sirloin steak, medium rare, with a baked potato and asparagus. Water to drink.

We talked while we ate. The girls kept urging me to leave right after the meal, but I kept teasing that I was going to order coffee and dessert, which drove them crazy. I didn't, of course.

By a little after 6:00 PM, my shoes were off, and I was in my recliner watching *The Andy Griffith Show* and journaling about my day. I might even turn in early.

That's all for now.

273: Mike

I'm an "old soul." I know this because people have been telling me that my whole life.

I act now pretty much the same way I acted when I was eight years old. Being born with a disability will do that to a fella; we have to grow up quick. And most of my friends are older than me. Much older.

One of my friends now lives in a nursing home after having a stroke. He was in the hospital when it happened, which, in a way, was probably a blessing. I haven't been able to visit him since the start of the pandemic.

Don't get me wrong, I have some younger friends, too. A couple live in Huntsville, and one in Chattanooga. We text, email, talk, and meet up when we can. But outside of them, just about every other friend I have is older.

One of those friends is "Mike." Right now, he's in the hospital—ICU, on a ventilator. I'm guessing he's about seventy years old, though we've never talked about our ages.

We've had long talks about the movie *O Brother, Where Art Thou?*—he's the one who introduced me to it. What a great film. If you haven't seen it, you should. You'll watch it more than once, I promise. *Hi-lar-i-ous.*

We've also talked at length about Jesus and Heaven. Like me, Mike has a brother in Heaven, and he misses him deeply. More than once, he's told me, "Lynn, I'm ready to go whenever the Good Lord takes me."

I'm not ready for him to go, though.

When I was baptized, I invited only two friends outside my family—my best friend Lee and his wife from Huntsville, and Mike and his wife. They both came, along with most of my family. If you invite someone to your baptism, they're important to you. And now Mike is lying in ICU on a ventilator.

Like I said, I'm not ready for him to go.

I've been praying for him and asked my preacher to put his name on our church prayer list.

I've also been riding by his house to pray for him right there in front of it. I guess part of me thinks the prayer will work better from that spot, though I know prayer works from anywhere. Still, I feel better doing it that way.

When I'm there, I see the shop, his pride and joy, that he built himself. We've sat inside it many times, talking about life while he showed me every detail of his handiwork. I'm not ready to give up those talks.

If praying is all I can do, then I'm doing all I can.

And that's the latest.

274: Subconsciously

Yesterday, I drove over to my hometown of Fultondale, Alabama.

I went to Fulton Road—at least, I think that's what it's called. Back when I was younger and driving, we had a little game we played there. We'd put the car in neutral at the top of the hill and try to coast all the way to the stop sign at the bottom. I think it's over a mile long, with a few hills you have to roll over, but the goal was to make it without touching the gas.

I also drove past my old house on Leora Avenue.

Later, I texted my nephew to wish him a happy birthday.

Today, I went to Gardendale—the next town over from Fultondale—and picked up some sandwiches from Pasquale's Pizza.

Growing up, Pasquale's was a treat. We usually went after playing ball at the park or swimming at the city pool. The place still looks the same inside, even down to the arcade games, probably the very ones I played as a kid.

To me, Pasquale's is real pizza. Chain pizza joints make chain pizza. Pasquale's makes *pizza*. And their stromboli steak sandwich? Best there is. My late brother could make a good one too, but outside of him and Pasquale's, no one else comes close.

I ordered two stromboli steaks, two hoagies, and a couple of gravies on the side for dipping. While I waited, I had a large Diet Coke.

On the way home, I called Mom to tell her I was bringing the food and that we could eat on the front porch.

When I walked in, she was heading toward me. I said something, and she teared up.

Then it hit me. Yesterday was Tony's birthday. He would've been fifty. The big 5-0. We probably would have thrown him a party if he were still here.

I realized that for the past two days, yesterday and today, I'd been back in my hometown, visiting all our old haunts. Subconsciously, I guess I'd been remembering him. How did I not see it? I even got food from one of our favorite spots.

That's the thing about losing someone you truly love. Sometimes, without even knowing it, you start doing the things that bring them close again.

We sat on the porch, ate our stromboli steak sandwiches, and talked about Tony.

275: Frogs

The year was 1963.

He and his friends were at the local bar, drinking.

He told them he'd been out frog gigging earlier that night.

Frog gigging is something we Southerners proudly do from time to time. We don't even have to be taught how it's built into our DNA. I could take you out tonight and show you exactly how to do it… and I haven't been in over thirty years. But I digress.

"Got over thirty frogs in the trunk of the car!" he boasted. "Come over Friday, and we'll fry 'em up."

Back then, people drank and people drove. There was no such thing as a "designated driver." No public service announcements warning about drinking and driving.

The man telling me the story said, "We knew it was wrong. But it's what you did. Heck, officers would follow you home just to make sure you got there safe. Sometimes they'd even drive you themselves. It was a different time..."

But that night would turn out different.

After knocking back a good bit of Jack, he paid his tab and headed for his car.

A mile from home, he got pulled over.

This particular officer wasn't the "give you a ride home" type. One thing led to another, and well, Jack Daniels will make a man mouthy.

"The next thing I remember," he told me, "is getting thrown into the backseat of the squad car—handcuffed somehow..."

He spent the night in jail. His wife had to come post bail the next day. Money like that wasn't easy to pull together, so he stayed behind bars most of the day before she could get him out.

"Where's my car?" he asked the officer at the front desk.

"It was impounded. You'll have to pay to get it out."

They paid the fee and headed to retrieve it.

It was August in Alabama, the dog days of summer. Stepping out into that heat, they caught a whiff of something foul.

"What is that godawful smell?" his wife asked.

He froze. "Oh no. No, no, no." He sank to his knees.

Looking up at her, he said, "Honey, I know you're already mad at me. Please... don't get madder."

And then... they opened the trunk.

276: Tiny Car

The sun had set, but the sky still glowed blue. The air had cooled off a bit.

I pulled into Sonic for something small from their snack menu. My blood sugar was low, and I didn't want to go for ice cream to bring it back up.

I ordered a corn dog, cheddar peppers, and a Diet Coke, then pulled up to the window.

Across the lot came a larger-than-usual minivan, not quite a full-size van, but longer than most. White with black trim.

Behind it, though… was the smallest car I'd ever seen. I swear it looked like it could only hold one person. Same white-and-black color scheme as the van.

The cashier opened the window to take my money just as I burst out laughing.

"What's so funny?" she asked.

"It looks like that minivan had a baby," I said, still laughing uncontrollably.

She called the rest of the crew over to look.

"Aww, it's so cute," one said.

"I want one," said another.

"He said it looks like the minivan had a baby," she told them. And they all cracked up.

I paid for my food, turned on some Bob Seger, and took the back way home.

It was a good drive.

277: The Porch

Today was one of those days worth writing about.

It started with me putting seventy-four dollars' worth of gas in my truck. That's when the pump cut off. Seventy-four dollars exactly. Didn't even fill the tank. I'm guessing the bank has a limit set for debit card purchases at the pump. (And no, it's not because I only had seventy-four dollars in my account.)

But the highlight of the day was my trip to my aunt and uncle's house.

There's something special that happens on their porch. We sat there for two hours and fifty minutes, talking and laughing without a single lull. Not once.

My uncle is the storyteller. My aunt is the fact-checker. Their rhythm is magic.

My Uncle: "Tommy. you know Tommy, Lynn. He's, I guess, thirty-six…"

My Aunt: "He's not thirty-six. He's thirty-eight now."

My Uncle: "Well, yeah, you're right. But anyway, he was driving to work when—"

My Aunt: "He wasn't going to work. He was going to see his mother."

My Uncle: "Well, yeah, you're right. He was going to see his mother. Anyway, he got to the train tracks—"

My Aunt: "You left out the part about the gas station."

My Uncle: "Well, yeah, he had stopped at the gas station…"

And on and on it went. I wish I could capture the way they do it—the timing, the back-and-forth, the affection between them—but words can't quite do it justice.

That porch isn't magical because of the wood and nails. It's magical because of the people sitting there.

To my aunt and uncle, I hope you don't mind me posting this. I love you. I'll be back soon.

278: Turkey Creek

I recently visited the famous Turkey Creek.

The water is clean, cold, very cold, and it's been part of my family's life for generations.

My granddaddy Rock's house sat close to the creek. My Tot Tot's house did too. Back then, my dad's family didn't have their own well water, so they used the neighbor's. Every day, Dad would wash off with water poured into a bowl—water drawn from that neighbor's well. A washcloth, a bar of soap, a bowl of water—that's all he needed.

Once a week or so, they'd heat water on the stove, fill a big metal tub, and take turns bathing. Five boys, one tub. Dad said he always went first. Oldest privilege.

In the warmer months, he'd take a bar of soap and a towel down to Turkey Creek and bathe right there in the flowing water.

My mother and her siblings also grew up along Turkey Creek. Unlike Dad's side, they had their own well, but the creek was still where they swam, played, thought, and sometimes made big life decisions.

For so many in our family, the creek was part playground, part bathroom, part sanctuary.

These days, a small portion of it is preserved as the Turkey Creek Nature Preserve. Some of my relatives helped make it happen, along with other local families. I'm glad it exists—something this precious deserves to be protected.

The Preserve has gravel parking spots, picnic tables, benches, and hiking trails. You can swim there too. No entry fee, it runs on donations.

When I was little, the creek was pure freedom. I could take my diaper off, hop in an inner tube, and float to my heart's content. Snakes didn't even bother me back then. (They might now.)

A lot of our family still lives on the creek.

Recently, I'd been in a bit of a funk, so I went back. Sat there. Thought. Listened to the water and watched it flow. It worked—the funk lifted.

Turkey Creek is special. Always has been. Always will be.

279: Downton Abbey: A New Era

At 9:00 AM, I began shaving and trimming my beard.

"This has to go smoothly, Lynn," I told myself as I worked up the lather.

"It's gotta be perfect."

After shaving, I stepped into the shower.

When I'm happy, I sing in the shower. I often make up words and try to make them rhyme.

♫♫ "Oh, we're going to the movies, we're going to see the show, we're going to the movies… I need a word that rhymes with 'show.'" ♫♫

By 10:00 AM, I had my attire picked out, tried on, and confirmed it fit.

After that, I hung it back up, sat in my boxers and socks, and waited until it was time to get ready.

At 11:00 AM, I got dressed and met my date for the day in the living room for pictures—Papa was the photographer.

I was taking my date to the movies, more specifically, to see the new *Downton Abbey* film.

And my mother looked beautiful.

A fella's never too old to take his momma out on a movie date.

To pull off today's schedule, everybody in the family had to pitch in.

Mom was having cataract surgery this morning. She had to be there at 5:45 AM—first surgery of the day.

Mom, Papa, and my dad have all had cataract surgery recently, about a month apart each.

The girls still needed to be at school at their regular times, though they were getting out early. That meant it was up to me to get them there on time.

My nieces go to two different schools in two different counties. We live right on the Blount/Jefferson County line. Today, both girls were riding with me. I braced myself for morning whining, but to my surprise, there wasn't any.

At 6:55 AM, we pulled out of the driveway, and I'm happy to say both girls got to school on time.

Now came the tricky part—picking up my oldest niece at 9:30 AM. That left me with about an hour and a half to kill, so I headed to Cracker Barrel for breakfast.

My sweet waitress came to take my order.

"Yes, ma'am, I'll have the Granny's Breakfast special, and add a biscuit and gravy to that, please."

She smiled. "Does my heart good to see a body eat well."

"Yes, ma'am."

I had coffee and water with breakfast and ate slowly to pass the time.

By 9:00 AM, I got my ticket, paid, and made my way to the car. At 9:30 sharp, I picked up my niece.

We got home around 10:00 AM. I was supposed to get my other niece from school at 11:00 AM, but Mom and Papa walked in just then.

Mom's surgery had gone well, and Papa said he'd get the other niece.

Before the door even shut behind them, I was back in bed, sound asleep.

281: Snakes

I hate snakes. Period.

For over twenty-five years, I've had night terrors related to something I haven't even shared here yet, and many of those terrors involve snakes.

The mountain where we live used to be called "Rattlesnake Mountain" by the older generation. For years, that's the only name anyone knew.

Then a realtor came along and thought, *I wonder why I can't sell any houses on 'Rattlesnake Mountain'?*

Now, it's called "Smoke Rise," and the housing market does much better under that name.

Today alone, I ran over two rattlesnakes driving up the mountain. And no, running over them doesn't kill them. To do that, you have to stop, press the brake, skid the tires over the snake's body, and take its head off. I never do that. I always worry the thing might find an opening into my floorboard and end up inside my vehicle, so I don't stop for snakes.

I also spotted a black racer in the neighbor's driveway. They're fast and have been known to chase people, but they're not poisonous. Non-poisonous snakes often kill the poisonous ones, so it's best to leave them be.

When I pulled into our driveway, I scanned for movement. I actually sat in the vehicle for a good thirty seconds, wondering absurd things before opening my door:

Can a snake be stuck to the bottom of my vehicle and strike me as I hop out?

Could one get in through the tailpipe… or the A/C vents?

What if one's already inside with me?

That last thought had me flinging the door open and jumping out.

This summer, I'll have to pay extra attention to the Disabled Garden while watering Mom's flowers or even just walking outside.

It's going to be a long summer…

282: Heart of Dixie Railroad Museum

H.O.D. Railroad Museum

I've wanted to visit the Heart of Dixie Railroad Museum ever since I learned it existed.

I love trains. Always have.

The first years of my life were spent living right next to the tracks. My brothers and I used to hop on a train and catch a ride to our friend's house or the nearby park.

As a kid, I was sure I'd grow up to be a train engineer.

Then… life happens. You end up doing something entirely different, and in my case, I ended up in the IT field, which I enjoyed very much.

So today, Dad and I finally made the trip to the Railroad Museum.

If you love being able to walk right up to old trains and touch them, this place is for you.

The museum is outdoors.

Some trains are protected under a roof, others are out in the open.

There are active tracks running nearby, with plenty of train traffic. While walking through the museum, you can hear trains and horns in the distance, adding to the atmosphere.

With a grin plastered on my face, I kept saying, "Look at this one! Look at that one over there!" as I bounced from train to train. I felt like a kid again. It's like wandering around a small train yard where you're allowed to touch and explore every single engine and car.

Many of the trains have signs explaining their history. Some are open for visitors to climb aboard.

There's even a section displaying the different types of railway light signals, complete with buttons you can push to see them light up and hear them operate.

They also have a working train on site. On Saturdays, you can buy a ticket and ride.

While we were there, Dad and I had the chance to ride along with a private group who had chartered the train. It would've cost us $10 each. Dad was all for it, but I didn't feel right about crashing their event. It could've been a birthday party for all I knew. Plus, I wasn't entirely sure about the restroom situation on board. I imagine there was one, but I didn't know how big it was or whether it was ventilated. Yes, I think about things like that. So, I passed on the ride.

The gift shop was fun to browse, but I only had one thing in mind, a wooden train whistle like the one I had as a child. Mine had been lost years ago, and I wanted to replace it. They had one for six bucks. Worth every penny.

If you get the chance, visit the Heart of Dixie Railroad Museum. You might just find yourself feeling like a kid again, too.

After taking photos and inspecting every train, we got back into the truck and headed for our next stop, the Alabama National Cemetery. But that's a story for another post.

283: 5/28/2022

I'm bachelor'ing it this weekend. Yep, I've got the place all to myself.

I stayed behind to take care of the animals, plus I've got a busy June and July ahead, and needed to save some money.

First thing I do when I've got the place to myself is stock up on supplies. So, off to Dollar General I went.

Shopping list:
- Totino's pizzas
- Bologna
- Bread
- Chips

Total: Around $21.

Between those supplies and what I already had at home, I'm set.

Normally, I'm in bed by 8:30 PM. Last night, though, I didn't get in bed until after 10:30. You know how sometimes, if you miss the moment you're hungry, you just don't feel hungry later? That's how I am with sleep. Miss the window, and I'm wide awake. I'm pretty sure I got less than two hours of sleep last night. So, I'll probably be napping today.

Since I couldn't sleep, I got up at 4:00 AM, took a shower, and went for an early-morning drive.

I saw several rabbits and had to stop to let a duck family cross the street. I think they watch for my vehicle. As soon as the momma duck sees me coming, she gathers the little ones, and they waddle across. I can't help but giggle watching them. I've heard "Why did the chicken cross the road?" jokes all my life, but here I am wondering why the ducks are doing it.

It's been raining here for three or four days straight, and my little garden is overdue for weeding. I'll take care of that today. The plants are doing exceptionally well, and I'm proud of it. I'll try to post pictures soon.

It's now 6:21 AM, so I'd better get started before the heat kicks in.

That's all for now.

284: On This Day – 2009

My phone likes to bring up "Memories."

It does this by showing me a picture with the title, *"On this day in such-and-such year"*, using the original date on the image.

I smiled as soon as I saw the photo. Then I forwarded it to my two best friends, who also happened to be in it.

It was taken in 2009, three younger versions of ourselves, camping together. In the picture, I'm playing my acoustic guitar, "Charlie," while my friends strum theirs. We're gathered around the campfire, and a few other people had stopped by to watch, listen, and hang out. I remember handing my camera to one of them and asking them to take the shot.

My truck—visible in the background—was less than a year old at the time. I still drive it today. The Honda Ridgeline came with a built-in trunk that doubled as an ice chest, complete with a drain plug at the bottom.

We were playing Johnny Cash when that picture was taken. Cash is always a hit around the campfire. My friends had to remind me of the chords—I can never seem to remember them for Johnny Cash songs—but once they told me, I played them with ease.

Back then, I didn't have a colostomy or a urostomy. I simply had a Foley catheter running to a leg bag, and I wore a diaper. My health was otherwise great, and I didn't even consider myself disabled. I just happened to pee and poop differently than my friends, and life was good.

On the table sat my Coleman stove and Coleman lantern. We had each brought food for every meal—breakfast, lunch, and dinner.

I drank back then, though I don't now. In the truck's ice chest were three cases of beer on ice—light beer for me, "Pabst" for my friends.

My tent was brand new, chosen because of how easy it was to set up. Just pull a cord, and it pops right up.

We had a camping rule: no drinking until your tent was up. So, I pulled the cord, my tent popped open, and I popped the top on my beer—then sat back and watched them wrestle with tent poles.

The campground had a bathhouse, which was my one requirement: bathrooms and showers. I still needed to keep germs to a minimum.

I did, however, enjoy walking into the woods, opening the valve on my pee bag, and letting it drain. That was about as close as I could get to actually peeing in the woods. I'd open the valve, sigh with relief, and feel oddly satisfied.

When it came time to leave, I couldn't get my tent to collapse. I ended up tying it to the truck bed and driving home with it still fully upright. I gave that tent away afterward.

That picture brought back all those memories and more. I couldn't help but smile when I saw it.

285: Bachelor'in It

The bachelor life has been good to me these past few days—and I've eaten like a King. "King" with a capital "K."

The first night, I made my favorite meal:

- Kraut and weenies
- Mashed potatoes (not instant—Mom doesn't allow that in the house, though I secretly like instant)
- Sweet peas
- Corn on the cob

Maybe my liking for instant mashed potatoes comes from school lunches as a kid, they always served instant. Still, I made the real kind from the Piggly Wiggly.

The next day, I browned a pound of ground beef and made sloppy joes. I warmed the hamburger buns in the microwave, then added jalapeños and shredded cheese to each sandwich. Golden Flake "Hot" Chips were the side—top chip brand in this part of the South. Coach Paul "Bear" Bryant ate Golden Flake Chips. Enough said.

On Monday, I cooked another pound of ground beef with taco seasoning, heated refried beans, and made Mexican rice. I chopped onions, opened a bag of lettuce I bought for $1.25, and set out toppings for tacos and burritos. I enjoyed tacos, burritos, and bell burgers—jalapeños on everything, of course.

In between all that, I baked a pecan pie. Yes, I've eaten like a King— "King" with a capital "K."

Every day, I've watered all the plants, including the garden, and even repotted three of them. One plant in particular—a "Ponytail Palm" I thought was dead—has come back strong after lots of watering. I've named it "Momma." When I repotted it, I discovered a huge base hidden under the soil. I'm hoping it thrives in its bigger home.

"Sparkey," our Roomba vacuum, runs every morning at 6:30 now that everyone's away.

I've also been slowly tidying the house so it'll be clean when everyone gets back. One day, I dedicated myself entirely to germ-killing. I moved all the cats to the garage or outside, and put the dogs outside, too. Then I ran my germ-killing lamp for an hour in every room. It took until 8 PM to finish. Afterward, I ran the lamp in the garage for good measure. I'm not a germaphobe, but I do my best to keep them at a minimum.

So yes, I've been busy—taking it slow, but still busy.

And I've eaten like a King— "King" with a capital "K."

That's all for now.

286: Alabama National Cemetery

The Alabama National Cemetery, located in Montevallo, Alabama, is one of the nicest cemeteries I've ever visited.

It spans 479 beautiful acres and has enough burial space to serve veterans for at least the next fifty years.

With so many veterans laid to rest there, you might think it would be difficult to find the grave of the person you've come to visit, but it isn't.

Inside the main building, there's a kiosk where you can look up the burial plot. Once you enter the name, the system prints a map with clear directions to the grave. You can also look up the location through the VA website.

A few peaceful ponds dot the property, each well-maintained.

The grass is neatly cut, the landscaping trimmed, and American flags wave proudly throughout the grounds. The place radiates peace.

During the COVID pandemic, a close family member passed away in the hospital from COVID complications.

We were in quarantine ourselves and couldn't attend the funeral.

On this trip, Dad and I were finally able to visit his grave.

Dad spoke a few words to him, and I'd like to take a moment to do the same here.

His name was John Thomas, though everyone called him "Big Daddy."

Big Daddy was a beautiful human being, kind, funny, and generous enough to give you the shirt off his back without hesitation.

I grew up with John and his family woven into my life. We were always around each other.

While John and his wife played cards with my mom and dad, my brothers and I would be outside playing chase or hide-and-go-seek with his kids.

John served in Vietnam, and there's a story that's been told in our family ever since he returned home, a story I know he wouldn't mind me sharing.

It was in Vietnam, and John was on guard duty.

It was nighttime. The moon was out.

Quiet, eerily quiet.

I've heard that sometimes the scariest part of war is when the quiet sets in.

I can't imagine what must have been going through his mind. Fresh out of high school, thousands of miles from home, dropped into the middle of a war, those were surely some of the hardest days of his life.

I think "hell on earth" isn't too strong a phrase for what soldiers endured there.

That night, John lit a cigarette and took a few drags, letting the nicotine calm his nerves.

Then, just as he inhaled again, a bullet whizzed past his head. He dropped for cover instantly and snuffed out the cigarette.

The faint orange glow had been enough for an enemy soldier to see his position, take aim, and pull the trigger.

John never smoked outside again for the rest of his tour.

After Vietnam, he was honorably discharged. But he never forgot his time there.

He was loved deeply and will be missed greatly.

As I mentioned earlier, Dad spoke a few words at his grave that day. And I hope John wouldn't mind me taking this time to say mine here.

At the Alabama National Cemetery, husbands and wives are buried together—one resting above the other. That means John's wife will one day be laid to rest in the same spot, on top of him. Many couples are buried together like that here.

While we were there, another funeral was in progress.

We later learned the service was for my aunt's cousin on her side of the family.

Many in our family have served in the military. Many have fought in wars.

If you ever have the chance, I urge you to visit the Alabama National Cemetery. Even if you don't have family there, go.

The men and women buried there did so much for you and me. Some never made it home alive.

They gave all they could be so you and I could be all we can be.

287: Spaghetti

I found myself standing in the pasta aisle at *The Pig*.

They have every type of noodle you can imagine—spaghetti, fettuccine, lasagna, angel hair.

I had set a spending limit for myself: make spaghetti with garlic bread for under twenty bucks.

Over the store speakers, *"Wanted Dead or Alive"* by Bon Jovi started playing.

I sang along quietly: ♪ *I'm a cowboy, on a steel horse I ride. I'm wanted... dead or alive.* ♪

I grabbed the noodles I wanted—about $2.50—and put them in the buggy. Next stop: sauce.

In our house, we use Prego spaghetti sauce, then doctor it up. I picked the variety with mushrooms.

♪ *And I walk these streets, a loaded six-string on my back. I play for keeps, baby, 'cause I might not make it back... oh yeah.* ♪ (Yes, sometimes I make up extra lyrics.)

From the produce section, I grabbed one Vidalia onion and one bell pepper. Then I headed to the meat section.

♪ *Wanted... dead or alive...* ♪

One pound of ground beef—$4.50.

Finally, in the frozen bread section, I grabbed a box of Garlic Texas Toast and made my way to the register.

"Did you find everything you needed today, sir?"

"Yes, ma'am. I'm on a mission—this has to come in under twenty bucks."

"Alright, let's ring it up and see."

Total: a little over $18.50.

Mission accomplished.

I headed home to make spaghetti for dinner. But that, as they say, is another post.

288: Vet Appointment

We have three dogs. Jet, Cooper, and Tommy.

Jet and Cooper are Australian Shepherds, and Tommy is a Black Lab.

This morning, I had to take Jet and Cooper to the vet for an 8:00 a.m. appointment.

Yesterday, I cleaned out my truck to make room for them and made sure everything was ready for the trip.

This morning, I let the dogs out to do their business, then took a shower and got ready.

I grabbed the dog leash and headed outside to get Cooper first.

When he came over, I realized he'd lost his collar. I knew it had to be somewhere in the backyard, but I didn't have time to search for it.

So, I set the leash down on the back porch table and went inside to grab one of the extra collars we keep.

Collar in hand, I stepped back outside and found all three dogs sitting side by side on the porch, looking at me with matching guilty expressions.

I glanced at the table.

The leash was gone.

"Where is it?!" I demanded.

They just stared.

"I know you hid it! Where is it?"

Still nothing.

"Where. Is. It?!"

At that point, Tommy looked to his right—my left.

I followed his gaze and spotted the leash in the corner of the fence, covered with a thin layer of straw, like someone had tried to camouflage it.

I retrieved the leash, clipped it onto Cooper, and got him into the back seat of the truck. Then I went back for Jet and loaded him in beside Cooper.

A quick glance at the clock: 7:21 a.m.

"I've got to get going. The appointment's at eight," I told myself. "Still on schedule."

I buckled up, cranked the engine, and turned the A/C on high to keep the dogs cool.

A few minutes into the drive, I felt a breeze coming from the back.

I glanced over my shoulder—Jet had rolled the rear windows all the way down. My heart jumped; I quickly used the driver's controls to roll them back up, then hit the child lock so they couldn't do it again.

We arrived at the vet.

"Yes, ma'am, my dogs Jet and Cooper have an 8 o'clock appointment. Can I get some help bringing them inside? They're pretty hyper."

"Yes, sir, I'll help you. If you'll give me your cell phone number, we'll call you when they're ready for pickup."

"Yes, ma'am, that sounds great."

We got the dogs inside and handed them over to the vet staff. Then I headed home to wait for the call to pick them up.

So far, a smooth morning.

289: Sunshine

I walked back into the house after dropping Jet and Cooper at the vet.

The moment I stepped inside, a smell hit me.

"Oh, no. What is that? I've spent all week cleaning this house and making it smell good—now this? I don't have time for this."

I followed the smell into one of the rooms… and there it was.

Two piles of "Sunshine."

"Oh, no, no, no, no, no! Mom and Papa are on their way home, and now this!"

I grabbed a roll of paper towels, medical gloves, and some warm water.

Dropping to my knees, I muttered, "Those little balls of joy have been plotting this all week. They probably heard me telling Papa to drive carefully, and they knew—now or never."

One pile would have been bad enough. But two? Two!

"This was intentional. They're not cute little dogs, they're dive bombers. I hope they get twenty-four shots apiece at the vet today."

I'd worked hard to get the house spotless and smelling fresh. I'd even run my germ-killing lamp through every room.

"I should throw one of my colostomy bags on their bed. That'll show 'em."

I cleaned up the Sunshine, then mopped the floor. Thankfully, the wood floors made it easy.

"Thank goodness, Sparky, the Roomba, didn't wander in here. That could've been ugly…"

I brought the germ-killing lamp back in, set it in the "attack zone," and turned it on. Then I made a quick run to Dollar General for big candles, the five-dollar kind.

Now, the candles are lit, the lamp is running, and I'm crossing my fingers that the house smells fresh again before Mom and Papa get home.

290: Gibbs Garden Center

Mom and I made our way over to *Gibbs Garden Center*, located off Exit 304 on I-65, today.

Gibbs is by far the best garden center I've ever visited.

And today was actually my first time there.

I don't know exactly how many acres it covers, but Mom and I guessed it's about the size of four football fields.

The place is simply amazing. I couldn't count how many greenhouses they had, but it was definitely more than seven—each one enormous. Gigantic.

Plants were everywhere—inside, outside, everywhere you turned.

They also sold clay pots, ranging from small to extra-large.

Just when I thought I had seen it all, I stumbled upon rows of wooden swings and chairs of all different styles. Fancy swings too, at least in my opinion.

The place is so large, it even has its own gift shop. I didn't make it there, though—I was too worn out. I ended up taking a break in the car, sitting with the A/C running for half an hour.

They were having several sales today, the main one being: *Buy one hanging basket plant, get one free.*

Normally, when I grocery shop, I like to lean on the cart for support. That wasn't an option at Gibbs. The entire lot is gravel, and instead of carts, they supply wagons that you load your items into and pull behind you.

I'll admit, Gibbs can be expensive.

But the good thing is this: if you buy a $60 plant at Gibbs, it *looks* like a $60 plant.

So if you're ever near Exit 304 on I-65—*Gibbs Garden Center.*

291: Where is "It"?

Wearing a diaper as an adult is embarrassing. And diapers aren't perfect—they have their flaws.

I was in my thirties at the time, working full-time as an I.T. Manager.

One day at work, I'd been up and down ladders all morning, running cable throughout the building. It was part of my job to maintain the I.T. equipment *and* install the lines—miles and miles of cable.

At some point, I went to the restroom to change my diaper.

But when I pulled it off, I discovered something terrible: an empty diaper. And poop tracks running down my leg where "it" had fallen out and rolled away.

Crap. It's in the hallway. Or worse—in someone's office. It must've fallen when I was on the ladder, I thought to myself.

I cleaned up quickly, stuffed some napkins in my pocket, and left the restroom on a mission to find "it."

Office after office, I poked my head in and casually asked, "Everything okay in here?" all while scanning the floor. No luck.

Finally, in one of the hallways, I spotted it. Relief washed over me.

I pulled out my napkins, picked "it" up, cleaned the area as best I could, and rushed into the nearest restroom to dispose of the evidence.

"Phew," I muttered to myself as I washed my hands.

On my way back to my office, I passed the maintenance man—Dicky—standing right where I'd found it.

Crap. Did I miss something? I thought, walking over to him.

"What's up, Dicky?" I asked.

"Lynn, you're not going to believe this," he said. "There was some crap on the floor right here, and now it's gone."

"Huh?" I replied, playing dumb.

"Yeah. It was right here. I went to grab what I needed to clean it up, and when I came back, it had disappeared."

I gave him a shrug and said, "You're right—I don't believe it." Then I walked away.

292: Garden Update

You may remember that I planted a garden this year.

We have a raised flowerbed at the house, and I used it for the garden. It comes up to my waist, making it easy to maintain—I don't have to bend over at all.

Bending is an issue for me because of my spina bifida, tethered spinal cord, and colon problems. Even something as simple as leaning down to pick something up could cause an obstruction in my bowel or colon. Honestly, it's scary how fragile the body can be. But I digress.

The garden isn't very big, but this year I planted:

- Tomato
- Squash
- Eggplant
- Broccoli
- Sweet Basil
- Strawberries

The strawberries didn't produce this year, but I've been told that's common in the first year.

The tomatoes, on the other hand, are doing great—we'll have plenty. We may even pick a few green ones to fry up.

The squash is thriving. I've already harvested three, enough to slice and fry with onions. I love fried squash.

The eggplant has blooms but hasn't started producing yet. Fingers crossed.

The sweet basil is doing incredibly well—I have loads of it. I'll need to look up how to properly harvest basil.

The broccoli plants—five in total—keep growing taller and fuller but haven't produced heads yet.

I water the garden every day and pull the weeds as I go. It gives me something to do, keeps me busy, and honestly, I enjoy it.

And that's the latest update on the garden.

293: Return To Gatlinburg – June 2022

This morning, I pulled out my suitcase, dusted it off, and opened it up to begin packing.

I'm headed back to the cabin in Gatlinburg, where I'll stay until the 30th.

Today I'll get my oil changed at the local mom-and-pop garage, then wash and vacuum the old truck.

This time, I'm buying my supplies here and carrying them with me up to the cabin. My goal is simple: not to spend any more money up there than I would down here.

Yesterday, I stopped by our local Dollar General. It was early morning, and I was the only customer in the store. The Coca-Cola delivery guys were unloading case after case of Cokes, while I was alone in the chip aisle.

From the other side of the aisle, one of the delivery guys hollered, "Hello... Is there anybody in there?"

Naturally, I hollered back, "Just nod if you can hear me..."

And he answered, "Is there anyone home?"

We both laughed and laughed.

If you didn't get that, it's a Pink Floyd reference. I enjoy little moments like that, when everything just falls into place.

Later today, I'll stop by our family-owned pharmacy to pick up my prescriptions. Then I'll pack all of my medical supplies. They fill up a large tote box on their own, but it's crucial that I have everything I might need while I'm away.

Once I've loaded up the truck, I'll straighten my bedroom and bathroom. I always like coming home to a clean space.

I'll also set up my "Ring" camera, which I call my "Travel Cam." I take it with me so Mom and Papa can check in on me while I'm gone.

If everything works out, I'll be on the road by about 3 a.m. tomorrow.

So here we go. We leave at 3 a.m.

294: Gatlinburg Update

I tried to get some rest around 5 p.m., but had to get up to take my dog, Tommy, out. While I'm up, I thought I'd give a quick update on the trip prep.

Today I got my oil changed and spent a good bit of time shopping for food. I even picked up condiments like Bama mayonnaise and French's mustard since the cabin doesn't keep any of that stocked.

I bought two coolers, one mid-sized and one small "Playmate." They're packed with sandwich meats, bacon, sausage, milk, cream, and Diet Cokes. My insulin is in there too, right alongside the groceries.

I filled a tote box with other supplies: cereal, bread, chips, cookies. Another tote box holds my medical supplies, including a bottle of antibiotics for emergencies.

I also packed my hospital bag—just in case.

Clothes were last on the list. I tossed them into my suitcase quickly, maybe too quickly. That might come back to bite me, but clothing is easy to replace on the road. Medical supplies, on the other hand, are not. Most pharmacies don't carry ostomy supplies.

It'll be 3 a.m. before I know it, so I'd better get back in bed.

295: Cabin – Arrival

I pulled into the cabin around 10:00 a.m. Eastern time.

The drive up was depressing. Rain poured down the entire way, the sky heavy and gray. For the first couple of hours, I was the only one on the interstate. Remember, I had left before 3 a.m. The rain just wouldn't let up, and I was glad when the drive was finally over.

I hauled in my supplies, food included, and set up my bed on the couch. That's where I always sleep when I'm here—the couch is soft and easy on my back.

I turned on the TV, pulled up the Philo app, and flipped through the shows I'd set it to record: everything from *Everybody Loves Raymond* to *The Golden Girls*. Of course, I landed on *The Andy Griffith Show*.

Around 4 p.m., I woke up to sunshine. Just seeing the sun after that gloomy drive lifted my spirits.

For tonight, I'm staying in. Tomorrow morning, I've got bacon and cheese toast planned for breakfast.

That's all for now.

296: Cabin – 6/10/2022

When I arrived yesterday, I found the couch in the upstairs living room moved around.

The last guest had rearranged the furniture to suit their needs and never put it back. I suppose they figured the cleaning crew would handle it.

The problem is, our "crew" was really just one lady named Lucy, and Lucy recently quit. She found a better job in another town. That's one of the reasons I came up here—to hopefully find someone new to clean the cabin.

For now, though, I'm stuck with the furniture out of place. And I hate change.

This morning, I woke up around 6:30 a.m. Eastern. I got up disoriented, bumped into the couch, and let out a dirty little word.

I've made my coffee now. Speaking of coffee, I discovered a Snickers candy bar flavored creamer. Not bad at all—I actually like it.

At eight, I'm planning to run down to the station at the bottom of the hill to say hello to the fellas. I'm hoping they might know someone who cleans cabins.

That's all for now.

297: Cabin Update

I've never had to slowly stick my head out the cabin door and look both ways before stepping outside—until today.

The bears are roaming the mountain.

Meanwhile, the search for a new cleaning crew continues. Nobody I talked to today knew of anyone available.

I did make a trip to the store to buy laundry detergent, dryer sheets, and dishwasher detergent. I also picked up a case of Diet Cokes.

The town is jam-packed with summer tourists. Because of that, I probably won't head out again this weekend. Thankfully, I've got everything I need here at the cabin.

Mom might come stay with me for a few days, and I really hope she does.

For lunch today, I made some microwave BBQ and paired it with two sides: hot chips and BBQ chips.

For dinner, I think I'll splurge and make a pimento cheese sandwich.

298: Cabin – 6/11/22

I got up this morning around 6 a.m. Eastern time.

The cabin has four sets of sliding glass doors—two upstairs and two downstairs. This morning, I noticed smudges on the upstairs doors. Looking closer, I realized the bears had been standing on their hind legs, peering inside. Their noses and paws left prints all over the glass.

I checked the downstairs doors and found the same thing.

I already keep the doors locked, and we always ask guests to do the same. Seeing those smudges was just more proof of why we stress that rule.

The sun came up, and it looks like a beautiful day. But with the town swarming with summer tourists, I'll probably stay in. I'll wait until Monday before venturing out.

I spoke with Mom today. She's not coming up just yet, but hopefully soon.

My plans for today are simple: do some laundry and fit in a nap.

For lunch, I'll make either a ham sandwich or a potted meat sandwich. I brought along a sweet onion to slice up and add to them. I love onions. I also packed some Bama mayonnaise and a few fresh tomatoes for a tomato sandwich.

Whatever I end up making, I know it'll be good.

That's all for now.

299: Cabin – 6/12/22

I've seen more bears on this trip than on any other.

I wouldn't be surprised if the Park Service trucks start coming around soon to collect and relocate them.

I don't know if you remember "Gladys" or not, so I'll tell you about her.

Gladys was a momma bear who had four cubs.

I gave her the name "Gladys" myself, and I called the poppa bear "Grady." I suspect Grady was the father, but I always saw Gladys alone with the cubs.

I once heard that one of those cubs originally belonged to another mother bear that had died. Gladys took that little one in and raised it with the others. That was the word going around anyway.

I went back through my journals and found that I'd been writing about Gladys and her cubs since 2018. Wherever Gladys went, the cubs followed right behind her.

Now, I suspect the bears I'm seeing are those same cubs, grown but still young. They're out on their own now, and Gladys taught them well.

They know how to walk up to a vehicle and check if the doors are unlocked.

They know how to pull the top off a hot tub to drink the water inside.

And they even know how to open "bear-proof" garbage containers.

Okay, that last part I said mostly as a joke.

But in all honesty, I feel like I got to witness something special—a momma bear raising her cubs.

300: Cabin – 6/13/22

I brought $190 worth of supplies with me to the cabin, which works out to about $9.50 a day for food. I still needed to replenish a few items like milk and bread, so off to Food City I went.

I parked the truck, got out, and started toward the entrance.

Out of nowhere, some guy whistles and yells, "Hey, nice legs!"

Crap. I'm about to get into a fight, I thought to myself.

But when I turned around, I saw he was whistling at a pretty girl walking behind me. Relieved, I kept going.

After grabbing a buggy, I headed to the produce section.

"I should've eaten before coming here. Careful, Lynn," I told myself. "Don't let hunger talk you into buying a hundred dollars worth of food."

At the bread aisle, I stopped.

"Seven dollars for that bread? Nope. I'll just grab this Sunbeam for a buck fifty."

On to canned meat—or so I thought.

"Chips. Two bags of plain Lays for seven bucks? I'll just get one. Oh, and I need some dip too. Now back to the canned meat."

"Paper towels. Sixty-nine cents each. I'll get three."

I spotted the drink section.

"Better grab some Canada Dry Ginger Ale for when my sugar goes low." Into the buggy went an eight-pack, along with a case of Diet Coke. "Now, canned meat."

"She does have nice legs…" I caught myself thinking again.

"Where is the canned meat in this place?"

I tossed two Totino's pizzas into the buggy—love those. Then I spotted lemon-flavored Oreos. "Gotta get those. Hard to find sometimes."

Finally, I found the oysters and Star-Kist products.

"And there she is again. And there's the canned meat. Thank you, Lord."

I picked up two cans. "Heard this stuff was good. I hope it is."

Adding it all up in my head, I figured it would cost about $35.

At the register, the total was $42. Not too bad.

Back at the cabin, I put everything away. Haven't opened the canned meat yet—that's for a special occasion.

Now, time for a nap.

301: Cabin – 6/14/22

I headed down to the station at the bottom of the mountain to check in with the fellas, see if they'd heard anything about a cleaning crew, and say hello.

On the way back, I ran into trouble. A diesel truck, a dump truck, and a tractor were blocking the entrance to the road leading up to the cabin.

I stopped and asked one of the workers if I could get through from the other end of the road. He said he wasn't sure and added, "God bless you, sir."

"God bless you as well," I said, then drove off to try another route.

The cabin isn't on a dead-end road, so I knew there had to be another way in. Problem was, GPS kept trying to send me through the blocked road, and I've always been worse with directions than I am with math.

I turned up one road and took a left. From there, I could see the road I needed, just below me.

"All I've got to do is get back down to that road," I thought.

At the next intersection, I was forced to turn right because left was a dead end, and straight ahead wasn't an option. That turn put me even higher up the mountain. From there, I could see the road I'd just been on below me, and even farther down, the road I needed. I was getting farther away instead of closer.

Finally, I stopped.

"Okay, Lynn, you can't afford to drive all over this mountain at five bucks a gallon," I told myself.

So I turned back toward the original entrance.

When I arrived, the diesel truck was gone, and the way was clear.

"I should've just waited here to begin with, you big dummy," I muttered.

Back at the cabin, I fixed breakfast.

I had planned on cheese toast and dry toast, since I forgot to bring butter. I also fried up some sandwich-sized bologna—larger in circumference than the usual kind.

The toast burned in the toaster oven, so I turned it into a bologna sandwich with mustard and onions. Pretty tasty, all things considered.

Now I'm enjoying a cup of black coffee and watching TV.

No big plans for the day.

302: Cabin 6/14/22 – Evening Meal

I'd been eating the food I brought with me, but I was getting tired of it. I wanted a Meat-and-Three plate for a change. This was last night.

"The Golden Corral" used to cost 17 bucks for the buffet and a drink before the pandemic. Afterward, it jumped to 19 bucks.

I had a twenty and seven dollars in my wallet. I figured I'd spend the twenty on the buffet and still have a couple of ones left for a tip. I took a shower and got ready.

When I arrived, there were about ten people in line ahead of me. Nobody struck up a conversation, and I didn't see anyone I could chat with. So, I just waited patiently.

Finally, I got to the register.

"One buffet and a tea, please."

"That'll be twenty-three sixty-five, please."

"Oh, wow. Prices went up. This is cutting into my tip money..."

"Uh-huh. We went up a little, sir."

I paid the fine—I mean the bill.

I tried to eat twenty-three dollars' worth of food, but I couldn't.

There was meat piled on every bar. "Ah, all this meat and veggies must've gone up in price," I thought.

Then I spotted the Steak Bar. Mounds of steaks. Just mounds. I had already loaded mashed potatoes and gravy onto my plate when I saw it, but I didn't care. I was getting a steak.

I asked for medium-rare, and the cook cut me a pretty generous slice. He even showed me the inside to make sure it was done how I liked. It was.

Next, I went for a plate of fried shrimp with steak fries. Before that, I had started off with a pretty good salad—I forgot to mention that earlier.

All in all, I had a salad and made three trips to the buffet. I tried hard to get my money's worth, but I came up short.

It was good, though.

I'm just not sure about the price.

Everything's getting too high for my blood.

303: Cabin 6/15/22

A short entry for today.

I woke this morning at 7:00 a.m. sharp—Eastern Time.

I took my meds, gave myself my insulin, and made a cup of black coffee.

A lady is supposed to stop by about cleaning the cabin, so I'm hoping we'll have a new cleaning crew soon.

Mom and I texted back and forth all morning. She's planning to try and come up next week. I really hope she can make it.

I have a video appointment with my psychologist today. I'm not shy about mental health—it's something that should be talked about. I truly believe mental health goes hand in hand with physical health.

And I love video appointments. They're so much easier and can be done anywhere.

That's all for now.

304: A Bear Story

I was sitting and watching TV when I heard a commotion outside.

It sounded like yelling—and a car alarm. Curious, I wandered out onto the back porch.

"Oh no! Not my apple fritters!" a lady cried.

"He's eating my Doritos!" a man shouted.

"Uh… excuse me… is the bear over there by chance?" I asked.

"Yes! We left the trunk open while unpacking, and he got into our car."

"Oh, I'm sorry."

"It's our fault. We shouldn't have left the trunk open."

"Um… sir… that bear can hit thirty miles an hour. I wouldn't do what you're about to do…" I warned the man who had walked outside onto the ground floor. He was slowly edging toward the bear with his phone out, recording.

"They don't chase people, do they?" he asked.

"I wouldn't find out if I were you. He's only four years old, in his prime, and his momma taught him well. Trust me, he can hit thirty."

"You local?" they asked me.

"Um… I'm here a lot."

"Oh, not that! He's eating all our food!" another lady exclaimed.

"He's eaten over ten thousand calories by now. He's gotta be full."

They asked me, "When can we go to the car?"

"After he leaves…" I said.

At that point, I decided I shouldn't get too involved. If that man got himself mauled trying to take pictures, I didn't want to be part of it. I wished them good luck, went back inside, and left them to it.

Gladys taught her cubs… well. I guess.

305: Cabin 6/16/22

I woke around 7 a.m.

I made a cup of coffee and stepped out onto the back porch to see if I could spot the bears, "Gladys" or "Gary."

Sure enough, Gary was across the road in the neighbor's yard, which meant he'd already passed through ours. He was sniffing around garbage cans and nibbling on a few leaves from a bush before wandering on down the mountain.

"See ya this afternoon, Gary," I said.

I noticed the neighbor's car was back in the driveway, so they must have returned. Probably had to go buy more food. (See earlier posts.)

I don't have any plans today—and honestly, with all the action I get just from sitting here at the cabin, why would I go anywhere?

Note to Reader: My camera battery died, and I didn't get a single picture this trip.

Yesterday, I drove to Cosby, TN. My oldest brother had told me about the place.

Cosby is a rural area full of beauty—rolling scenery, old homes, farms, and a lot of bikers passing through. It's the kind of place you want to slow down and take in.

There were lots of stops I didn't get the chance to make, like antique stores and craft shops.

To get to Cosby from Gatlinburg, you take 321 for about twenty miles until you reach a "T." Turn left there, and you'll run right into Cosby.

I stopped at *Janice's Diner* for a bite.

Janice's serves good country cooking. All the locals eat there—I could tell because when I walked in, the place went quiet, everyone looked at me, and instantly knew I was a tourist. Once I sat down, though, they went right back to their conversations.

The crowd was made up of hardworking folks on their lunch breaks—sweaty, dirty, and real, much like my own family.

The menu had everything from wings to fried mushrooms for appetizers, plus sandwiches, burgers, and the classic "meat and two" plates with a roll or cornbread.

There was also a board with $5 deals, including beef vegetable soup with crackers or cornbread.

On the counter sat six homemade cakes under glass domes—everything from chocolate to butter pecan.

The main menu had beef liver and onions (a family favorite of mine) and country fried steak with gravy. I had a hard time choosing but went with the country fried steak. Don't worry, though—I'll be back for that liver and onions before this trip is over.

Honestly, I want to spend more time in Cosby. I feel like I barely scratched the surface.

If you're ever near Cosby, TN, take the drive—and make sure you stop at Janice's Diner.

That's all for now.

306: Cabin 6/18/22

The birds outside are chirping.

From the back porch, I watch a chipmunk darting through the woods, hopping and running around like he's having the best time. I sip my coffee and just take it in.

In the distance, over Gatlinburg, fog is rising.

A bad storm rolled through last night, but now everything is peaceful. And at this moment, I'm reminded why I love coming to the mountains—why I love this cabin.

I have no plans today.

This, right here, is all I need.

307: Father's Day 2022

Happy Father's Day to all the Fathers, Dads, Daddies, Pops, Papas, Poppas, and Pas out there.

We love you.

And just for you, here's a picture of a sweet ride I spotted at the station at the bottom of the mountain. Look close—you'll see another sweet ride in the background.

308: Technology Part 1

The '80s and '90s still feel like yesterday to me.

Lately, I've been using Audible to have books read to me, and I like it. Yes, that's what I'm doing—listening while someone else reads me a book. So if someone asks, *"Read any good books lately?"* I'm not sure how to answer.

I've been preparing for this for years, really—listening to old-time radio shows like *Johnny Dollar* and *The Whistler.*

Recently, I started *The Three Musketeers.* It runs over twenty hours, which makes it perfect for long drives. On my way up here, I made it to Five. I did have to restart a few chapters because I was driving through Chattanooga traffic and couldn't concentrate.

Technology really has caught up with *The Jetsons.* We've got robot maids that vacuum our floors, people reading us books through our phones, and Bluetooth connections piping it all through our car radios.

Then at 8 p.m. Eastern, I logged into my Monday night podcast—on the very important subject of *The Andy Griffith Show.*

Not too shabby, if you ask me.

309: Cabin 6/21/22

I got up just after 7 a.m. Eastern and headed to the Log Cabin Pancake House. They've got some solid breakfast.

The place wasn't busy at all. I also noticed Crocketts Breakfast Camp wasn't busy when I drove by.

At the Log Cabin, I ordered two eggs over easy, two sausage patties, and hashbrowns, with coffee and water.

On the way back to the cabin, I stopped at the gas station and chatted with the fellas. We talked about the lack of tourists in town. Even for a weekday, this time of year should've been busier. We figured it had to do with gas prices all over the country.

While I was there, I grabbed a case of Diet Cokes and headed back to the cabin.

I planned to flip through the TV for something to nap to, but then I realized I was out of bread and milk—again.

So I drove out toward the Gatlinburg Bypass. First, I stopped for ten gallons of gas. Prices had dropped from $4.98 to $4.89 a gallon here.

Once I got onto the bypass, I had to stop almost immediately. There was a long line of cars—stretching a quarter mile or more around the curve. This wasn't just folks pulling over to watch a bear. Something was wrong.

Right then, my FreeStyle Libre diabetes alarm went off, telling me my blood sugar was low. I didn't have any sugar or carbs in the car, and I knew I couldn't just sit stuck in traffic. So I made a U-turn back to Red Light #10 and stopped at *Dad's General Store.*

I figured I'd grab a quick drink, some bread, and make a sandwich back at the cabin. But they were out of bread.

The food counter, though, was open for supper. I thought it was only for breakfast and lunch, but apparently not.

The burgers at Dad's are no joke—they take them seriously.

I ordered a double cheeseburger with bacon and pepper jack cheese, plus an order of fries. The total was just over nine dollars, which felt like a steal for a restaurant-quality burger.

I also picked up a gallon of milk and headed back to the cabin.

Now I've had my supper, stretched out on the couch, and I'm ready to settle in for the night.

That's all from me for today.

310: Cabin 6/22/22

Whenever I come up to the cabin, I try to repair or upgrade anything I'm physically able to handle. So, off to *Ace Hardware* I went.

I needed two outside floodlights to replace the ones that were out, and I picked up some single Philips head screws while I was at it. Knowing it would be hot today, I also grabbed some bottled water.

One nice thing about being up here alone in the mountains is that I can take my shirt off. That may not sound like much, but it's a big deal to me.

Since getting "Lenny" and "Squiggy"—the names I gave my colostomy and urostomy—I've developed a new appreciation for women and their bras. Sometimes you just have to take your top off and be yourself. With the heat, I wanted to minimize any chance of overheating.

I also knew that if I overdid it, my urine would turn the color of tea. So, I paid close attention to how my body was doing.

Back at the cabin, the first thing I did—after shedding my shirt—was drain the hot tub and replace the two floodlights. Then I slowly cleaned the hot tub and refilled it.

I took my time. So much time that a job that might take someone else an hour stretched from 9 a.m. until 3:45 p.m. for me.

But in the end, I got all the little jobs done and felt good—mentally and physically. It's always satisfying to finish your chores.

That's all for now.

311: The Lone Cub

Last night, around midnight, I wandered out onto the back porch because I couldn't sleep.

It was quiet, but I could hear something moving through the woods, easing its way toward the cabin. To me, it sounded like a hog. I've heard that sound before, and it usually turns out to be a hog.

Bears, on the other hand, are nearly silent. They're hard to hear.

Whatever this was, it was getting closer and closer. I had turned on the floodlights, ready to catch a glimpse when it got near.

And then I saw it—my heart sank.

It was a baby cub, only a few months old, out all alone. No mama bear in sight. That's never a good sign. The little one was only about the size of a fat raccoon.

I rarely see bears after dark. Usually they're tucked away in their dens, caves, or wherever they bed down. A cub wandering around at midnight wasn't right. If his mama were okay, she'd never have let him roam out that late.

He wandered under our porch, into the driveway, then down the mountain. I never saw or heard the mother.

In truth, I think he was out looking for her.

I went to bed saddened that night.

312: Cabin 6/24/22

Yesterday, I puttered around the cabin doing "this and that."

I may or may not have mentioned it before, but when I first got here, a bear had torn the top off the hot tub and tossed it into the yard.

And, as luck would have it, hot tub covers are on backorder all over the country. We might not have a replacement for eight weeks.

So, I bought a tarp at Ace Hardware to use as a cover. It's a good one too—8x8 with a drawstring sewn into the edges. I threw it over the tub, pulled it tight, and tied it down with straps. Easy to take off, easy to put back on.

Of course, I've already considered the possibility that the bear might tear the tarp off as well. What can you do?

While at Ace, I also stocked up on hot tub chemicals, including a floater. You put a chlorine tablet in it, and it just drifts around in the water. That little shopping trip cost me over $150. The sales lady said chlorine and bromine prices have gone through the roof. The chlorine alone was $80.

I bought test strips too. Once the water tested perfect, I set the temperature to 95 and covered it with the tarp. For the record, our hot tub runs anywhere from 80 to 104 degrees.

It was plenty hot yesterday, so I took my time. I started at 9 a.m. Eastern and didn't finish until about 4 p.m. I made sure not to overdo it.

For dinner, I kept it simple—Campbell's chicken noodle soup and three slices of cheese toast. I love dipping cheese toast into soup. And honestly, you can't go wrong with Campbell's.

That's all for now.

313: Life

It happens to everyone.

Second by second, minute by minute, hour by hour, day by day, month by month, year by year—it happens.

We see ourselves in the mirror every day, sometimes multiple times a day. Yet, we never notice it.

Then one day, while flipping through old photos, you stumble across a picture of yourself. And suddenly, you see it.

I thought about everything that happened between two such photos of me. Key family members passed away. I went through surgeries, procedures, and sickness. In one picture, I wore diapers; in the other, I had a colostomy and a urostomy. I spent over a hundred days in the hospital between those photos. And in one, 9/11 hadn't even happened yet.

The younger man in the first picture would've gotten angry if you dared call him "disabled."

The older man in the second picture has accepted the truth.

As I said, you don't see it in the mirror day by day. But it's happening all the same.

Some call it "aging."

I call it life.

And I try to live it to the fullest.

314: Cabin 6/25/22

I got a surprise visit from Mom and my Aunt.

Yep. They drove up to the Cabin and surprised me.

We had talked about them coming up sometime while I was here, but no dates were ever set.

So, I was pleasantly surprised.

I want to take them over to Cosby, TN., visit some of the shops, and maybe grab a bite to eat. I'm already thinking Liver and Onions.

This morning, I brewed a cup of coffee and sat on the porch, listening to the sounds of the mountain waking up. Chipmunks scurried through dry leaves, birds called back and forth, and the tram rumbled by with passengers on their way to Ober Gatlinburg. I sipped my coffee slowly, taking it all in.

Mom poked her head out the door and said, "I'm heating up the fried apple pies for breakfast. Do you want me to heat one up for you?"

"Yes, please. Thank you," I answered.

And quietly to myself, I thought: *It's gonna be a good day.*

315: Cabin 6/26/22

Yesterday, as we walked out to Mom's vehicle to head out for dinner, we noticed something odd—her back door was wide open. Turns out she had unlocked the car but never re-locked it. Long story short: the Bear had gotten into her vehicle.

Luckily, we had already carried in all the food and their bags. The Bear didn't get anything—just snooped around and left. Still, muddy paw prints covered the seats, and we had some cleaning up to do.

Once the car was in decent shape, the three of us went to eat at *A Taste of Italy* off Highway 321. If you've never been, you really should. It's owned by a husband-and-wife team, and they're some of the kindest people you'll meet.

She's from Brooklyn, with that thick accent that could cut through concrete. He wears a big cowboy hat, vest, and boots—the whole western getup. He swears his food is better than "that other Italian restaurant." Personally, I think both places have their own charm.

We ate well, laughed plenty, and ended the night with a few pictures.

316: Storms

Sunday evening, storms rolled through—thunder and lightning cracking across the sky. Most of the Southeast got hit, and some places even took damage.

Me? I was asleep.

I put on *Everybody Loves Raymond*, pulled a blanket over myself on the couch, and drifted off. But the thunder was fierce, shaking the cabin. It woke me more than once, and each time I shot up screaming. Thunder tends to stir up my night terrors.

Now the storms have passed, and silence has settled back over the mountains.

It's 1:45 AM Eastern, and I'm wide awake. Thought I'd sit here and write a bit in my journal.

317: Bear Names

We had another visitor today at the cabin. A big one.

No cubs followed, so I'm guessing this was a male. And since I can't really tell bears apart, I stick with the names I've made up:

- All grown males are "Grady."
- All grown females are "Gladys."
- Cubs are "Gary."

This one? Definitely a Grady. And a big 'ol boy at that.

318: Cabin 6/28/22

It dawned on me today that this trip has really been about the wildlife.

There's a rabbit I named "Bugsy" who seems to live nearby. The chipmunk who darts around the porch is "Monk." Of course, the bears all fall into the Grady/Gladys/Gary system.

I finally got the hot tub cleaned out and covered—at least until the proper lid arrives. The last one got torn up when a bear tossed it off the porch like it was nothing. For now, a heavy-duty tarp will have to do. Not glamorous, but it works. Since I drained the water, the bears seem to have lost interest. None have wandered onto the porch since.

Another task I had this trip was hiring a new cleaning crew. That got done early on. Prices have gone up—like everything else lately.

Before the trip is over, Mom, my Aunt, and I want to eat at *Janice's Diner* in Cosby. I've heard their Beef Liver and Onions are worth the drive.

Today, though, I scheduled a meeting with the new cleaning lady so Mom and my Aunt could meet her.

That's all for now.

319: Cabin – Last Day

I've been here since June 8th—almost a month.

Mom and my Aunt came up seven days ago, and I've enjoyed having them here. Tomorrow, we all leave.

So what do you do on your last day at the cabin? Pack? Nope. Mom decided it was the perfect time to rearrange the entire upstairs. On the last day.

I'll admit, it does look better. But we had a whole week, and it still ended up happening today.

After that, we went to *Cracker Barrel*. I ordered a steak—my first one from there. Not bad at all. My Aunt and Uncle surprised us by picking up the check.

I haven't packed a single thing yet, so tomorrow morning will be a rush. The plan is for Mom and me to caravan home, with my Aunt riding shotgun in Mom's car.

I didn't get out much this trip. That was the plan—I wanted to save money for my July trip to Mt. Airy, NC, for the "Mayberry Meet-Up." That's only a couple of weeks away now, and I'm really looking forward to it. Mom and my Aunt will join me for that one, too.

Tomorrow morning, July 1st, we'll head home.

It's been a great trip.

That's all for now.

320: Home

I arrived back home at 5:30 PM Central Time today.

I'm going to hit the sack for now—maybe tomorrow too.

Thanks for going along with me on the trip.

321: A Haunting

I don't believe in haunted houses or anything like that. That's just me. Some folks in my family do, but I never have.

Now, I do believe in the Holy Spirit—don't get me wrong there.

People used to say the house that Mom and Papa built was haunted. My oldest brother swears the house we lived in was haunted too. But I never believed it.

On my way home from the Cabin, though, my beliefs got tested.

My phone hooks to my vehicle's radio through Bluetooth. That way everything is hands-free. Out of the blue, my phone started calling people. My radio started playing music I didn't even have on my phone. I rebooted it.

Back to listening to XM Old-Timey Radio—"Johnny Dollar," to be exact. Then suddenly, bands I'd never listened to started playing. Looked like they were coming from my phone, but I knew better. Then my phone dialed my oldest brother. I hit "hang up" and rebooted again.

This time, a preacher's voice came over the radio, telling me about Jesus.

I said out loud, "Okay, Jesus. You obviously want me to hear something. I'll listen." Then my phone dialed another number. I said,

"I ain't talking to a stranger, though, Jesus. You gotta give me who, what, when, and where."

So I sat there, convinced I was caught up in something supernatural.

Then I pulled up the "Settings" on my radio. And there it was: Mom's cell phone had connected to my radio. Since I was following her home from Gatlinburg, I was close enough for her Bluetooth to latch on. And my phone? Connected to her radio in her car.

I was kinda bummed. Thought I'd been part of something supernatural.

Unpaired her phone from my radio and mine from hers. Problem solved.

But still—bummed.

(Oh, and the same thing was happening in Mom's vehicle. Except she was listening to "Johnny Dollar.")

322: 4th of July 2022

This year's 4th of July was a good one.

My Aunt and Uncle came over, and we grilled hamburgers and hot dogs.

Afterward, my Aunt and Uncle broke out the homemade ice cream maker. If you've never had homemade ice cream, you're missing out. It's as American as apple pie. (Don't spoil it by Googling where ice cream or apple pie really came from.)

Her recipe called for heavy cream. Mom said half-and-half would work, but it really needed the heavy cream. Still turned out delicious. We also had banana pudding. My diabetes alarm went crazy after that dessert.

Later, Papa, my Uncle, and I watched two funny movies back-to-back: *St. Vincent* and *Murder Mystery*. Both rated PG-13, but back when I was growing up, they would've been rated "R."

Then I headed to our "Small Town, USA" fireworks show in front of the middle school. About a thousand people showed up. The local wrecker company had a big American flag waving. Kids ran around chasing each other. A live band played old songs like "Little Red Riding Hood" from 1966.

The crowd counted down from ten, and the fireworks began.

In that moment, I was proud to live in a small town. Proud to be an American.

Happy 4th of July.

323: *The Shopping List*

Mom emailed me a shopping list, and I volunteered to go to "The Pig" for her.

I opened it up. "Oh. This is a lot. I thought you just needed milk and maybe eggs."

"You can un-volunteer if you want to."

"No, I'll get it. Just a lot more than I thought," I said, running my hand through my hair.

Honestly, I volunteered because I enjoy listening to podcasts and old-time radio while I drive. With gas prices the way they are, I don't get out and just drive anymore. Too expensive. So whenever I can justify it, I do.

Now, Mom would take two hours with this list. She browses, compares. I don't. I figured I could do it in 30 minutes flat.

I left the house at 5:45 PM CST, pulled into "The Pig" at 5:58, and was inside by 6:00.

From there, it was poetry in motion. Bananas in the bag, into the buggy. Lemons, carrots, celery, asparagus. People stepped aside. One lady whispered into her phone, "Honey, it's over. I just found the one."

An old man told his wife, "That's how you shop, honey."

Dairy aisle: two hunks of extra sharp cheese, six sticks of cream cheese. Bakery: fresh bread. Buggy wheel locked, but I muscled through.

Two boxes of strawberry Jell-O. Broccoli. French onion soup. Spinach. Strawberries.

I was lightning. A machine.

Checkout time. Two teenage girls working. One on the register, one bagging. The cashier was mid-breakup with her boyfriend Chad. Everything slowed to a crawl.

I tapped my fingers, tapped my foot, hummed along with the overhead music.

Finally, "$143.75, sir."

"Yes!" I swiped my card, pushed my buggy out the door, and loaded up.

Back home by 6:30 CST.

And that's how I shop.

324: A Stye in My Eye

♪There's a stye in my eye,♪ sung to the tune of Hank Williams' *There's a Tear in My Beer*.

I've never had a stye in my eye—or even pink eye—until today.

I woke up around 5 a.m. and couldn't open my left eye. It was swollen shut.

Naturally, I panicked. I hurried to the mirror, and what I saw didn't help. I panicked more.

"Mom! Wake up! My Spina Bifida has gone to my eye!" I said in a half-joking tone. I think I tried to laugh it off just to calm myself, but honestly, it didn't help.

By 8 a.m., I managed to get a telehealth video appointment with my doctor.

The appointment went smoothly. I leaned right into the camera so he could get a good look.

"It feels just like a sprained ankle—except in my eyelid," I told him.

He laughed, but I meant it. That's exactly how it feels. The same pain I sometimes get in my left foot, only this time it's parked on my eyelid.

Anyway, the doctor confirmed it was a stye and sent a prescription over to my pharmacy.

I thought about posting a picture here, but trust me—it looks rough. Maybe even a little scary.

For now, I've been pressing a hot wet rag on my eye throughout the day. The heating pad too—the doctor said that was fine.

That's all for now.

325: Stye Update

Here's the latest on me.

The combination of everything I've been doing actually seems to be working.

A hot teabag, a warm washcloth, the heating pad, and the antibiotics together are finally making a difference.

With a little luck, I should be better in time for my upcoming trip to Mt. Airy, NC.

Here's a picture that isn't too bad to look at. I won't show what my eye really looks like, it's pretty rough and maybe even a little frightening.

That's all for now.

326: '80s Christmas Party

The 1980s.

My late brother Tony and I once had to attend a Christmas party hosted by one of Mom's friends.

In our minds, this particular friend was rich. At least, she seemed that way to us.

She and her husband drove what looked like a 1940s-style car—if I had to guess, maybe a Triumph Roadster.

Their home was old and elegant, surrounded by tall trees with stone walkways winding through the yard, leading everywhere, even to a swimming pool. A pool! To us, that sealed it: they were rich.

The yard itself was like a flower garden, colorful blooms lining the paths.

It was Christmas, 1980-something, and inside the house were several Christmas trees. I had never seen a home with more than one tree before.

The house was two stories with multiple fireplaces—one in nearly every bedroom and another in each sitting room. To us, it was as fancy and "rich" as it got.

We were served tiny crystal glasses filled with warm apple cider and cinnamon. People in suits and ties mingled as Christmas music floated through the rooms, though I never once saw a speaker. The music just seemed to exist in the air.

Tony and I wandered around, wide-eyed. That's when I spotted it.

"Look! Rich food!" I whispered to Tony.

On a tray were neatly arranged vegetables, cut into perfect little pieces and circled around a bowl of thick, white dip.

I watched carefully as a man used tongs to put vegetables on his plate, then a spoon to scoop the dip. Nervous but determined, I followed his lead exactly—tongs first, then spoon. My hands shook a little as I loaded my plate with broccoli and a spoonful of that mysterious dip.

"Rich food," I told Tony. He nodded in agreement.

I dipped the broccoli, took a bite, and nearly shouted.

"Holy cow! You gotta taste this!"

Tony hurried to get his own plate.

"Mmm-mmm!" he said after trying it. "That's great! I wonder what it's called."

Curious, I went over to our hostess.

"Ma'am, what's this dip called?" I asked.

"It's called Ranch Dressing," she said with a smile. "It's good, isn't it?"

"Yes, ma'am. It's delicious."

And from that moment on, Tony and I were hooked.

To this day, in my mind, Ranch Dressing will always be "rich people's" dressing.

327: Mt. Airy 2022

My trip to Mt. Airy, NC, is just around the corner.

This Wednesday, around 1 p.m., Mom, my Aunt, and I will head out for this year's *Mayberry Meet-Up*. I'm really looking forward to it.

Most of you know I'm a big fan of *The Andy Griffith Show*, or as we fans call it, "TAGS." Each year, fans gather in Andy Griffith's hometown of Mt. Airy to celebrate the show and the world of Mayberry.

At night, over a hundred of us set up lawn chairs and watch episodes of TAGS projected on a big outdoor screen. There's even a gazebo on the property where, late at night, groups gather to sit and talk all things TAGS.

The drive is about nine and a half hours, so we usually split it into two days. I can usually make it to Dandridge, TN, the home of the Bush's Baked Beans factory, before stopping.

This year, I've been told we *will not* be staying at any $79-a-night motels. Personally, I don't mind the cheap ones. I grew up that way and actually like them—the big old A/C unit under the window that runs all night, the temperature cranked into the 60s while I drift off to its steady whirl. I sleep great that way. But not this trip. I've been informed we'll be staying in places with "quiet" A/C units and breakfast in the morning. At least a Continental one.

The Mayberry Motor Inn, where we stay once in Mt. Airy, is an older motel, but to me that's part of the Mayberry experience. Out front sits a '60s Ford Galaxy patrol car, and one of the rooms is dedicated entirely to Aunt Bee. Many of the items inside came from the estate auction of Frances Bavier after she passed. Looking around that room feels like stepping into another time—Mayberry, USA.

The property itself is charming, with a well-kept lawn and, of course, the gazebo. That gazebo is the icing on the cake. A quiet place to sit, to talk, or just to think. Some people bring board games—like the official TAGS game, and play into the evening. I usually prefer just sitting and soaking it all in.

There's always plenty to do in Mt. Airy, and I'll try to hit the highlights during the day. But the real magic happens at night, under the stars, when we gather together to watch one of the greatest television shows in American history. We arrive as strangers but leave as friends, and isn't that the heart of Mayberry?

328: Mt. Airy – 7/14/22

We pulled into the Mayberry Motor Inn later than I expected.

The Motor Inn is the main place where us TAGS fans stay when we come to Mt. Airy. I had hoped to arrive around noon, but traffic on the interstate had other plans. Backed-up lanes and long delays turned the trip into a test of patience.

At one point, I felt like Malcolm Tucker in the "Man in a Hurry" episode, honking my horn, slamming the brakes, muttering under my breath at other drivers. I was in a hurry! A hurry to get to… Mayberry. And then, just like the preacher's words that startled Gomer awake, it hit me: *What's your hurry?*

So I eased off the gas, slowed my mind, and, just like that, everything seemed to work itself out.

Near Fancy Gap, I exited the interstate, and within thirty minutes, I was easing into the parking lot of the Mayberry Motor Inn.

We checked in, got our room key, and unpacked. Then I made a quick run to the local Dollar General for supplies—Duke's Mayonnaise and Wonder Bread, the essentials.

The room is nice. I'm told it was renovated last year. I unpacked my laptop, tested the internet, turned on the TV to MeTV, and settled in.

All is well in Mayberry.

329: Mt. Airy – 7/15/22

The Mayberry Meet-Up has been a wonderful success.

Not many people know this about me, but I'm naturally shy in social situations. It takes me a while to warm up and even longer to start conversations. But there's something different about this place.

Here in Mayberry, I come out of my shell. I think many others do, too.

Tonight I talked with so many people. Some I walked over to myself, others who came over to me. Either way, it was easy, natural. In high school, I always felt out of place at gatherings, too nervous to say much. Here, it's the opposite. Here, you can walk up to anyone, start talking, and be welcomed.

And so tonight, under the stars, I found myself at one of the best "get-togethers" I've ever attended. We laughed, shared stories, and enjoyed one another's company while *The Andy Griffith Show* played in the background.

I don't know if it's something in the dirt or the air, but there's a certain magic in this place. And I know it's real, because I felt it tonight.

330: School Pranks

Seventh grade.

Back then, I didn't tell anyone I had Spina Bifida—or, more importantly to me—that I wore a diaper. I also had zero feeling in my butt cheeks.

At school, kids loved pranks. I'm sure they still do.

One of the classics was taping a thumbtack to someone's chair. This time, my desk was the chosen one.

As I walked down the aisle, I could hear the giggling. I sat down. Nothing. No pain, no reaction. I didn't feel a thing because, well, I had no feeling back there.

"Must've split the cheeks," Jerry whispered to another kid.

I pulled out my books and faced forward, but I could sense all the guys staring at me.

"What?" I asked.

"Lynn, can you stand up?" one said.

I knew then that I must be sitting on something.

"Nope. Not getting up. What is it?"

Jerry grinned. "It's not what you're sitting *in*—it's what you're sitting *on*."

"What is it?"

"A thumbtack," he replied.

I reached under, and sure enough, there it was—right in my cheek. I pulled it out without showing anyone my backside. Luckily, no blood.

Then I held the tack up in the air and proudly announced, "Split the cheeks, fellas! Better luck next time."

331: The Flora-Bama

I ran across a photo from 2013 and remembered the day instantly.

I was at the Flora-Bama, a bar-slash-club that sits right on the Alabama–Florida line. That's where the name comes from: Flora-Bama.

That day, I was eating oysters with my niece—and maybe a nephew, too. Between us, we polished off eight dozen oysters. At nine dollars a dozen, it was a feast.

The wooden tables inside were all covered in signatures. The walls, too. Everyone seemed to carve or write their name somewhere.

So, of course, I signed the table.

I sometimes wonder if my name is still there, waiting to be found.

332: Unpacking

I haven't posted since July 20th. I guess the trip wore me out more than usual. It was a great trip, though.

This morning I woke up just before six. Breakfast was four pieces of cheese toast and a cup of coffee, eaten out on the front porch while listening to the birds.

Last night I did the same—sat on the porch—but listened instead to crickets, locusts, and bullfrogs. We've got a fountain out back where a giant bullfrog lives, along with a bunch of little ones. At one point, even a hoot owl called in the distance.

I've rested up now, but tomorrow I'll finally start unpacking my luggage. Yep—still haven't done it. Like I said, that trip really took it out of me. But it was worth it.

333: A Round To It

Lately, I've been sticking close to home.

The little garden I planted earlier this year has given all it's going to give—better luck next season.

Summer heat has been steady in the 90s, so we've been bringing the dogs inside during the day. My dog, Tommy, doesn't care for it. He'll tolerate being indoors for a bit, but he'd rather be outside.

Today I treated myself and went to Jack's, the local fast-food joint. I ordered a Number 2: bacon burger, fries, and a drink. I even large-sized it. The bill came to just under ten bucks. That's when I realized just how much fast food prices have climbed.

Afterward, I drove the back roads home, taking in the countryside. I try to do that often—living in the country, I like to soak up the scenery. "Broadway Is My Beat" was playing on XM's Old Time Radio station, which made the ride even better.

Now I'm back home. My suitcase is still unpacked, but I'll get around to it.

That phrase makes me think of Paw Paw. He once had a round piece of steel with the words *To It* printed on the front. On the back, it read: *Now that you have a Round To It, do it!*

I have plans to hang out with a friend soon, and I'm looking forward to that.

That's all for now.

334: I'm Outta Here

I've always had a hard time making friends. I have my reasons.

Growing up, I kept my Spina Bifida a secret. I kept the fact that I wore a diaper a secret. I tried to keep *everything* a secret. And now, I'll try to explain why.

First, let me say this: nobody reading this knows the person in this story. He's not from my hometown, and he's not from yours. He shall remain nameless. In fact, I'll just call him "Nameless."

"Nameless" and I became friends fast, almost overnight. Have you ever met someone and felt like you'd known them forever? That's how it was. I was on cloud nine just to have this new friend.

He came over to my house nearly every day, and we'd hang out. We both played guitar, so we'd jam together.

I hadn't told him about my Spina Bifida, and I wasn't planning to.

One day, I made the mistake of leaving him alone in my bedroom while I walked out to the mailbox. As I was flipping through the mail, he walked out of the house, heading for the road. He passed me at the mailbox, and the words he spoke have echoed in my night terrors ever since.

"You wear diapers, and I'm outta here."

And he kept walking.

I raced back inside, dreading what I'd find. My medical supplies—usually carefully hidden—were laid out in the middle of the floor. He'd found them all.

We never spoke again.

That moment altered my life. I hated myself. I hated my Spina Bifida. I hated people. And worst of all, I turned my anger toward God. I vowed never to tell anyone about my condition.

For years, I blamed myself for that broken friendship. If only I'd hidden my supplies better, maybe we'd still be friends. I carried guilt and shame, and resentment toward God, for a long time.

As an adult, he probably doesn't even remember saying those words. But I never forgot them:

"You wear diapers, and I'm outta here."

Later in life, once I began having night terrors, those same words found their way into my dreams again and again.

That's why I've always struggled to make friends.

In fact, I was friends with my best friend for ten years before I finally told him about my diapers. Ten years. I don't drink anymore, but back then I did. One night after we'd both had too much, I told him.

I'll never forget his reaction:

"You waited TEN YEARS to tell me? TEN YEARS? Lynn, you should've told me long ago. We're friends."

Those words changed me. They may have even saved me and set me back on the right track. Because of him, I eventually learned to be open. Today, I tell people within the first hour of meeting them.

Sometimes I'm *too* open. Once, on a first date, before the appetizers even arrived, I blurted it all out:

"I have Spina Bifida. I have a colostomy and urostomy. I hear the fried pickles are good. Want to order an appetizer? Oh, and by the way, I can't have sex."

So yes, I struggle with friendships and dating. And it all traces back to that one moment.

Words can be stronger than a nuclear weapon. I know that firsthand. He probably wouldn't dream of saying such a thing today. Kids can be cruel. But I've never forgotten it.

And I don't think I ever will.

I know this story is a bit heavy, but it's part of my journey. It belongs here. This is *Walking with Spina Bifida.*

335: 7/28/2022

I got up early this morning around 6 a.m. and let Tommy out.

Then I ran to the gas station to pick up a few things for my outing today. I was heading out with two friends, a husband and wife.

I grabbed a couple of sugared drinks in case my blood sugar went low, and three boxes of Whoppers, one for each of us. I figured if I was buying some for myself, they ought to have their own, too. I tossed a couple Diet Cokes in the bag for me, and I filled my cargo pockets with medical supplies, just in case.

I noticed I really need a haircut.

Good morning, and have a great day.

—

Later that day…

I had a *great* time.

I met up with my friends, and together we headed to Jasper, Alabama, to visit the grave of George Lindsey. You might know him as "Goober" from *The Andy Griffith Show.* He was born and raised in Alabama, and when he passed, he was buried in his hometown of Jasper.

My friends picked me up at the Park and Ride off the interstate in Hayden, Alabama—right at the bottom of the hill where I live. From there, we took the Warrior–Jasper Road straight to Goober's grave.

After paying our respects, we walked the streets of Jasper, soaking in the beauty of the town. To me, it looked like a picture-perfect American town—full of mom-and-pop shops and local restaurants.

We stopped at Son's Smokehouse for lunch. If I'm not mistaken, the place was part of a larger building that also housed Son's Grocery and Son's Pharmacy. I'd like to learn more about that family and how they started and grew all three businesses. Maybe next trip. For now, I can tell you the BBQ sandwich and sweet tea were both delicious.

I was enjoying myself so much—just living in the moment—that I only took a couple of pictures.

My friend is just as big a Mayberry fan as I am, so we had plenty to talk about.

All in all, it was a beautiful day.

336: The Engagement Party

Oxford, Alabama was the city.

Hubbard's Off Main was the location.

The occasion? An engagement party.

Whose? One of my nephews and his beautiful fiancée. (They deserve their privacy, so I'll leave it at that.)

Hubbard's sits off Choccolocco Street, a name I love to say. Chocc-o-locco.

The party was in the banquet room, while in the main restaurant a two-person band played. One on guitar, the other on keys. As I walked in, they were playing Bob Seger's *Against the Wind.*

The restaurant was full of charm, decorated with antique furniture—some of it dating back to the '50s. The walls were exposed red brick, and the floor was worn wood that carried decades of footsteps.

Off to the side sat an old-fashioned phone booth. Dark brown wood, with a door you could close behind you for privacy. Inside was a wooden chair and a phone directory. I stepped inside, shut the door, and for a moment, it felt like another era. The payphone accepted nickels, dimes, and quarters.

And before you ask, no. I didn't try it. I was too nervous I might break it. Imagine being scared to touch a payphone because it was an antique! Yet there I was.

Back in the banquet room, people mingled at heavy old dining tables. I like restaurants that use real tables like that. It makes it feel more like home.

There was a cash bar, with one waitress running drinks like a pro. Two buffet tables offered finger foods: sausage balls, chicken nuggets, BBQ smoked wieners, a vegetable tray with ranch dip, and more. I made two trips. Even grabbed some broccoli with ranch, and let me tell you, I felt downright fancy eating it.

Games were played with the bride, groom, and guests. Laughter, applause, and cheers filled the night. We celebrated the young couple, all of us together.

And through it all, I could almost feel the spirit of my late brother Tony there with us.

337: Restroom Stalls

Back in my drinking days, a lot of bars had restrooms with no stall doors.

Now, changing a diaper in a stall is already tough enough. Take away the door, throw in strangers walking in and out—it can be overwhelming. Even managing a colostomy can get complicated in that situation.

That's when a true friend comes in handy.

I've been in restrooms with four stalls and not a single door, not even on the handicapped stall. In those moments, your buddy becomes the door. He stands guard, facing the other way, and says things like, "Nothin' to see here, keep it movin'."

And that's how you know if you've got a real friend.

338: The Bachelor

When I first moved out on my own, I had to learn to handle things myself, including shopping.

I'll never forget my first grocery trip.

There I was, pushing my buggy down the aisle when I spotted something I didn't know existed: cake icing. Sold right there in the store! I picked up a tub of chocolate icing and stared at it.

"You've got to be kidding me," I muttered. "All this time I've been licking the spoon, when I could've just bought the stuff outright? Toss it in the buggy. Grab some vanilla, too."

Back home, I decided to cook dinner. Ten minutes in, I was already lost. Like so many new bachelors, I picked up the phone to call Mom.

"Mom, I'm trying to make Hamburger Helper, and I'm confused…"

I could hear the disappointment in her sigh.

"Honey, Hamburger Helper should be easy. What's the problem?"

"Well, it says to brown the ground beef."

"Yes, you need to brown the beef."

"That's just it—the box doesn't have any ground beef in it."

Silence.

"Am I wrong? Did I already mess this up?"

"Son..."

"Yeah?"

"Ahem..."

"What?"

"It's called *Hamburger Helper*, son."

"I'm lost. What do you mean?"

"Do you really think they'd put raw ground beef in a box and sit it out on a grocery shelf?"

"OHHH. Hamburger *Helper*! Okay, I get it now. My bad."

She sighed again. "So what are you going to eat tonight?"

"Chocolate cake icing."

And honestly, it's no wonder I'm diabetic now.

339: The Dentist

This week I went to the dentist for my six-month cleaning.

I hate going to the dentist. Hate it. I fear it. The same goes for haircuts. Both make me anxious.

Once they put that smock around your neck, you're trapped until they're done. And that freaks me out.

As a kid, something must have happened to me in that chair, something my mind buried. It isn't the cleaning or the haircut itself I dread; it's being stuck there, unable to move until they finish.

The hygienist sat me down, put protective glasses on me, and leaned me back. I mentioned I have twenty screws in my jaw from surgery and warned her I might need breaks to close my mouth. My jaw aches when it's open too long.

On top of that, I have a tiny mouth, which makes her job harder. Sometimes she uses this little spring apparatus that props my mouth open wider. It helps.

I closed my eyes, and she began scraping my teeth. Top first, then bottom.

When I opened my eyes, her nose was two inches from my face. She looked like she was staring straight into my eyes, though I knew she was focused on my teeth. Still, it felt weird. I shut my eyes again.

My fists were clenched tight.

Then came the electrical tools, buzzing and whining like fingernails on a chalkboard.

"You doing okay, Mr. Thomas?" she asked.

"Uh-huh," I mumbled.

"We're almost finished."

I tried to relax, but my whole body was wound up tight. Tighter than a ten-cent top, as Andy Griffith would say.

"Almost done!" she promised.

In my head, I started singing: ♪ *She'll be comin' 'round the mountain when she comes…* ♪

"Wheee-eeeeee," the tool whined.

Finally, she said, "All done! I'll floss you now, then the dentist will take a look."

She flossed, I rinsed and spit, and then the dentist gave me a quick once-over. Everything looked fine.

I scheduled my next six-month visit, said goodbye at the desk, and walked out.

Next on my to-do list? A haircut.

But I'm not quite mentally ready for that yet. Maybe in a few days.

340: People Watching

10:57 p.m.

I pulled into the parking lot of a little breakfast place. Only five cars were there, including mine. I was craving steak and eggs—and some coffee.

Inside, I sat at the bar.

"You need a menu, sweety?" the waitress asked.

"Not tonight," I told her, ordering steak, eggs, hashbrowns, and coffee.

Ten minutes later, muddy Chevy and Ford trucks began filling the lot.

"Get ready!" one waitress yelled. "The concert's over. Here they come!"

And just like that, the quiet diner was packed. Cowboy hats and boots everywhere.

My food arrived, and I dug in while people-watching.

A man fed the jukebox, and soon Tim McGraw's *I Like It, I Love It* blasted out. The whole place sang along. I cut another bite of steak.

The waitress leaned in and shouted, "You need a refill?"

"Yes, please!" I shouted back.

Next up was Garth Brooks' *Friends in Low Places.* Again, the entire crowd sang at the top of their lungs.

I forked up some eggs and watched.

More people crowded in, but every booth and stool was taken. Some had to stand and wait.

"You gonna need that ketchup?" my neighbor asked.

"Nope, have at it," I said, sliding the bottle his way.

The jukebox switched to Hank Williams Jr.'s *A Country Boy Can Survive.* Glasses went up in the air as the crowd sang.

By now, I was wiping my mouth with my napkin.

"You through eatin', sweety?" my waitress asked.

I wanted to linger, but she needed my seat. A line of twenty people stretched to the door.

"Yes, ma'am, I'm finished," I said, handing her my card.

"You just came on a bad night," she apologized. "A big concert let out."

I smiled. I knew that. I had planned it. The same thing happened last year, and I promised myself I'd come back again just to people-watch.

I signed my check, stood up, and called out: "See ya next year!"

341: Spaghetti

Mom said she was making spaghetti for supper tonight.

A while back, I'd written about learning her sauce recipe. So this time I told her I'd handle dinner.

First stop: The Pig.

Like most Southerners, we put ground beef in our sauce. Into the buggy it went. Next, bell pepper, sweet onion, and a jar of Prego. We buy the sauce, then "doctor" it up with our own fresh ingredients. Herbs and spices, too—but I'll keep those a family secret.

I grabbed a loaf of homemade garlic bread from the bakery before heading home.

By the time Papa picked up one of my nieces from school, everything was nearly ready.

This niece is picky. The kind who wrinkles her nose at anything green.

As she walked in, I said, "Hey, I've been working like crazy in this kitchen, and you're gonna eat tonight. Turns out what Grammy does is really hard! You know those onions, peppers, and other 'stuff' that ends up in our food? Somebody has to chop it all up and cook it. Cooking ain't easy. So you need to eat whatever Grammy makes."

She shrugged. "Papa took me to get food on the way home."

So much for my speech.

The rest of us, though, enjoyed the spaghetti. And honestly, it was pretty good.

342: The Haircut

I made my way to Miss Margaret's today for a haircut.

No, not a barbershop. There isn't one close by where I live. Out here in the country, those are few and far between.

Miss Margaret has a little shop on the bottom floor of her house. A real, licensed "hair-cutting shop"—I'm not calling it a "salon." It even has a health inspection rating posted on the wall.

It had been so long since my last haircut that I forgot how I usually got it trimmed.

"Just use a three guard on the whole thing," I told her.

She quickly corrected me, shaking her head. "No, Lynn. We use a three on the sides and blend the top."

"Yes, ma'am. That. Do that."

The nice thing about Miss Margaret's shop is that she books one customer at a time. No waiting room, no audience. Just you and her.

Back when I lived in the city, I went to barbers. After moving out here, the choices dwindled. We had a "Quick Cuts" at one time, but it went under.

Margaret does hair for a lot of elderly and sick folks. I'm sure she's even done hair for the deceased, making them look good for their viewing.

Over the years, my Aunt Gail cut my hair, too. (Love you, Aunt Gail!) She's retired now.

I do miss the days of sitting in an old barbershop, but out here in the country, there just isn't enough demand.

Miss Margaret keeps up pleasant conversation while she works, which makes the whole thing easier.

So, the point is: I finally got my haircut today.

343: Feeling – The Furnace Grate Story

1978

I was three years old.

Now, I don't remember this myself, but I've heard the story all my life.

I was developing normally for a kid with Spina Bifida. Walking right on time. Everything seemed fine, except I couldn't feel my legs or bottom.

One day, Mom had just bathed me. She stood me up and said, "Let me grab a towel for my big boy."

While she was gone, I sat myself right down on the floor furnace grate.

Those grates get blistering hot. I sat there happily while it burned my skin, the skin I couldn't feel.

Mom came back, saw me, and screamed, "NOOO!" as she rushed to pull me up.

The grate had left marks like grill lines across my little backside.

My bottom was no longer "smooth like a baby's bottom."

At the ER, Mom explained Spina Bifida, and the doctors bandaged me up, sending her home with medicine.

Do I still have the marks? I'll let you wonder. (They're gone.)

That brings me to today:

Papa and I went to Wild Wings for supper. We love wings around here.

We ordered thirty—bone-in. On the drive home, I set the bag on my lap.

About five minutes in, Papa touched the bottom of the bag and said, "Get that off your legs. It's scalding hot!"

Sure enough, it was. I moved it quickly.

Life in this body is different sometimes. But one thing's for sure: it's never boring.

344: Friday Night Drive

Highway 160, Blount County, Alabama—the country.

It's dark out as I drive back home.

My speed? 50.

The speed limit? 55.

The speed everyone else drives? 70.

Luckily, not many others are on the road tonight.

"Dragnet" is playing on the radio.

I pass big country yards, three acres or more per home. Cows graze in fields, and small fishing ponds reflect bits of moonlight as I roll by.

The windows are down, my arm resting on the sill, the night air rushing through.

On the way, I come to a roundabout. Our area fought hard over putting it in. Some for it, some against it. Me? I don't see the problem. A roundabout's a roundabout.

A deer appears ahead. I slow down. Sure enough, it darts across the road. Luckily, I've already eased up on the gas, so it crosses safely. Once it's clear, I speed back up.

On the radio, Joe Friday is after "smack dealers." The wind runs through my hair, and for a moment, I don't feel like a forty-something-year-old man headed home. I feel like a teenager again, out on a Friday night with freedom ahead.

Life's good like that sometimes.

345: The Piggly Wiggly

August 15, 2022.

Tonight, my brother and his family are coming over. Nothing big, just a small get-together. I decide to make a cheese tray. So, off to *The Pig* I go.

As I head inside, a little old lady is pushing her buggy out. She smiles and says, "If I'd been a little quicker, you could've used my buggy. Only got these two bags."

"I'll take your buggy, ma'am," I say, and she hands it over.

"God bless you, sir."

"God bless you too, ma'am."

I roll inside.

The Piggly Wiggly in my town has a nice little section for meats and cheeses. I grab some peppered salami, pepperoni sticks, and four different cheeses. Next goes a jar of olives stuffed with garlic, a jar of sweet gherkins, and a jar of pickled okra. Then I head to the cracker aisle.

A lady there is looking hard for a certain brand. She asks if I can help. We look together, but the shelf is empty.

"Out of stock, ma'am," I say.

"Oh, shucks! Thank you for helping me, sir."

"Well, ma'am, maybe you can return the favor. If you were making a meat and cheese tray, which crackers would you get?"

Her face lights up. "Oh, that's easy!" She grabs four boxes and drops them into my buggy.

"These!"

"Perfect," I grin. "You just made my job simple."

"You're welcome. God bless you, sir."

"God bless you too, ma'am."

That's small-town living for you.

346: Morning Drive

I went for an early morning drive today.

The fog hung low over the mountain, beautiful and still. From the top, I looked out and saw peaks poking through like little islands. The fog stretched between them like an ocean.

Further down, I passed the duck pond. The lead duck suddenly took off, flying right alongside my truck as if he were escorting me. He stayed with me until I reached the stop sign, then turned back toward the pond.

"Thanks for the escort!" I laughed.

I thought to myself, *It's gonna be a good day.*

Good morning, everyone.

347: The Kid

A diner.

I'm sitting alone.

I scan the room and notice a young guy, also by himself.

He looks maybe 18 to 22 years old. Thin, with an oily face and long hair—like Axl Rose in the '80s, just without the headband and hat. Tough-looking, hardened.

He leans on the table, arms crossed, his eyes darting. First to the left, scanning the room. Then to the right. Distrust written all over him. He doesn't trust the world, and it shows. You can tell when someone has carried too much, too young. His shoulders sag with it.

The waitress sets down his plate: eggs, bacon, hashbrowns, and toast. A cup of coffee.

That's when I notice the tattoo on his right arm.

It says *Mom*.

Underneath are two dates—her birth date and… her death date.

In that moment, I know. He isn't a kid at all. He grew up a long time ago.

348: High School Football Game

Tonight, Papa, the girls, and I went to a local high school football game. Mortimer Jordan versus Leeds.

High school games sure have changed since I was in school. Back then, you walked up to the gate, and a lady with a little cash box would take your money. Cash only. That was it.

Tonight? Tickets were bought online. Nine dollars each, through an app on a smartphone, and all you do is flash your phone at the gate. Technology has even reached Friday night lights. I was impressed.

We arrived about 45 minutes early so Papa could find a good parking spot and we could grab seats near the bottom of the stands. First stop for me: concessions. No line yet, so I pounced. Nachos with jalapeños and a hot dog, because you can't go to a game without having a hot dog. That's practically un-American. Later, during the fourth quarter, I even treated myself to a slice of pepperoni pizza.

The girls met up with their friends and spent most of the game doing what kids do best—walking around, laughing, and being teenagers.

The game itself was solid, though Mortimer Jordan lost:

Leeds—21

MJ—7

Still, it was a good night. Knock on wood, my blood sugar stayed steady, too.

Next up for me will be a Hayden High game. Another local school, another Friday night under the lights.

It's 11:45 p.m. now, and I think I'll call it a night.

That's all for now.

349: Local Sports

As I mentioned earlier, I went to a high school football game this past Friday night. And it reminded me how much I love living in a small community.

Everywhere I looked, there were familiar faces. The local pharmacist walked over, shook my hand and Papa's, and chatted for a moment. The owner of a local painting company stopped by too—someone we've hired for both house and cabin jobs. He shook our hands and caught up with us for a bit.

Local businesses were woven into the game itself. Time-outs and touchdowns were "sponsored" by them. The announcer up in the press box would call out, *"Mortimer Jordan calls a time-out. This time-out is brought to you by [Local Business Name]."*

Even the announcer was a local face. He was my oldest brother.

I saw people from my church, and Papa talked with folks from his Bible study class.

At one point, I looked around the stands, really taking it all in. Families, friends, and neighbors all gathered together to cheer on the kids and support the community.

It was beautiful.

Tony riding Smoke

Lynn and his brother Tony

Lynn with his Paw Paw just before his Baptism

Lynn with his Mom

Lynn's snow globes.

Tony and Lynn holding the gun

Lynn with Ms. Betty Lynn

Lynns home in Huntsville, AL

Lynn TAGS Award

Lynn with Pop, Mom, and nieces Summer and Brooklyn.

Lynn with Nephew Luke and his wife Kylee

Tony's three children that he left behind.

Lynn's late brother, Tony.